Critical Pedagogy and Teacher Education in the Neoliberal Era

Small Openings

EXPLORATIONS OF EDUCATIONAL PURPOSE

Volume 6

Series Scope

In today's dominant modes of pedagogy, questions about issues of race, class, gender, sexuality, colonialism, religion, and other social dynamics are rarely asked. Questions about the social spaces where pedagogy takes place - in schools, media, and corporate think tanks - are not raised. And they need to be.

The *Explorations of Educational Purpose* book series can help establish a renewed interest in such questions and their centrality in the larger study of education and the preparation of teachers and other educational professionals. The editors of this series feel that education matters and that the world is in need of a rethinking of education and educational purpose.

Coming from a critical pedagogical orientation, *Explorations of Educational Purpose* aims to have the study of education transcend the trivialization that often degrades it. Rather than be content with the frivolous, scholarly lax forms of teacher education and weak teaching prevailing in the world today, we should work towards education that truly takes the unattained potential of human beings as its starting point. The series will present studies of all dimensions of education and offer alternatives. The ultimate aim of the series is to create new possibilities for people around the world who suffer under the current design of socio-political and educational institutions.

For other titles published in this series, go to
http://www.springer.com/series/7472

Susan L. Groenke • J. Amos Hatch
Editors

Critical Pedagogy and Teacher Education in the Neoliberal Era

Small Openings

 Springer

Editors
Susan L. Groenke
Department of Theory and Practice
  in Teacher Education
University of Tennessee
Knoxville TN
USA

J. Amos Hatch
Department of Theory and Practice
  in Teacher Education
University of Tennessee
Knoxville TN
USA

ISBN 978-1-4020-9587-0   e-ISBN 978-1-4020-9588-7

Library of Congress Control Number: 2009920157

Printed on acid-free paper

springer.com

Joe Kincheloe passed away as this book went into production. The book would not have been possible without Joe's support and encouragement, and his chapter is a key element in the case we are trying to make. We dedicate this volume to Joe's immense generosity, his amazing contributions to the field, and his passionate commitment to making the world a better place for all.

Foreword

Susan L. Groenke and J. Amos Hatch

It does not feel safe to be critical in university-based teacher education programs right now, especially if you are junior faculty. In the neoliberal era, critical teacher education research gets less and less funding, and professors can be denied tenure or lose their jobs for speaking out against the status quo. Also, we know that the pedagogies critical teacher educators espouse can get beginning K–12 teachers fired or shuffled around, especially if their students' test scores are low. This, paired with the resistance many of the future teachers who come through our programs—predominantly White, middle-class, and happy with the current state of affairs—show toward critical pedagogy, makes it seem a whole lot easier, less risky, even smart not to "do" critical pedagogy at all. Why bother?

We believe this book shows we have lots of reasons to "bother" with critical pedagogy in teacher education, as current educational policies and the neoliberal discourses that vie for the identities of our own local contexts increasingly do not have education for the public good in mind. This book shows teacher educators taking risks, seeking out what political theorist James Scott has called the "small openings" for resistance in the contexts that mark teacher education in the early twenty-first century.

As we conceptualized this book, we wanted to give teacher educators committed to doing critical pedagogy a place to tell their stories, but we also wanted to provide the contextual backdrop describing the contemporary sociopolitical conditions within which their narratives can be understood. We divided the book into two parts. Part I, "Contexts for Critical Pedagogies in Teacher Education," describes and critiques the neoliberal and neoconservative forces that impact higher education and aim to commodify teacher education and standardize the experiences of teacher educators and the beginning teachers they prepare. Part II, "Enacting Critical Pedagogies in Teacher Education," shares hopeful accounts of the "small openings" critical pedagogues working in teacher education programs in places as diverse as Kentucky, Oregon, and Wyoming find to resist and counter the discourses described and critiqued in the first part. The book concludes with an Afterword, which synthesizes the work presented in the book and offers future considerations for those who attempt to practice critical pedagogy in the challenging contexts of the early twenty-first century.

S.L. Groenke and J.A. Hatch
University of Tennessee

We believe this edited collection is well suited for university educators, critical scholars, and students in the fields of teacher education, cultural studies, foundations of education, educational leadership, and critical studies. Education professionals, such as teachers, principals, and policymakers, who are interested in critiquing the contexts of contemporary schooling, should also find the book to be of value. Following are some of the features that make this book unique:

Critical Pedagogies in Teacher Education in the Neoliberal Era: Small Openings

- The book is by and for those interested in applying critical perspectives in higher education settings.
- Chapter authors represent scholars from diverse backgrounds, institutions, and levels of experience.
- The book is divided into parts focused on (a) sociopolitical contextual influences that impact the development and teaching of critical perspectives and (b) ways to enact critical pedagogies in real teacher education settings.
- The book adds to the theoretical, empirical, and practical knowledge base of multiple disciplines, including teacher education, critical pedagogy, foundations of education, and educational policy.
- A chapter is included that traces the roots of critical pedagogy to the early social reconstructionists, bridging the gap between past and present teacher education efforts on behalf of social justice.
- A chapter reporting findings from a recent study of critical teacher educators' perspectives on the issues they face and how they deal with them is featured.
- A comprehensive bibliography of materials for working with preservice teachers is presented.
- Volume editors conclude with a synthesis of themes, conclusions, and applications woven throughout the book.

Overview

Part I, "Contexts for Critical Pedagogies in Teacher Education," charts the contextual territory in which critical teacher educators are forced to operate in the first decade of the twenty-first century. We are concerned that the small openings available for critical teacher educators may be becoming even more constricted in the current climate of neoliberal economics, neoconservative education policy, and standards-based reform. We invited scholars to address some of the powerful forces impacting possibilities for doing critical teacher education in the current social, political, and economic climate. Contexts addressed in Part I range from historical influences to the impact of No Child Left Behind (NCLB), and the section concludes with a report of a research project designed to capture what those currently doing critical teacher education in a variety of places perceive to be the factors that influence their work. We believe the chapters in this section provide a powerful backdrop for contextualizing the narratives of practice in Part II, and they stand individually and collectively as important, with often troubling statements about the current state of affairs in teacher education and schooling.

The part opens with Chapter 1, "Social Reconstructionism and the Roots of Critical Pedagogy: Implications for Teacher Education in the Neoliberal Era." In this chapter, Susan Groenke of the University of Tennessee traces the history of the social reconstructionist movement of the 1930s, showing this movement's influence on contemporary critical thought and the evolvement of teacher education in the United States. Groenke makes a powerful case that the capitalist policies that the original reconstructionists resisted so strongly have been reincarnated in the neoliberal assault on contemporary schooling—and teacher education in particular. She argues that lessons from those who fought for social justice in the past should not be forgotten by those engaged in critical teacher education today.

Before he passed away in December of 2008, Joe Kincheloe authored Chapter 2, "Contextualizing the Madness: A Critical Analysis of the Assault on Teacher Education and Schools." Kincheloe was one of the leading advocates for using critical approaches to understand and change how schools work. His chapter builds on the historical context in Chapter 1, providing a prescient critique of what he terms "the recovery movement" of the past 30 years—that is, efforts by right-wing conservative forces to "recover" White supremacy, patriarchy, class privilege, and heterosexual normality. The chapter exposes both the madness and the impact of the recovery movement on education in general and teacher education in particular, arguing that change will not be possible unless critical pedagogues reframe the "commonsense" that right-wing political, economic, religious, and cultural forces have successfully created over the past three decades.

Chapter 3, "Standards Talk: Considering Discourses in Teacher Education Standards," is authored by Nikola Hobbel of Humboldt University. Hobbel's project is to deconstruct national standards discourses to examine the complex social and political processes that both enable and constrain teachers and teacher educators, especially in terms of preparing teachers for effective, culturally relevant practices. She provides an overview of standards proposed by National Council for Accreditation of Teacher Education (NCATE) and Teacher Education Accreditation Council (TEAC), with the purpose of explicating the kinds of discursive themes that are present within them. She explores the frames of reasoning that act as the NCATE and TEAC standards' underlying assumptions, arguing that understanding the political symbolism of the standards movement allows us to envision alternatives to the status quo.

Kate Menken of the City University of New York, Queens College & Graduate Center, has written Chapter 4, "Policy Failures: *No Child Left Behind* and English Language Learners." Menken provides a comprehensive overview of NCLB and the controversies surrounding it, then explores its impact on English language learners (ELLs)—the fastest-growing population in US schools—and on teachers and teacher educators. She concludes that teacher educators have the responsibility to inform future teachers that they have the final say in how policies like NCLB are implemented in classrooms and to take an active role in advocating for ELL students and informing policymakers of the impact of failed policies on schooling.

Part I concludes with Chapter 5, "Issues in Critical Teacher Education: Insights from the Field," by Amos Hatch and Susan Groenke of the University of Tennessee. The chapter is a report of findings of an open-ended, Web-based survey sent to critical teacher educators, asking them to identify issues they face in their work, ways they address those issues, and the major critical texts they find useful with teacher education students. Based on data from 65 respondents, the findings use the words of critical teacher educators to bring to life their perspectives on issues related to students, colleagues, and expectations. The chapter includes an extensive bibliography of materials critical teacher educators have used successfully with preservice teachers. The insights offered by study respondents offer an empirical bridge that connects the contexts described in Part I to the stories in Part II.

In Part II, "Enacting Critical Pedagogies in Teacher Education," we include ten narratives of practice written by critical educators working in a wide variety of roles and institutions. As we planned this part of the book, we invited abstracts from individuals with different levels of experience in higher education, who work in different kinds of college and university settings in different parts of the United States, who teach in programs preparing teachers for different grade levels and subject-matter areas within the K–12 system, and who represent a variety of ethnic and racial backgrounds. We selected chapter authors who share the experience of attempting to do critical pedagogy as part of their teacher preparation activity, but who bring unique and interesting perspectives to the task because of who they are and how they adjust to the contexts in which they do their work. Some chapters are single-authored, some are written with colleagues, and others are by professors and graduate students who share the experience of introducing critical pedagogical approaches to future teachers. The first set of narratives in this part (Chapters 6–10) are grouped together because they represent teacher educators working across the spectrum of grade levels and subject specialties; the latter set (Chapters 11–15) includes diversity in terms of grades and subjects, but emphasizes the impact of a variety of settings on critical pedagogical work. We believe the stories collected across the part create a narrative mosaic that can give a sense of solidarity to those who do critical pedagogy in teacher education and provide a source of insight for those imagining their own "small openings" in the future.

Chapter 6, "A Critical Pedagogy of Race in Teacher Education: Response and Responsibility," is authored by Jill Flynn, Tim Lensmire, and Cynthia Lewis of the University of Minnesota. The chapter presents stories of the authors' experiences implementing a critical pedagogy of race with predominantly White preservice teachers. Lessons learned related to positioning the students as "responsible" but not necessarily "guilty" are explored.

In Chapter 7, "Anti-oppressive Pedagogy in Early Childhood Teacher Education: A Conversation," Beth Swadener, Cristian Acquino-Sterling, Mark Nagasawa, and Maggie Bartlett of Arizona State University frame their stories of practice as a conversation among a professor and three graduate students. Authors recount their personal/professional journeys to critical pedagogy, discuss tensions and contradictions in their work with early childhood teacher candidates (especially around issues of high-stakes testing and accountability), and explore the place of "radical love" in teacher education experiences that aim to be anti-oppressive and critical.

Chapter 8, "Integrating Macro- and Micro-level Issues in ESOL/Bilingual Teacher Education," is by Maria Dantas-Whitney of Western Oregon University and Karie Mize and Eileen Waldschmidt of the University of New Mexico. The chapter focuses on the authors' efforts to develop critical sociocultural consciousness in students preparing to teach English language learners (ELLs). The authors use examples of ESOL/Bilingual teacher education students' written reflections following an interview with an immigrant to the United States to make the case that preservice teachers can learn to see connections between macro- and micro-level issues faced by ELL students and their families.

Glenda Moss, who teaches at Indiana University Purdue University Fort Wayne, has written Chapter 9, "Standards, Critical Literature, and Portfolio Assessment: An Integrated Approach to Critical Pedagogical Development." Moss describes how she encourages critical reflection in her students around state requirements that teacher candidates complete a portfolio based on standards developed by the Interstate New Teachers Assessment and Support Consortium (INTASC). She uses extensive quotations from her students' written reflections to show the development of analytic skills when students are asked to apply critical pedagogical lenses to understanding standards-based approaches to education, concluding the chapter with lessons learned about critical teacher preparation.

Venus Evans-Winters of Illinois Wesleyan University has authored Chapter 10, "Leaders-Cloaked-As-Teachers: Toward Pedagogies of Liberation." Writing as an African-American foundations of education professor, she discusses the challenges and possibilities of teaching critical pedagogy frameworks to majority White, middle-class, female students. She uses the concept of "leaders-cloaked-as-teachers" to describe her approach to encouraging the transformative process preservice teachers must undergo in order to view themselves as change agents in classrooms, schools, and communities.

Chapter 11, "Regulation, Resistance, and Sacred Places in Teacher Education" is written by David Greenwood, Sean Agriss, and Darcy Miller of Washington State University. Using the NCATE review process as an example, these authors discuss the debilitating effects of the "hidden curriculum" of regulation on teacher educators' thoughts, feelings, and imaginations. Although they remain committed to teaching as a subversive activity, they acknowledge the difficulties of developing transgressive pedagogies in the heavily regulated secondary teacher education program in which they work. They describe "place-based" approaches to help students envision ways to transform their own thinking and the communities where they reside. Their emphasis on the importance of place sets up the last set of chapters in Part II.

Exploring Web-based teacher education experiences, Susan Groenke and Joellen Maples of the University of Tennessee have authored Chapter 12, "Small Openings in Cyberspace: Preparing Preservice Teachers to Facilitate Critical Race Talk." One of the objectives of the authors' Web Pen Pals project is to provide a safe space where preservice English teachers can practice taking a critical stance toward literature in online discussions with middle-school students. In this chapter, they explore their experience of trying to facilitate critical race talk, using excerpts from chats between future English teachers and adolescents around Walter Dean Myers's young adult novel *Monster*. Groenke and Maples conclude with a description of what they have learned using computer-mediated communication tools to help future teachers challenge current definitions of reading processes, instruction, and teacher agency.

Chapter 13, "Teaching for Democracy and Social Justice in Rural Settings: Challenges and Pedagogical Opportunities," describes the experiences of two African educators, Lydiah Nganga and John Kambutu, who are professors at the University of Wyoming/Casper Center. These authors see implementing critical pedagogical approaches as especially difficult in rural settings they characterize as isolated, individualistic, conservative, lacking diversity, and generally resistant to the advancement of democracy and social justice work. The chapter explores their experiences as educators of color collaborating across teacher education courses to confront the sometimes-debilitating resistance they find in the communities where they teach.

Lane Clarke writes of her experiences teaching literacy courses at Northern Kentucky University in Chapter 14, "Adjusting to Rose-Colored Glasses: Finding Creative Ways to Be Critical in Kentucky." She tells the story of her discovery of critical theory as a way to understand her own privileged upbringing and her place as a teacher in perpetuating structures that keep oppressed peoples in the margins of society. She then describes the many challenges she faced as a new faculty member, including those emanating from her university, her state, federal legislation, and her students. Clarke shares descriptions of projects she has used to build the critical consciousness of her literacy students and concludes with questions that continue to trouble her as she moves forward in her career as a critical teacher educator.

In Chapter 15, "Becoming Critical in an Urban Elementary Teacher Education Program," Amos Hatch and Wendy Meller describe the ups and downs of taking on a critical stance in their work preparing urban elementary teachers at the University of Tennessee. The authors use data from different qualitative studies of the same cohort of preservice urban elementary teachers to bring to life the difficulties, paradoxes, and rewards of becoming critical in the midst of powerful conservative forces. Examples of instructional activities are presented, as are lessons learned along the way to encourage critical pedagogical development in future teachers.

In conclusion, an Afterword authored by editors Susan Groenke and Amos Hatch synthesizes the contributions made by all the featured authors toward a collective awareness of, and resistance to, neoliberal forces, and offers future considerations for other, more locally collaborative forms of collective resistance against the current neoliberal forces fast at work dismantling public schools and university-based teacher education programs.

Critical Pedagogies and Teacher Education in the Neoliberal Era

Our goal for this project was to collect under one cover a set of readings that describes the current sociopolitical contexts of critical pedagogy and reveals the complexity, quality, and depth of work being done by critical teacher educators working in a wide variety of settings. Because so many critical educators work in relative isolation, and some are forced to apply their critical perspectives in quiet and subversive ways, we hoped to provide evidence that colleagues in diverse settings are finding ways to confront the many challenges of critical pedagogical work. We believe we have accomplished our goal. The chapters that follow have informed and inspired us, and we think they will do the same for readers interested in critical approaches to teacher education.

We want to express our appreciation to all those who submitted abstracts when we began this project. We are sorry that space limitations made it impossible to include many of the quality proposals we received. We are especially grateful to the authors whose chapters are included in this book. They have been professional and good-spirited, as we have asked for two, three, and sometimes four revisions. Of course, the book would not exist without their hard work and willingness to share what they have learned. Finally, we honor Joe Kincheloe's memory. We are truly grateful for the opportunity we had to work with him and be included in this important series.

Contents

Abbreviations

ABCTE	American Board for Certification of Teacher Education
AYP	Adequate Yearly Progress
AACTE	American Association of Colleges of Teacher Education
ABCTE	American Board for Certification of Teacher Education
ASCD	Association for Supervision and Curriculum Development
CP	Critical Pedagogy
EBI	Educational Benchmarking, Incorporated
ECE	Early Childhood Education
ESEA	Elementary and Secondary Education Act
ESL	English as a Second Language
ESOL	English for Speakers of Other Languages
ELLs	English Language Learners
IDEA	Individuals with Disabilities Education Act
IPSB	Indiana Professional Standards Board
IEP	Individualized Education Plan
IRE	Initiate-Respond-Evaluate
INTASC	Interstate New Teachers Assessment and Support Consortium
NBPTS	National Board for Professional Teaching Standards
NCATE	National Council for Accreditation of Teacher Education
NCSS	National Council of Social Studies
NCTE	National Council of Teachers of English
NCTM	National Council of Teachers of Mathematics
NRP	National Reading Panel
NCLB	No Child Left Behind
TEAC	Teacher Education Accreditation Council
UCEA	University Council for Educational Administration
WTEP	Wyoming Teacher Education Program

Part I
Contexts for Critical Pedagogies in Teacher Education

Chapter 1
Social Reconstructionism and the Roots of Critical Pedagogy: Implications for Teacher Education in the Neoliberal Era

Susan L. Groenke

1.1   Introduction

When people hear or see the term "critical pedagogy," they might think of Paulo Freire, whose work with Brazilian peasants in the 1970s led him to see education as inseparable from individual empowerment and social change (1970/2000). Joe Kincheloe (2008) suggests anyone working in critical pedagogy today must reference Freire's work; Peter McLaren, another prominent figure in critical pedagogy, has called Freire the "inaugural philosopher of critical pedagogy" (2000, p. 1).

Others might associate critical pedagogy with Henry Giroux, who first coined the term in the 1980s (1983). Giroux drew on Freire's work to criticize a Reagan-era educational "culture of positivism" that used schools as forms of social regulation to preserve the status quo. Still others may associate critical pedagogy with Frankfurt School critical theorists Max Horkheimer (1937, 1972) and Herbert Marcuse (1968), or more contemporary critical theorists like Michael Apple (1979, 2006), Ira Shor (1980, 2000), and bell hooks (1994)—all prominent figures in the emergence and implementation of critical pedagogy in teacher education as we know it today. But the roots of critical pedagogy in teacher education may go further back, to the early 1900s when teachers' colleges were first being formed, and beliefs about what teachers should be and do were first being debated.

This chapter describes a group of radical progressive teacher educators who, in the 1930s and 1940s, encouraged teachers to have critical perspectives on the relationships between schooling and societal inequities, and a moral commitment to correcting those inequities through the classroom and school activities. Educational historians call these radical progressives—people like George Counts, Harold Rugg, William Kilpatrick, and Theodore Brameld—"social reconstructionists," as they ultimately desired a total "reconstruction" of society and schooling that could only be brought about if teacher education itself was "reconstructed" (Stanley, 1985; Zeichner & Liston, 1990).

Thus, long before Paulo Freire encouraged the development of "critical consciousness," and Henry Giroux coined the term "critical pedagogy," the social

S.L. Groenke
University of Tennessee

S.L. Groenke and J.A. Hatch (eds.), *Critical Pedagogy and Teacher Education in the Neoliberal Era: Small Openings,*
DOI 10.1007/978-1-4020-9588-7_1, © Springer Science + Business Media B.V. 2009

reconstructionists were describing and acting on what Kincheloe (2008) explains are some of the central characteristics of critical pedagogy today, namely that education and educational reform are often aligned with the capitalist marketplace rather than democratic values, and schools often work to reproduce the dominant culture and status quo, but teachers and students can work together in schools to transform culture and institutions (Stanley, 1985).

The early social reconstructionists were working in teacher education at a time when support for public schooling and university-based teacher preparation was strong. Acting on beliefs that public schools and teachers' colleges were places that could affect social change, they implemented what have come to be foundational elements of teacher education programs claiming to do critical work today.

In what follows, I outline some of the major tenets of "social reconstructionism" and provide descriptions of what kinds of teaching and teacher education the social reconstructionists envisioned and implemented. Then—to present some of the contextual struggles that today's critical teacher educators face—I consider the social reconstructionists' earlier historical work in light of the current neoliberal assault on teacher education that threatens the demise of public schools and many of the foundational elements the social reconstructionists worked to put in place, including social foundations courses in teacher preparation programs, and critical and equity-oriented teacher education programs themselves.

1.2 Characteristics of Social Reconstructionism

1.2.1 Anticapitalism

It was the early 1930s, not long after free public high schools had been established[1], thus influencing the need for well-trained teachers. Teachers College in New York, founded by philanthropists who believed education should play a role in ameliorating poverty and other societal ills, was on its way to becoming the premiere teaching college in the country. Against the backdrop of the stock-market crash, and long unemployment lines on New York's city streets, the term "critical theory" had just been coined by Max Horkheimer (1937), a member of the Frankfurt School, in exile at Teachers College[2]. Horkheimer and other Frankfurt School members had experienced widespread economic depression and unemployment in Central Europe, and witnessed Hitler's rise to power in an advanced, industrialized Germany. Wary and weary of liberal capitalism's promise of equality and social freedom, they criticized America for its reliance on a class structure that put the production and distribution of goods, and decisions about societal priorities, in the hands of powerful capitalists.

---

[1] See Cremin (1953) for more on history of American state public school systems.
[2] The Frankfurt School emerged from the Institute for Social Research, originally a center for Marxist study at the University of Frankfurt, in Germany. In 1934, as Hitler's concentration camps were being established across Europe, several sociology professors urged Teachers College president, Nicholas Butler, to invite members of the Institute to New York (Marcus & Tar, 1988).

To the critical theorists, consumer capitalism created "a marketable mass man who is told by the advertising media what he needs and desires; subsequently, this atomized individual sings the praises of the corporation" (Brosio, 1980, p. 17). Man should be more than "cogs in factory wheels, more than manipulable, interchangeable parts in the production of class society" (Marcuse, 1968, p. 86). In a "good society," peoples' worth would not be determined by what they earned, but by their contribution to the betterment of society for all. Schools were not immune; rather—as the critical theorists suggested—schools "asserted the legitimacy of capitalism and class structure" by preparing students to "become workers who considered their entry into the consumer market a substitute for real democratic power" (Brosio, 1980, p. 3).

While it is not clear if any collaboration occurred between members of the Frankfurt School and professors at Teachers College, or to what extent, if any, professors at Teachers College embraced critical theory, it seems likely that the new theory was influential[3]. For it was during the "Horkheimer era" at Teachers College that Professors George S. Counts, William Kilpatrick, and Harold Rugg called on teacher education to "[redress] … and [correct] the 'social injustice and evils of capitalism'" (Kliebard, 1986, p. 183).

The social reconstructionists believed that the Depression demonstrated the bankruptcy of a liberal capitalistic political economy, and capitalism's reliance on individual self-interest promoted a disregard for public welfare (Cohen, 1976). The "age of individualism is closing, and … an age marked by close integration of social life … collective planning and control is opening," wrote Counts in the journal *Social Frontier*, which the social reconstructionists founded for their cause. (Cremin et al., 1954, p. 146).

In his 1932 manifesto *Dare the School Build a New Social Order?* Counts described a "cooperative" or "collectivistic" economy that should replace capitalism. A cooperative economy would not produce and distribute goods essentially for the sake of private gain, but for the purpose of serving the needs of all the people. Only when the nation's wealth was distributed equitably, and full employment and adequate incomes for fair standards of living ensured, would citizens be motivated to come together to work toward a more democratic future.

Accordingly, the social reconstructionists also found public schooling's emphasis upon economic success to be problematic. They—like the critical theorists—believed schools function to help reproduce dominant culture and institutions, and the dominant culture's beliefs in "progress and optimism [masked] … problems of social and economic injustice and inequality" (Stanley, 1985, p. 386).

Counts and his like-minded colleagues believed schools should assume responsibility for the negative effects of capitalism, and teachers should help to broaden and deepen student's aspirations beyond "economy and work" (Brosio, 1980, p. 12). Kilpatrick (1933, p. 71) explained that education should

---

[3]While Maier (1988) explains that Horkheimer and his colleagues remained "outsiders" at Teachers College (they continued to write and publish in German, limiting their readership), Maier suggests "the presence of the institute on American soil did make a difference. There was … always a group of intellectuals … who did mine the gold in [Horkheimer's writings]" (p. 34).

prepare individuals to take part intelligently in the management of conditions under which they will live, to bring them to an understanding of the forces which are moving, and to equip them with the intellectual and practical tools by which they can themselves enter into the direction of these forces.

With capitalism's collapse, the US culture was in crisis, but education could fix it. Central to this mission was indoctrination.

1.2.2 Indoctrination

The social reconstructionists called on teachers to consciously indoctrinate their students with socialist and collectivist values. Counts (1932, p. 19) wrote in his manifesto:

There is the fallacy that the school should be impartial in its emphases, that no bias should be given instruction. We have already observed how the individual is inevitably molded by the culture into which he is born. In the case of the school a similar process operates and presumably is subject to a degree of conscious direction. My thesis is that complete impartiality is utterly impossible, that the school must shape attitudes, develop tastes, and even impose ideas.

That the "school must shape attitudes, develop tastes, and impose ideas" was a hotly debated idea in education at the time. Some educators believed "core cultural values" should be emphasized in schools, while others believed only the skills required to make policy decisions, rather than social or political goals, should be emphasized (Newmann, 1975, p. 72). John Dewey, an influential educational philosopher at the time, believed social and cultural values might be learned by individuals through their own reflective inquiry rather than through imposed, previously determined social programs[4].

Counts and other social reconstructionists took issue with these stances, wondering "whose cultural values" should be taught, and criticizing what they saw as Dewey's "spectator" position (Counts, 1932, p. 8). The social reconstructionists believed students had to be taught to "care" about certain values or issues if they were to develop a commitment to reflecting and acting on social problems (Stanley, 1985). Counts exclaimed in his manifesto that "the good society is not something that is given by nature: it must be fashioned by the hand and brain of man. This process of building a good society is to a very large degree an educational process" (1932, p. 15).

So what was this indoctrination to look like in schools? Brameld (1947, p. 133) proposed that schools implement courses on the history of the labor movement and the place of labor in American life for students in junior and senior high schools:

[W]hether they like it or not, the vast majority of the young men and women who graduate from the public schools will be compelled to decide whether to become trade unionists.

---

[4]John Dewey's beliefs about the role of schooling in developing democratic participation was an early influence on the social reconstructionists, but Dewey eventually became a harsh critic of Counts and the social reconstructionist movement (see Bowers, 1969, and Kliebard, 1986, for more on the history of their relationship).

Therefore, the least the public schools can do is to provide familiarity with the structures, responsibilities, and problems of these crucially important organizations. Also, if unions are to operate democratically ... young people should learn how to take part in them effectively.

Brameld (1947, pp. 137–138) also proposed the use of discussion in classroom instruction:

The aim should be to arrive at group decisions by social consensus by which I mean (a) awareness of as much evidence as possible; (b) open testimony and communication of that evidence; and (c) reaching agreement among the largest possible number, upon the basis both of that evidence and its communication.

Brameld believed that to facilitate this process, teachers should make explicit their own beliefs and the reasoning processes they used to clarify and develop their own views on controversial issues (Stanley, 1985).

In addition, Teachers College professor, Harold Rugg (1929–1932), wrote a multivolume series of social studies textbooks entitled *Man and His Changing World* for teachers' use in classrooms. Social reconstructionists like Rugg envisioned education to be "functional," with a "social aim," and broadly contextualized, rather than "scientific" or "essentialist," and narrowly focused on single, decontextualized subjects and disciplines (Cohen, 1976, p. 309).

Discouraged by what he saw as "curriculum fragmentation and unnecessary compartmentalization" in social studies curriculum, Rugg envisioned a new curriculum "organized around real social problems" (Kliebard, 1986, pp. 200–201). In Rugg's textbooks, these "social problems" included an emphasis on America as a nation of immigrants, the disparity between rich and poor, and the changing role of women in society. The textbook series proved popular, and by 1939, over a million copies of Rugg's textbooks had been distributed to public schools all over the country (Kliebard, 1986).

While the social reconstructionists certainly envisioned nontraditional classroom techniques and curriculum materials as part of the "reconstruction" of schooling and therefore of society, they also believed teacher educators themselves had an important role to play in the process. In essence, the social reconstructionists believed teachers must become "political statesmen ... zealous in the improvement of present conditions [and] capable of educating citizens to study social problems earnestly, think critically about them and act [accordingly]" (Brown, 1938, p. 328). The social reconstructionists believed that for this to happen, teacher educators would have to provide teachers a "thoughtful and systematic study of the economic and industrial problems confronting us today" (Brown, 1938, p. 238).

1.2.3 Preparing "Political Statesmen"

1.2.3.1 Education 200F: Social Foundations

To better consider what such study should entail, Harold Rugg, George Counts, William Kilpatrick, and others formed a bimonthly Discussion Group at Teachers College, whose purpose was to "cooperatively study ... the foundations of education"

(Rugg, 1952, p. 225). As a result of their discussions, Rugg and his colleagues decided to "give up our academic individualisms and unify our … prima-donna departments into one organic Division of the College—that is, the Division of Social and Philosophical Foundations" (Rugg, 1952, p. 225). The Division eventually became a two-semester course which represented the collectivist ideals the social reconstructionists held dear: by combining the liberal arts fields of the history of education, economics, and sociology—what the social reconstructionists deemed the "social foundations of education"—the course represented a move away from the traditional "outmoded individualistic emphasis on discrete courses in different, unrelated fields" (Cremin et al., 1954, pp. 145–146).

Rugg, Kilpatrick, and others envisioned the course as a cross-disciplinary study in which students would view social institutions, processes, and ideals with a critical orientation that would help them to develop a more informed perspective about the relationship between society and schooling (Tozer & McAninch, 1987). Such a course would serve as a "firm foundation for educators," and "aid in the development of a social and educational philosophy by prospective teachers that would enable them to assume a leadership role in the making of educational policy" (Zeichner & Liston, 1990, p. 14). And so it was that Education 200F, or the Social Foundations course, was born. Although the course was never widely popular at Teachers College, it became what some historians consider one of the most influential innovations in American teacher education in the twentieth century (Cohen, 1976). By the 1940s, social reconstructionists working at the University of Illinois—William O. Stanley, Kenneth D. Benne, B. Othanel Smith, and Archibald Anderson—were considered the "philosopher-kings of American education" (Cohen, 1976, p. 313), and by the 1950s, the social foundations textbooks they wrote became seminal works in the curriculum and foundations fields. In the 1970s, Greene (1976), the first woman philosopher to be hired at Columbia University, argued that the foundations course is the area best suited to foster critical understanding among teachers:

> The responsibility for critical understanding of the language of functional reality, its premises, its origins, its distortions fall heavily upon the educator. Perhaps its falls most heavily on the foundations specialist in teacher education, since he/she is distinctly obligated to equip teachers-to-be to reflect critically upon and identify themselves with respect to a formalized world. … There must be efforts made to reflect critically on the numerous modes of masking what is happening in our society—the numerous modes of mystifying, of keeping people still. (p. 10)

Today, social foundations courses are taught in university-based teacher education programs all over the country, and in some cases, they are the only courses in university-based teacher preparation where students have opportunities to consider the history of public education; the relationship between academic success and race, class, and gender; and what the purposes of education should be in a democratic society (Carlson, 2008; Morrison, 2007).

Finally, in addition to the emergence of an integrated social foundations component in teacher education, the social reconstructionists also heeded early educational reformers' calls for "practice" schools for teachers (Cremin, 1953). New College at

Teachers College (1932–1939) and the Putney Graduate School of Teacher Education in Vermont (1950–1964) were two such schools, dedicated to applying to teacher education the major tenets of social reconstructionism, especially the idea that teachers could—with the right preparation—be leaders for social change.

1.2.3.2   New College and Putney Graduate School of Teacher Education

Everything at New College and Putney School seemed to revolve around the idea that future teachers of a *new social order* "required contact with life in its various phases and understanding of it—an understanding of the intellectual, moral, social, and economic life of the people" (Cremin et al., 1954, p. 222). *Contact with life* at New College took various forms. Students participated in weekly industrial seminars, where students returned from jobs to discuss "industry as they were experiencing it against a background of study of current industrial conditions and their origins" (Education of teachers, 1936, p. 12). At other times, New College students were expected to live on student-operated farms where they built and repaired their own housing, grew their own food, and laid pipes to bring water to farmlands.

To help students "understand their own country better by contrast with another, to give that greater understanding of people and things that only new scenes can stimulate," students traveled to Europe and lived abroad (Education of teachers, 1936, p. 8). Scholarships were awarded to students who went "furthest beyond academic neutrality in active participation in life outside the walls of the university" (Cremin et al., 1954, p. 226). Students were also encouraged to debate and participate in political issues, attend faculty meetings, and be involved in community activities. Some of these activities included the formation of a nursery school, a camp for teens where New College students served as counselors, and an adult high school program in an urban community.

At Putney Graduate School, students were expected to participate in "study tours" that required a diverse mix of multiracial and international students to "live, travel, and make decisions together as a community" (Rodgers, 2006, p. 1283). One such tour took place in the Deep South, in 1956, not quite 2 years after the Supreme Court's *Brown vs. Board of Education* decision ruled that legally sanctioned racial segregation of schools was unconstitutional. White students saw acts of racial hatred and violence committed toward their African and African-American peers while on tour, and this helped them "see" the oppression and societal inequity they theorized in their classes. The school leaders' intent for the tours was to "radicalize" students through experience and interaction, by "[pushing] the borders of the groups' understanding" (Rodgers, 2006, p. 1284).

More recent examples of university-based teacher preparation programs that enact the early social reconstructionists' goals include Center X, in UCLA's Teacher Education Program, first conceived in 1992 "out of the upheaval and self examination stemming from Los Angeles's Rodney King verdict uprisings" (Olsen, 2005, p. 34). Candidates participate in dialogic, inquiry-focused classes and teaching projects embedded not only in schools, but urban community centers. Other examples include the University of Indiana, Bloomington's Program for Democracy, Diversity, and Social Justice, and Sacramento State University's Bilingual and Multicultural departmental program.

1.3   Support for Social Reconstructionism Wanes

By the late 1950s, —with war and McCarthyism as cultural backdrops—the radical social reconstructionists began to lose many supporters. It was anti-American to be anticapitalist. Rugg's textbooks came under challenge, for "[casting] aspersions upon our Constitution and our form of government," and for "[condemning] the American system of private ownership and enterprise" (Kliebard, 1986, p. 206). John Dewey had long attacked social reconstructionists for "reducing education to an exercise in inculcating a class point of view" (Bowers, 1969, p. 154). R. Bruce Raup believed the social reconstructionists did not understand the Marxian terminology (e.g., "class struggle") they used (Bowers, 1969). Others criticized the social reconstructionists' failure to understand the labor movement was primarily interested in obtaining more wealth for workers than overturning capitalism. Perhaps more importantly, practicing teachers—predominantly women who lacked job security and power—did not feel they could advocate social changes that were unacceptable to the people who paid their salaries (Bowers, 1969).

Schools were blamed for Sputnik, whose launch was represented in the media as a sign that Soviet Russia's educational system was superior to America's. As Kliebard (1986, p. 265) explains:

> While American schoolchildren were learning how to get along with their peers … so the explanation went, Soviet children were being steeped in the hard sciences and mathematics needed to win the technological race that had become the centerpiece of the Cold War.

Because of Sputnik, public support for federal aid to education grew (Kaestle & Lodewick, 2007).

It was soon made clear to all—as money for curriculum revision was funneled through the National Science Foundation—that science and mathematics were to be given greater priority in the public schools, and that henceforth the schools themselves were to play an important part in national policy. The National Defense Education Act was passed in 1958, declaring that the "security of the Nation … depends upon the mastery of modern techniques developed from complex scientific principles" (Kliebard, 1986, p. 266).

In teachers colleges, emphasis moved from integrated teacher education—as the social reconstructionists had envisioned—to specialization in academic disciplines (Carlson, 2008). College teacher educators were encouraged to consider education less as a "social aim," and more as a "science, in the form of psychology, tests, and measurements" (Cohen, 1976, p. 306). At Teachers College, faculty were warned against "left-wing ideals" (Cremin et al., 1954).

The social reconstructionists, however, especially Theodore Brameld, continued to write about teacher preparation and the quality of teachers; Brameld's writings about teachers' responsibilities in shaping the good society (cf. *Education as Power*, 1965, and *The Teacher as World Citizen*, 1976)—in conjunction with the Civil Rights movement and a 1960s counterculture disillusioned with war—helped pave the way for critical pedagogues like Paulo Freire in the early 1970s, and Henry Giroux in the 1980s.

1.4   Social Reconstructionism's Contributions to Critical Pedagogy in Teacher Education

At an unstable economic time, the early social reconstructionists looked to schools and teachers' colleges to reform the ills of capitalism and work for social change. To enable teachers in this reform, they created and implemented many of the foundational elements considered "standard" in today's critically oriented, university-based teacher education programs. As example, they wrote curriculum for teachers and advocated radical ideas (e.g., dialogue, critical literacy) that continue to be encouraged in teacher education programs (see Chapter 6, Flynn et al. and Chapter 12, Groenke & Maples, this volume). They created the "foundations of education" course, which has become a standard requirement in teacher education programs (see Chapter 10, Evans-Winters, this volume). Long before Freire and other contemporary critical theorists called for "praxis," or the "complex combination of theory and practice resulting in informed action" (Kincheloe, 2008, p. 120), the social reconstructionists created "practice schools" where beginning teachers engaged in multiple and diverse interactions and experiences, and used such experiences as lenses through which to view teaching and social justice frameworks. This tradition continues in several critically oriented teacher education programs in the United States (see Chapter 7, Swadener et al., this volume).

But much of what the social reconstructionists worked to put in place in teacher education is being threatened, in large part by the unregulated, liberal capitalism the social reconstructionists once critiqued. Capitalism did not go away as the social reconstructionists had hoped, but instead has taken on the shape of neoliberalism, which operates on the idea that a totally unregulated capitalist system (a "free-market economy") "embodies the ideals of free individual choice, and achieves optimum performance, efficiency, economic growth, and distributional justice" (Kotz, 2002, p. 64).

Neoliberals believe the government should have very little control of the economy—outside of regulating the money supply and enabling free-trade markets—and would like to see the "deregulation of corporations, the privatization of public services, and the elimination of social welfare programs that benefit the working class and other popular groups" (Kotz, 2002, p. 65). Indeed, as Carlson (2008, p. 107) suggests, neoliberalism has as its goal the "conquering" and "dominating" of all public sites and services to "ensure their participation in the new global relations of power and domination."

Unlike the capitalism of the social reconstructionists' time, which needed schools to prepare workers for US jobs (and/or to compete with Russia), and left control of schools in the hands of local school districts, neoliberalism has had a devastating impact on public schools and university-based teacher education programs, especially in the form of the No Child Left Behind Act (NCLB), signed into law by President George W. Bush in 2002. Sleeter (2008, p. 1948) explains that NCLB represents a neoliberal "tool for restoration of elite power in which education serves as a resource for … private wealth accumulation."

As example, NCLB mandates federal standardized testing of all students in reading and math in grades 3–8, and requires schools to meet annual "Adequate Yearly Progress" (AYP) measures. To help schools meet these mandates and requirements, the Bush administration established federal funding to support "scientifically based" commercial curriculum programs. Two such reading programs—Reading Mastery [Direct Instruction (Engelmann et al., 1995)] and Open Court (SRA/ McGraw-Hill, 2000)—are published by President Bush's long-time friend, Harold McGraw, of McGraw-Hill, which has recorded billion dollar sales annually since NCLB went into effect (see Chapter 2, Kincheloe, this volume). These programs have been criticized for their sole emphasis on phonics-based instruction, a "white male ideology" at work in the program texts, and the undue burden they place on poorer urban school systems that rely heavily on federal funding[5] (Altwerger et al., 2004; Jordan, 2005).

Thus, in place of Rugg's textbooks—which encouraged students to think critically about the world in which they live—corporate reading programs are supported with federal funds. In place of Brameld's vision of open dialogue in classrooms, little to no authentic discussion occurs in classrooms (Applebee et al., 2003; Jordan, 2005). If teachers share their political views or encourage students to think critically about controversial issues, or resist routinized, scripted teaching, they risk losing their jobs (Achinstein & Ogawa, 2006; Meyer, 2004; O'Quinn, 2005–2006).

In addition, tied to federally mandated standardized testing and annual accountability measurements are the neoliberal goals of school privatization and school "choice," which intensifies market competition between schools (Hursh, 2005). When schools fail to reach AYP goals in 2 years, students must be given the option to transfer to another school; when schools fail for 3 consecutive years, students

---

[5]Other NCLB critics describe its deleterious effects on high-poverty communities. Sleeter (2008, p. 1952) explains that NCLB reflects a "narrowing in how equity is discussed, away from the need to address high-poverty communities' chronic lack of basic resources, including education resources." McNeil (2000) suggests that disadvantaged students often receive test-prep "drilling" that does not transfer well to literacy requirements outside of school. Thus, disadvantaged students fall further behind other culturally advantaged students. See Chapter 4, Menken, and Chapter 8, Dantas-Whitney et al., this volume, for negative effects of NCLB on English language learners (ELL), including how they are repeatedly retained (and thus encouraged to drop out of school) to lessen low-score impact on school accountability systems.

must be provided supplemental community services (e.g., tutoring, after-school programs), paid for with federal funds. When schools continue to fail to make AYP, they may be reopened as charter schools, or taken over by private, corporate, for-profit organizations like Edison Schools, Inc., that run schools like "businesses," where students are "consumers." This opens the door to voucher programs and faith-based sponsorship of schools with federal dollars. Thus, in the neoliberal age of "it's your responsibility," instead of public education, "it's your personal responsibility to try to get your child admitted to the right charter or private school" (Jones, 2008, para. 7). Many critics argue that failing public schools are indeed the goal of neoliberalism, that neoliberalism *relies on failing public schools* (Hursh, 2005; Nelson & Jones, 2007).

Public college-based teacher education programs are not immune. Rather, as Sleeter (2008, p. 1952) suggests, teacher education is "under assault" from neoliberal pressures to (1) move away from explicit, multicultural, equity-oriented programs, and toward preparing teachers as technicians who can "teach to the test"; (2) define teacher quality in testable, content-centered ways, rather than in terms of professional knowledge; and (3) shorten university-based teacher education programs or do away with them altogether.

As example, university-based teacher preparation programs have been pressured to align their programs with the professional standards of powerful accrediting agencies, the National Council for Accreditation of Teacher Education (NCATE)[6] and the Teacher Education Accreditation Council (TEAC), which claim as their mission the preparation of "professionals" (see Chapter 14, Clarke and Chapter 11, Greenwood & Agriss, this volume, as examples of programs struggling with realignment pressures).

These standards are closely aligned with NCLB and other national neoliberal reform efforts. As Carlson (2008, p. 108) explains, behind the language of these standards lies a

> project of conquering and further administratively dominating teacher education ... to make sure that it prepares the kind of teachers the system wants in the age of NCLB, which is, docile, uncritical, technically skilled "professionals" who will not question what is really going on in the schools.

(See Chapter 3, Hobbel, this volume, for critique of professional teacher standards.)

College-based attempts to align with accrediting agency standards has led state teacher licensing boards to require other college courses to better meet these standards. As Morrison (2007) explains:

> When more courses are required, teacher education programs, which are allowed to mandate only a certain number of credit hours for teacher candidates, must make difficult decisions to eliminate or reorient courses that do not seem to explicitly meet the professional standards. (para. 15)

---

[6]Under pressure from conservative organizations and right-wing think tanks, NCATE dropped "social justice" as a disposition teacher educators should help develop in their students in 2006 (Morrison, 2007).

One area of professional teacher preparation threatened by this is the social foundations course/program. Since the 1980s, social foundations courses have been abolished as required or even recommended courses in the professional preparation of teachers (Shea & Henry, 1986). At some universities, entire foundations departments have been eliminated and their faculty dismissed (Carlson, 2008; Parker, 1984; Morrison, 2007).

In 2005, Virginia's Advisory Board on Teacher Education and Licensure proposed to delete the three-semester "Social Foundations" course and replace it with semester hours in "Instructional Design Based on Assessment Data" and "Classroom Management" (Morrison, 2007). In 2006, the University of Tennessee's College of Education, Health, and Human Sciences deleted, with no discussion or input from faculty, the three-credit hour cultural foundations requirement and replaced the hours with additional coursework in special education and educational psychology.

Finally, with the help of NCLB's deregulated, content-based definition of "highly qualified" teachers, and "crisis" media rhetoric aggrandizing nationwide teacher shortages[7], neoliberal market forces are forcing teacher education programs to compete with private degree-granting and alternative licensure programs, and corporate professional development organizations outside the university. As Carlson (2008, p. 108) explains:

> Internet university is one extreme example of this competition in higher education that is leading public universities to reduce professional preparation to a series of modules that can be "delivered" through the Internet.

Thus, the very places the social reconstructionists looked to as sites for political struggle, resistance, and social change—public schools and public university-based teacher education programs—are under threat and in danger of disappearing. Indeed, the openings for resistance are small, and are getting smaller. Modern public schools are near ruin, public universities are in "chains" (Giroux as quoted in Carlson, 2008, p. 97), and "democracy has taken a back seat in teacher education" (Sleeter, 2008, p. 1955).

So what are those of us who still believe public schools and teachers colleges can be sites of struggle and social change to do? Perhaps we can learn from the early social reconstructionists, who took advantage of the economic crisis in the 1930s to garner public support for social change in educational settings, and called on schools to take responsibility for the negative effects of capitalism. The United

---

[7] Darling-Hammond (2001) suggests there is a *surplus* of teachers, but a *shortage* in their *distribution*, as few teachers are both qualified and willing to teach in urban and rural schools, especially those serving low-income students or students of color. Also, Ingersoll (2002) suggests, teacher shortages occur not because of teacher retirement, as many educational policymakers suggest, but because of teacher migration/attrition due to low salaries, teachers' feelings of having little influence in school policies/decision making, and student discipline problems/concerns about school safety. The overemphasis on fast-track, alternative licensure programs to account for teacher shortages distracts attention away from the reasons teachers leave teaching, and the resources needed by high-poverty schools to attract and retain high-quality teachers.

States is once again in economic "crisis,"[8] and world economic leaders are calling for a "new financial order" and a "capitalism based on morality and transparency" (Beardsley, 2008, para. 6).

Perhaps it is time for teacher educators to call once again for a "new social order," as George Counts did in 1932, at the height of the Great Depression. Counts wrote in his manifesto that the capitalist crisis presented the teaching profession with an opportunity to introduce a "new vision of American destiny" in schools (p. 54). In this vision, people would not be

> permitted to carve a fortune out of the natural resources of the nation … organize a business purely for the purpose of making money … build a new factory or railroad whenever and wherever … [or] throw the economic system out of gear for the protection of [their] own private interests. (p. 49)

Counts encouraged teachers and teacher educators to "bequeath" the "legacy" of this new American vision to children—"a priceless legacy which it should be the first concern of our profession to fashion" (p. 54).

What "new vision of American destiny" might today's teacher educators propose? What legacy will today's teachers and teacher educators bequeath to tomorrow's children? Perhaps the process of shaping this vision and legacy should include engaging in dialogue with the public and policymakers over the purposes of schooling in a democratic society (Hursh, 2005). Perhaps through such dialogue critical teacher educators can help others imagine a new "public" that regrounds public schools and public universities within the democratic goals and purposes of a civil society (Carlson, 2008).

The consequences of not doing so could be disastrous. If teacher educators continue to have as little impact on school practices outside of academia as the early social reconstructionists have had (cf. Cremin, 1988; Kliebard, 1986; Zeichner & Liston, 1990), it is not reconstruction of public schooling and university-based teacher preparation we will be hoping for, but resurrection.

Acknowledgments The author wishes to thank Eileen Galang and Shannon Coulter, doctoral students at the University of Tennessee, for their help on earlier drafts of this chapter.

References

Achinstein, B., & Ogawa, R.T. (2006). (In)fidelity: What the resistance of new teachers reveals about professional principles and prescriptive educational policies. *Harvard Educational Review, 67*(1), 30–63.

Altwerger, B., Arya, P., Jin, L., Jordan, N.L., Laster, B., Martens, P. et al. (2004). When research and mandates collide: The challenges and dilemmas of teacher education in the era of NCLB. *English Education, 36*(2), 119–133

---

[8] At the time of this writing, US corporations' and banks' unregulated financial dealings have left them bankrupt and the world economy in collapse. American consumers wait to see what the repercussions of the government bailout of these corporations and banks will be. American economists compare the current financial crisis to the Great Depression of the 1930s (Uchitelle et al., 2008).

Apple, M.W. (1979). *Ideology and curriculum.* New York: Routledge.

Apple, M.W. (2006). *Educating the "right" way: Markets, standards, God, and inequality.* (2nd ed.). New York: Routledge.

Applebee, A.N., Langer, J.A., Nystrand, M., & Gamoran, A. (2003). Discussion-based approaches to developing understanding: Classroom instruction and student performance in middle and high school English. *American Education Research Journal,* 40(3), 685–730.

Beardsley, E. (2008). Financial turmoil deepening in Europe. National Public Radio. http://www.npr.org/templates/story/story.php?storyId=95420466. Accessed 6 October 2008.

Bowers, C.A. (1969). *The progressive educator and the depression: The radical years.* New York: Random House.

Brameld, T. (1947). Workers' education in America. *Educational Administration and Supervision,* *33,* 129–140.

Brameld, T. (1965). *Education as power.* New York: Hold, Rinehart, & Winston.

Brameld, T. (1976). *The teacher as world citizen: A scenario of the 21st century.* New York: ETC Publications.

Brosio, R.A. (1980). *The Frankfurt School: An analysis of the contradictions and crises of liberal capitalist societies.* Muncie, IN: Ball State University Press.

Brown, H. (1938). A challenge to teachers colleges. *The Social Frontier,* 4(37), 327–329.

Carlson, D. (2008). 2007 AESA Presidential Address. Conflict of the faculties: Democratic progressivism in the age of "No Child Left Behind." *Educational Studies,* 43, 94–113.

Cohen, S. (1976). The history of the history of American education, 1900–1976: The uses of the past. *Harvard Educational Review,* 46(3), 298–330.

Counts, G.S. (1932). *Dare the school build a new social order?* New York: Stratford Press.

Cremin, L.A. (1953). The heritage of American teacher education, Part I. *Journal of Teacher Education,* 4, 163–170.

Cremin, L.A. (1988). *American education: The metropolitan experience 1876–1980.* New York: Vintage.

Cremin, L.A., Shannon, D.A., & Townsend, M.E. (1954). *A history of Teachers College, Columbia University.* New York, NY: Columbia University Press.

Darling-Hammond. L. (2001). The challenge of staffing our schools. *Educational Leadership,* 58(8), 12–17.

Education of teachers in New College: The first four years. (1936). *Teachers College Record,* 38(1), 3–15.

Engelmann, S., Bruner, E., Hanner, S., Osborn, J., Osborn, S., & Zoref, L. (1995). *Reading Mastery.* Columbus, OH: SRA/McGraw-Hill.

Freire, P. (1970/2000). *Pedagogy of the oppressed.* New York: Continuum.

Giroux, H. (1983). *Theory and resistance in education: A pedagogy for the opposition.* South Hadley, MA: Bergin & Garvey.

Greene, M. (1976). Challenging mystification: Educational foundations in dark times. *Educational Studies,* 7(1), 9–29.

Hooks, b. (1994). *Teaching to transgress: Education as the practice of freedom.* Boston, MA: South End.

Horkheimer, M. (1937). Traditionelle und kritische Theorie. *Zeitschrift für Sozialforschung,* 6, 245–292.

Horkheimer, M. (1972). *Critical theory: Selected essays.* New York: Continuum.

Hursh, D. (2005). The growth of high-stakes testing in the USA: Accountability, markets, and the decline in educational equity. *British Educational Research Journal 31*(5), 605–622.

Ingersoll, R.M. (2002). The teacher shortage: A case of wrong diagnosis and wrong prescription. *NASSP Bulletin,* 86(631), 16–31.

Jones, B. (2008). Script change for neoliberalism. Socialist Worker. http://socialistworker.org/2008/09/23/script-change-for-neoliberalism. Accessed 2 October 2008.

Jordan, N. (2005). Basal readers and reading as socialization: What are children learning? *Language Arts,* 82(3), 204–213.

Kaestle, C.F., & Lodewick, A.E. (Eds.). (2007). *To educate a nation: Federal and national strategies of school reform.* Lawrence, KS: University Press of Kansas.

Kilpatrick, W. (Ed.). (1933). *The educational frontier.* New York: Appleton-Century-Crofts.
Kincheloe, J. (2008). *Critical pedagogy primer.* (2nd ed.). New York: Peter Lang.
Kliebard, H. (1986). *The struggle for the American curriculum 1893–1958.* Boston, MA: Routledge & Kegan Paul.
Kotz, D.M. (2002). Globalization and neoliberalism. *Rethinking Marxism, 14*(2), 64–79.
Maier, J.B. (1988). *Contribution to a critique of critical theory.* In J. Marcus & Z. Tar (Eds.), *Foundations of the Frankfurt School of Social Research.* (pp. 29–54). New Brunswick, NJ: Transaction Books.
Marcus, J., & Tar, Z. (Eds.). (1988). *Foundations of the Frankfurt School of Social Research.* New Brunswick, NJ: Transaction Books.
Marcuse, H. (1968). *Negations: Essays in critical theory.* Boston, MA: Beacon Press.
McLaren, P. (2000). *Che Guevara, Paulo Freire, and the pedagogy of revolution.* Lanham, MD: Rowman & Littlefield.
McNeil, L. (2000). *Contradictions of school reform: Educational costs of standardized testing.* New York: Routledge.
Meyer, R. (2004). Shifting to political action in literary research and teacher education. *English Education, 36*(2), 134–140.
Morrison, K. (2007). Shaking foundations. Rethinking Schools Online. http://www.rethinking-schools.org/archive/21_04/shak214.shtml. Accessed 4 October 2008.
Nelson, T., & Jones, B.A. (2007). The end of "public" in public education. *Teacher Education Quarterly, 34*(2), 5–10.
Newmann, F.M. (1975). *Education for citizen action: Challenge for secondary curriculum.* Berkeley, CA: McCutchan.
O'Quinn, E. (2005–2006). Critical literacy in democratic education: Responding to sociopolitical tensions in U.S. schools. *Journal of Adolescent & Adult Literacy, 49*(4), 260–267.
Olsen, B. (2005). *Center X: Where research and practice intersect for urban school professionals: A portrait of the teacher education program at the University of California, Los Angeles.* In P.M. Jenlink & K.E. Jenlink (Eds.) *Portraits of teacher preparation: learning to teach in a changing America,* pp. 33–51. Lanham, MD: Rowman & Littlefield.
Parker, L. (1984). Henry Giroux's tenure decision. *Psychology and Social Theory, 4,* 68–70.
Rodgers, C.R. (2006). "The turning of one's soul"—Learning to teach for social justice: The Putney Graduate School of Teacher Education. *Teachers College Record,* 108(7), 1266–1295.
Rugg, H. (1929–1932). *Man and his changing society: The Rugg social science series of the elementary school course (vols. 1–6).* Boston, MA: Ginn.
Rugg, H. (1952). *The teacher of teachers: Frontiers of theory and practice in teacher education.* New York: Harper & Brothers.
Shea, C.M., & Henry, C.A. (1986). Who's teaching the social foundations courses? *Journal of Teacher Education, 37*(2), 10–15.
Shor, I. (1980). *Critical teaching and everyday life.* Chicago, IL: University of Chicago Press.
Shor, I. (2000). *Education is politics: Critical teaching across differences, K–12.* Portsmouth, NH: Boynton/Cook.
Sleeter, C. (2008). Equity, democracy, and neoliberal assaults on teacher education. *Teaching and Teacher Education, 24*(8), 1947–1957.
SRA/McGraw-Hill. (2000). *Open Court Teacher Edition.* Worthington, OH: McGraw-Hill.
Stanley, W.B. (1985). Social reconstructionism for today's social education. *Social Education, 49*(5), 384–389.
Tozer, S., & Mcaninch, S. (1987). Four texts in social foundations of education in historical perspective. *Educational Studies, 18*(1), 13–33
Uchitelle, L., Norris, F., & Olsen, E. (2008). Echoes of a dismal past. [Video File]. Video posted to http://video.on.nytimes.com/?fr_story=6e955c67a19791605b18eb8131fe31b4c0eb6252. Accessed 8 October 2008.
Zeichner, K., & Liston, D.P. (1990). Traditions of reform in US teacher education. *Journal of Teacher Education, 41*(2), 3–20.

Chapter 2
Contextualizing the Madness: A Critical Analysis of the Assault on Teacher Education and Schools

Joe L. Kincheloe

2.1 Introduction

I have never been particularly impressed with teacher education in the United States during its relatively short history. Make no mistake, there have been moments of brilliance with John Dewey, George Counts, Harold Rugg, the countless other luminaries that followed them, and the inspired teacher educators who operate with little appreciation in the contemporary era. At the same time that I make a sweeping indictment of too much of what has passed as teacher education, I would say the same thing about the history of American higher education in general. For many of the same reasons, teacher education and the liberal arts and sciences have often failed to engage their students in a rigorous and complex education that prepares them for professional and civic competence in a democratic society.

My criticism of higher education in general is important in this chapter and in this book, as much of the criticism leveled against teacher education by politicians and other members of the academy is patently unfair and elitist. While there is much to criticize about teacher education and higher education in general, many of the attacks on teacher education emanate from an impoverished view of teaching and learning and the complexity of the educational process in a democratic society. Its elitism comes from a condescending attitude toward teachers and the applied dimension of pedagogy. With these caveats delineated, a discussion of the contemporary assault on schools and teacher education can proceed.

This chapter will discuss those forces in the contemporary *Zeitgeist* that operate to undermine rigorous forms of teacher education and teaching. At the end of the first decade of the twenty-first century, critical pedagogical teacher educators who support a scholarly rigorous, practical, socially just, and democratic teacher education are not happy with what they see going on around them. Critical teacher educators live in a time when there are continuing efforts to destroy the very concept of a professional teacher education. In a Dickensian best-of-times, worst-of-times

J.L. Kincheloe
McGill University

S.L. Groenke and J.A. Hatch (eds.), *Critical Pedagogy and Teacher Education in the Neoliberal Era: Small Openings*, DOI 10.1007/978-1-4020-9588-7_2, © Springer Science+Business Media B.V. 2009 motif, we concurrently witness brilliant attempts to reform the field from within. In order to operate on such a rugged and dangerous landscape, critical teacher educators will need a nuanced understanding of the sociocultural and political economic forces attempting to deprofessionalize teaching. Such deprofessionalization efforts serve larger ideological goals in the culture wars that still rage in the United States. In this context, it is fascinating to appreciate the threat that a justice-oriented, scholarly, and professional teacher education poses to dominant power brokers in the society.

Following a narrow ideological agenda, the Bush Administration sought to undermine public education one piece at a time—always, of course, in the name of improving it. This deprofessionalization of teaching has been, and continues to be, a central dimension of a larger right-wing effort to, in effect, do away with any serious type of teacher education. Throughout the 1980s and 1990s, anti-public education groups worked for the deprofessionalization of teachers. The movement had made relatively little progress until the election of George W. Bush in 2000. As part of his larger plan for public education, Bush funded these groups with millions of dollars.

With new support at the highest levels of government and new financial resources, proponents of deprofessionalization formed the American Board for Certification of Teacher Education (ABCTE) to promote a simplistic form of teacher certification characterized by few requirements. At the same time that right-wing operatives claim that schools and teachers are failing and need higher standards to promote "educational excellence," they throw their full weight behind efforts to undermine high standards in the professional preparation and certification of teachers (Coles, 2003; WEAC, 2004). Such a schizophrenic scheme fits well larger efforts to standardize all knowledge taught in schools, reduce educational funding and support, test and measure, proclaim failure, and then work for the corporatization and privatization of public schools in America.

A grotesque form of not only anti-intellectualism but also anti-scholarly fervor is observable in twenty-first-century America. Critical pedagogy and critical teacher education are not only caught in the social tsunami of this impulse but also in the flood of antisocial justice assaults on social institutions and reform of any type. Of course, such tides have engendered a backlash from millions of Americans, but the response to such irrationality has yet to substantively affect teacher education, educational policy, and pedagogical practice in most US schools. This assertion in no way should be taken as an assault on teachers who are underpaid, underappreciated, and often inadequately prepared for what is unmistakably one of the hardest jobs imaginable. Those teachers who succeed in such a position, who reach students and bring them into a community of learners and cultural workers are truly heroic figures. This chapter examines the nature of the madness surrounding the assault on intelligence and thus teacher education and schooling from a critical pedagogical perspective. In the following section, I will historically contextualize the emergence of what I have referred to elsewhere as the recovery movement in American cultural politics and its impact on American education.

2.2 The Madness: Recovering Unconsciousness

Beginning in the first decades of the twentieth century and reaching its apex by the middle of the century, peoples around the world from the Middle East, India, Southeast Asia, and Africa began to rebel against their colonization by European and ultimately American power wielders. Such movements captured the imagination of many reformers in the United States and by the middle of the 1950s, the so-called liberation movements were taking shape especially around issues of racial oppression. Martin Luther King, who as a doctoral student at Boston University had studied the history of anticolonial tactics employed by Mohandas Gandhi against British colonialism in India, was emerging as a leader in the nascent Civil Rights Movement. A study of King's short career reveals the depth of influence the global anticolonial movements had on his vision of the Civil Rights Movement in the United States. Over the next 20 years the perceived success of the Civil Rights Movement would help initiate similar liberation movements among women, Latinos, Native Americans, gay rights advocates, those who opposed the war in Vietnam, and many other groups. Again, while progress was made by all of these movements, many Americans sensed that the movements were more successful than their reality and were, thus, severely threatened by the new social order they deemed to be taking shape around them.

By the mid-1970s, a conservative counterreaction—especially in the United States—to these liberation movements was taking shape with the goals of "recovering" what was perceived to be lost in these movements (Gresson, 1995, 2004; Kincheloe et al., 1998; Rodriguez & Villaverde, 2000). Thus, the politics, cultural wars, and educational and psychological debates, policies, and practices of the last 3 decades cannot be understood outside of these efforts to "recover" white supremacy, patriarchy, class privilege, heterosexual "normality," Christian dominance, and the European intellectual canon. These are some of the most important defining concerns of our time, as every social and educational issue is refracted through their lenses. Any view of education conceived outside of this framework becomes a form of ideological mystification. This process of ideological mystification operates to maintain present dominant-subordinate power relations by promoting particular forms of meaning making. In this colonial context, ideological mystification often involves making meanings that assert that non-European peoples are incapable of running their own political and economic affairs and that colonial activity *was* a way of taking care of these incapable peoples.

Right-wing educational policy was directly connected to this larger recovery movement, as it sought to eliminate the anticolonial, antiracist, anti-patriarchal, and diversity affirming dimensions of progressive education and curriculum development. Understanding the way some educators were using education to extend the goals of the worldwide anticolonial movement and the American liberation movements in particular, right-wing strategists sought to subvert the public and civic dimensions of schooling. Instead of helping to prepare society for a socially mobile and egalitarian democracy, education in the formulation of the right-wing recovery redefined schooling as a private concern. The goal of this private concern was not to produce socially informed teachers or graduate "good citizens," but to provide abstract individuals the tools for socioeconomic mobility.

The progressive idea of helping marginalized *groups* such as African-Americans become socially mobile was not the same goal as facilitating individual mobility. In fact the two attempts often came into direct conflict. In the right-wing recovery project, the promotion of the mobility of marginalized groups was a form of social engineering that perverted the basic goals of education. The promotion of the mobility of abstract individuals in this conceptual context was a tribute to the basic American value of meritocracy. Only the intelligent and virtuous deserved mobility and such individuals according to the recovery movement's cognitive theorists, Herrnstein and Murray of *Bell Curve* (1994) fame, tended to be white and upper-middle class. Employing the rhetoric of loss, the promoters of recovery spoke of the loss of standards, discipline, civility, and proper English. Because of the pursuit of racial/cultural difference and diversity, America itself was in decline. In the rhetoric of recovery, the notion of loss and falling standards was always accompanied by strategically placed critiques of affirmative action, racial preferences, and multiculturalism. Though the connection was obvious, plausible deniability was maintained—"we are not racists, we only want to protect our country from the destruction of its most treasured values."

With the emergence of this ideology of recovery in the last quarter of the twentieth century, the very concept of government with its "public" denotations began to represent the victory of minorities and concerns for the inequities of race, class, gender, and colonialism. "Big government" began to become a code phrase for anti-white male social action in the recovery discourse. Indeed, in this articulation it was time to get it off "our" backs. Thus, privatization became more than a strategy for organizing social institutions. Privatization was the ostensibly deracialized term that could be deployed to signify the recovery of white, patriarchal supremacy, as well as put unprecedented monies in the hands of the already well-to-do. In the same way, the word, "choice", could be used to connote the right to "opt out" of government-mandated "liberal" policies. Like good consumers, "we" (Americans with traditional values) choose life, privatized schools, the most qualified job applicants, and Christian values over the other "products."

In the grander sense, therefore, "we" (white male Americans) chose the private space over the disturbing *diversity* of the public space. In rejecting the public space, the right wing rejected the political domain—a choice that resonated with many conservative white Christians throughout the nation. Indeed, any political action on our part, the advocates of recovery asserted, will in effect be antipolitical. We will work to make sure that traditional "political types" be defeated by antigovernment agents who will work to undermine the public space with its social programs, infrastructures, and, of course, schools. Thus, we witness a decline in interest in the political and the academic. Indeed, politicians who are not born-again Christians working to dismantle the public space and academics who are not denouncing the academy are not our types of people. In the recovery, the institutions of public government and education must go. Both institutions, the right-wing argument goes, display the tendency to undermine the best interests of Christian white people—white males in particular.

2.3   The Recovery in Twenty-First-Century Education

Framing this phenomenon in historical context, we can better understand the right-wing use of programs such as No Child Left Behind (NCLB) in the twenty-first century as a legal tool to reconfigure the federal government's role as the promoter of equality and diversity in the educational domain. Though it was promoted as a new way of helping economically marginalized and minority students, such representations were smoke screens used to conceal its mission of recovery of traditional forms of dominant power. In this power context, NCLB has been quite cavalier about the inequity between poor and well-to-do school districts and even schools within particular districts. The right-wing public discourse about education successfully erased questions of race and class injustice from consideration. The fact that 40% of children in the United States live in poor or low-income conditions is simply not a part of an educational conversation shaped by the rhetoric of recovery. The understanding that students who are upper-middle class and live in well-funded schools and/or school districts have much more opportunity for academic and socioeconomic success than students from poor contexts is fading from the public consciousness in the twenty-first century.

The realization that inequality is deemed irrelevant even when we understand that socioeconomic factors are the most important predictor of how students perform on high-stakes standardized tests is distressing. In this context, we begin to discern that in a system driven by such high-stakes tests, it was not hard to predict who was most likely to succeed and fail. In the name of high standards and accountability, the recovery project scored great victories. "We can't let these 'incompetents' get by with such bad performance," right-wing ideologues righteously proclaimed, "it degrades the whole system." As they cried their crocodile tears for poor and marginalized students in their attempt to hide their real agenda and garner support of naïve liberals for their educational plans, they concurrently supported deep cuts in any programs designed to help such students. Such actions represented, of course, the antithesis of what critical pedagogy promoted and promotes.

During the George W. Bush presidency, for example, Americans witnessed cuts in food stamps, Temporary Assistance for Needy Families, nutrition programs for children, childcare, the enforcement of laws for child support, child health insurance, and the Low-Income Home Energy Assistance Program. And this does not include the education programs that helped poor and marginalized students that were summarily eliminated. The privatization-based voucher programs proposed as means of helping students from poor families avoid failing schools and gain access to a higher-quality education have not worked. The price of attending many private schools, especially the elite ones, is far more costly than the worth of the meager voucher. Most students from poor families even with their vouchers are still not able to afford private education, not to mention meet the high standardized-test score requirements such schools require. Such critical pedagogical issues of equity are, of course, not typically a part of the truncated public conversation about vouchers and private schooling.

Not one of the right-wing educational proposals has dealt honestly with issues of inequality. With a wink and a nod, they offer suggestions that have little to do with the committed work needed to help improve the possibility of academic success for poor and racially marginalized students. The Heritage Foundation (Karp, 2002; Hartman, 2002), for example, responding to the question, how do we improve marginalized student school performance and help get them out of poverty, has suggested as follows:

- Get rid of "progressive education" and in its stead demand basic skill teaching—progressive education is defined here as any pedagogy that starts "where students are" taking into account student needs rather than imposing a standardized curriculum from outside.
- Promote high-stakes testing.
- Replace principals who complain about not having enough funds with ones who do not.
- Fire staff who do not believe in the mission of such traditional forms of schooling.

Such suggestions serve the recovery ideology well, as they guarantee the underfunding of poor schools, the use of failed pedagogies, and the failure of marginalized students. With such policies in place, we can scientifically "certify" the inferiority of students from disenfranchised backgrounds. The "naturally superior" will take their proper places in the scientific, technological, academic, and professional marketplace. Meritocracywill have worked, right-wing ideologues will proclaim (Coles, 2003).

Such faux-meritocratic educational policies have been designed to "fix" the academic race. Standardized curricula and standards-based assessments not only censor diverse perspectives (read, critical), but they also make sure the culturally and socioeconomically privileged have their advantages officially validated. Indeed, several researchers have identified a tendency for poor and minority students to drop out at higher rates as standardized test scores rise (McNeil, 2000; Horn & Kincheloe, 2001). In the name of standards and quality education, minor and easily addressed intellectual characteristics of students of color take on monumental importance. Verb-ending usage by some African-American and Latino students becomes "empirical proof" of their writing problems and even English language deficiency (Fox, 1999). No matter how brilliant other dimensions of their writing and language usage may be, they are often described as not being "academic material."

I have known of, or have taught, scores of minority students who brought such writing tendencies to school with them but quickly dealt with them when given a chance in teacher education and other disciplines. Understanding such tendencies in a larger socioeconomic and cultural context, they came to appreciate how such cultural characteristics would be unfairly used against them and other African-American, Latino, and Native American students. In recovery-grounded educational contexts, existing forms of inequality have been allowed to continue and with the implementation of NCLB and standardization policies, new forms of inequity developed. Educators concerned with promoting rigorous academic work along with understanding and help for economically and culturally marginalized students have faced ever-expanding institutionalized obstacles. The recovery of white supremacy, patriarchy, and class elitism entered a new educational phase in the era of NCLB and other policies promoted during the George W. Bush administration.

2.4 The Madness of Positivism and Corporatization: Evolving Forms of Rational Irrationality

The educational reforms emerging from the recovery movement have reflected a worldview and a perspective on knowledge and teaching in particular that early critical theorists referred to as a form of rational irrationality. In 2002, NCLB, for example, specifically endorsed an educational research limited to evidence-based scientific methods—positivist science—and insisted that only teaching strategies "proven to work" by such methods be used in schools. Positivism is an epistemological position that values objective, scientific knowledge produced in rigorous adherence to the scientific method. In this context, knowledge is worthwhile to the extent that it describes objective data that reflect the world.

The term "positivism" began to be used widely in the nineteenth century. French philosopher August Comte popularized the concept, maintaining that human thought had evolved through three states: the theological stage, where truth rested on God's revelation; the metaphysical stage, where truth was derived from abstract reasoning and argument; and the positivistic stage, where truth arose from scientifically produced knowledge. Comte sought to discredit the legitimacy of nonscientific thinking that failed to take "sense knowledge" (knowledge obtained through the senses and empirically verifiable) into account. He saw no difference between the *ways* knowledge should be produced in the physical sciences and in the human sciences, and he believed one should study sociology just like biology. This had a dramatic impact on the way scholars would approach social, educational, and psychological research. Social knowledge and information about humans would be subjected to the same decontextualizing forces as the study of rocks. Social and behavioral scientists would pull people out of their cultural setting and study them in laboratory-like conditions (Kincheloe, 1993).

The incursion of the federal government under the George W. Bush administration into the legislative mandating of research methods marked the beginning of a new era in the politics of knowledge or the so-called science wars. Indeed, with these actions the United States moved into a new era where research methodology had become a legal issue with right-wing organizations attempting to exclude scientific methods attuned to the diversity, specificity, and contextualized dimensions of human experience. In this situation, government became an arbiter of what we are allowed to know. After the signing of NCLB into law in January, the Congress passed the Educational Sciences Reform Act in October 2002 to consolidate and expand the role of evidence-based, neo-positivist research in federal education policymaking. The epistemological insights of critical pedagogy were desperately needed in this new, mad politics of knowledge.

Again, the doublespeak of the right-wing agenda revealed itself, as in the name of a small and unobtrusive government, the Bush administration mandates not only standardized curricula but also regulated what research methods could be used to study schools. The nation had never witnessed such restrictive forms of federal governmental control in the sphere of education. Educators gained a new vantage point on the meaning of a science driven by dominant power. The right-wing educational strategy connected to this dominant power covered all its bases. At the same time, it plotted to create privatized corporate schools; it made sure that the public ones also towed the ideological line. No matter what way the struggle for privatization eventually works out, right-wing politicos know that because of the processes mandated in the Bush administration, they will continue to dominate schooling in America in the coming years with authoritarian, antidemocratic policies that strategically eliminate anyone or any knowledge that counters their right-wing, positivist agenda (Fleischman et al., 2003; Foley & Voithofer, 2003; Lather, 2003).

The positivistic authoritarian nature of such science policies can be seen clearly in the legacy of the Bush Administration's Reading First program. Educational leaders and researchers who raised questions about the scientific methods used to study the reading process and the performance of students and teachers in learning and teaching reading were excluded from even presenting their opinions to Congress or the Department of Education. In the public conversation about reading and the teaching of reading that developed around Reading First, ideological zealots established a McCarthy-like blacklist. Long-recognized experts on reading who use qualitative research methods were no longer welcome in the community of reading scholars. At the same time, particular journals, terms, and concepts were not allowed in the conversation, as federal monies were provided only to those who pledge allegiance to the flag of positivism and the exclusive teaching of, in this case, phonics-based reading methods (Murray, 2002; Coles, 2003).

The origins of the Bush federal educational policy that deployed a science of dominant power can be observed in right-wing educational movements of the last 3 decades (see Kincheloe, 1983). An immediate predecessor involves then Governor George W. Bush's educational policies in Texas in the 1990s. Numerous consultants were brought to the Governor's Mansion in Austin, most of who were authors of books published by McGraw-Hill. All of the scholars and political operatives who participated in the Texas conversation called for evidence-based research that led to standardized teaching and evaluation methods in Texas schools. Since most of the research pointed to the need for McGraw-Hill textbooks, the company made a fortune in the process producing phonics-based scripted programs to be read by teachers to their classes (Trelease, 2003). Throughout the Bush administration, this positivistic, standardized, financially lucrative process of educational research and reform was transmitted to the federal governmental level.

Thus, while operating in the name of objective science, the right-wing educational agenda is profoundly influenced by corporate money and power. Again, positivism, privatization, and corporate influence have joined together in a sordid ideological ménage à trois. In fact, the Bush administration's educational proposals looked like profit enhancement plans for McGraw-Hill and other corporations. In the first 8 years of twenty-first-century education, dollars were spent on testing, teacher manuals, and textbooks, and not on efforts to promote equity and equal educational funding between rich and poor districts. The need for such a shift in funding, of course, was promoted by an evidence-based science that claims objectivity and intellectual rigor.

Indeed, such positivist research proclaims that because of the low abilities of African-American, Latinos, and poor whites from these low-income districts, there is little that can be done to help them (Kincheloe et al., 1996). Educators, the argument goes, might as well forget trying to educate such students in such a way that they can achieve socioeconomic mobility and instead focus their attention on raising the test scores of those who *are* capable of learning. Thus, NCLB mandated the creation of over 200 new tests. The federal government spent $400 million over a 6-year period to develop such tests and another $7 billion to implement them in all states. The coffers of the corporate cronies runneth over.

The first day George W. Bush assumed the presidency in 2001, he invited a group of "educational leaders" to the White House. The leaders consisted mainly of Fortune 500 CEOs. A central player, of course, was Harold McGraw III, the chair of McGraw Hill. So central was McGraw to the educational reform process that he and his company were in collusion with the "objective" researchers producing the data used to justify particular Bush educational policies. A cursory reading of George W. Bush's educational policies as governor of Texas and as president always finds the McGraws at the center of decision making. Even before Bush became governor of Texas, Harold McGraw Jr. was a board member of the Barbara Bush Foundation for Family Literacy. Bush's first secretary of education, Rod Paige, was the "Harold W. McGraw Jr. Educator of the Year" during his tenure as superintendent of schools in Houston.

George W. Bush's educational relationship with the McGraws and McGraw-Hill was similar to his oil and gas relationship with the late Ken Lay and Enron. Indeed, the relationship between the Bushes and McGraws goes back three generations to the friendship that developed between grandfather Sen. Prescott Bush and publishing tycoon James McGraw Jr., the uncle of Harold McGraw Jr. The two met in the 1930s on Jupiter Island off the east coast of Florida, an exclusive vacation spot for the northeast elite of the day. George H.W. Bush maintained the relationship with Harold McGraw Jr. and the relation extended to the third generation with George W. Bush and Harold McGraw III. The first President Bush in the early 1990s awarded Harold McGraw Jr. the highest award in the promotion of literacy for his contributions to the cause of reading. Harold McGraw III was appointed to the Bush transition advisory panel after the 2000 election. The connections between the two families go on and on as numerous Bush administration officials traveled back and forth between service to the president and lucrative positions at McGraw-Hill.

The influence of McGraw-Hill on the National Reading Panel's (NRP) report is a compelling example of the impact of corporate power on knowledge production about education. The NRP was commissioned by Congress in the late 1990s to study the existing research on the teaching of reading in order to inform the contentious debate over reading pedagogy in the United States. While there were extensive problems with the report of the NRP around issues of methodology, the panel's dismissal of concerns with reading comprehension, and the panel's lack of theoretical/philosophical diversity, the most egregious problem involved the reporting of the panel's findings. The report was presented in three formats: (1) the report of the subgroups—500 pages of data including the studies on reading analyzed and the findings of the panel; (2) a 15 minute video that claimed to summarize the panel's findings; (3) a 32-page pamphlet that "summarized" the larger report. Importantly, it was this pamphlet that was used as the source employed by legislators to mandate reading curriculum and pedagogy.

The problem is that the short pamphlet presented recommendations for teaching reading that did not match the conclusions put forward in the report of the subgroups. The larger report warned that the teaching of phonics does not affect reading comprehension; the pamphlet in direct contradiction promoted phonics teaching maintaining that phonics instruction is the scientifically proven best method for teaching reading. It seems more than just a little suspicious that the NRP summary was composed in part by Widmeyer-Baker, the public relations company that McGraw-Hill employs to promote its phonics-based Open Court reading program. When positivism and scientific objectivity are the words de jour, such corporate influence is especially troubling.

The pamphlet, not the larger report of the NRP, was used as the basis for educational legislation at both state and federal levels concerning the teaching of reading. In this context, the Bush administration helped pass legislation that provided $1 billion a year for literacy education (the Early Literacy Initiative) for a 6-year period. To administer the allocation of such monies, President Bush picked McGraw-Hill DISTAR program promoter, Christopher Doherty—DISTAR is McGraw-Hill's scripted literacy program. In light of these dynamics, McGraw-Hill came to be known on Wall Street as a Bush stock and increased its valuation because of the policies described here. Obviously, corporate-driven educational policies produce significant profits for those with political influence (Karp, 2002; Scripted Learning, 2002; Metcalf, 2002; Eisenhart & Towne, 2003; Garan, 2004).

2.5 Christian Political Fundamentalism's Contribution to the Madness: Right-Wing Evangelicalism and Anti-Intellectualism

As we attempt to understand the madness behind the right-wing assault on intellect and schooling *that is not a form of indoctrination*, the rise of Christian political fundamentalism emerges as a key dimension of this process. Political fundamentalism emerges at different stages in the twentieth century with the convergence of a fundamentalist theological perspective with right-wing politics. While expressions of political fundamentalism can be observed from the 1920s through the 1960s, the most recent expressions of political fundamentalism dovetail smoothly with the aforementioned recovery movement. Political fundamentalism's textual literalism and black-and-white view of the world fit seamlessly into the recovery context with its efforts to protect "traditional values" and "America as a fundamentalist Christian nation."

Diversity and respect for the viewpoints of non-Western peoples, men and women oppressed by colonialism, individuals from differing social classes, genders, and sexualities, etc. demand that multiple perspectives be entertained and taken seriously. In such a situation, critical theoretical/pedagogical modes of complex comparative analysis, a sense of multiplicity, interpretative skills, and knowledge in diverse contexts and domains are needed. Recovery-based political fundamentalism offers a way out of this complexity and ambiguity for "true believers," as it promotes the simplicity of literalism. In this social and theological configuration, individuals no longer have to grapple with textual meanings or the historical and social contexts in which a text has been produced. All the believer has to do is trust in God and accept things as they seem to be on the surface. Objects in the rearview mirror are exactly as they appear. Thus, within fundamentalism and other social dynamics as well, we can observe the recovery of a naïve realism that simply ignores the deeper questions of meaning that attend any form of social, cultural, political, theological, and educational activity (Rycenga, 2001; Gresson, 2004).

Very importantly in this recovery context, the social and political influence of fundamentalist literalism is strengthening. Near the end of the first decade of the twenty-first century:

- Over 70 million Americans call themselves evangelicals, millions of others share beliefs with this group.
- Four out of ten view the Bible as the literal word of God.
- Eighty-four percent believe that Jesus is the son of God.
- Eight out of ten believe they will stand before God on Judgment Day and will face consequences based on the Creator's decision.
- One half believe that angels exist.
- Over 66% openly say they have made an allegiance to Jesus.
- Fifty-nine percent believe in the literal truth of the Book of Revelations description of the Rapture (Prothero, 2003; Hedges, 2006; Sheler, 2006).

My point here is not to condemn Christianity or any other religious tradition. There is great diversity under the mantle of Christianity and even evangelicalism. Instead, I am attempting to illustrate the political, theological, and educational relationship that perpetuates anti-intellectualism, fear of diversity of all forms, and a rejection of a critical multiperspectival teacher education in particular and teaching and learning in general. The literalism and fear of scholarship as a tool to undermine belief structures in contemporary Christian political fundamentalism reinforce the regressive politics and indoctrination-based education of the right-wing recovery movement.

Whenever any text is interpreted literally without the benefit of historical, social, and cultural contextualization and its relationship with other texts, much understanding and meaning is lost. The study of these dynamics of interpretation and meaning-making is simply not important in the collective consciousness of the political fundamentalists. Part of the explanation for this involves the vicious anti-intellectualism and even antirationality of many—certainly not all—of the political fundamentalists in question. A mature theology examines the process by which canonized and non-canonized religious texts were written, the lives and times of the authors, the multiple contexts of which they were a part, linguistic and sociopolitical factors in the translation process, and other such complex dynamics.

Rigorous scholars of Christianity, Judaism, Islam, Hinduism, Buddhism, and other religions understand that these are difficult and complex questions. The writers of the four Christian gospels, for example, took as all researchers do a variety of written and oral sources and synthesized them into a narrative about the life of Jesus. And as with all research, the gospel writers employed creative processes to transform their data into a narrative form. They left some information out and emphasized data that fit into the narrative format they had most likely unconsciously chosen for their presentation. Which texts were included in the Bible and which ones were left out is another profoundly complex issue, as theological scholars study the arguments and politics surrounding how such choices for inclusion or exclusion were made by early church leaders.

As individuals come to understand more and more of these factors, the depth of their understanding of the meaning of a theological tradition and their own investments in that tradition becomes more sophisticated. Such scholarly dynamics are not a part of the political fundamentalist universe and the evangelical tools they produce to win new converts to the fold. Critical observers find this tendency to be highly problematic and even frightening in the kinds of blind faith and zealotry it can produce. Thus, the very idea of dealing with the tough scholarly issues that always accompany theology is antithetical to the Dominionist (Christian fundamentalists who believe that God gave Christian fundamentalists the right to rule over all the world in the Kingdom of God on Earth) and political fundamentalist outlook. The seminaries and the "scholarship" that does take place in the political fundamentalist domain often amount to little more than an effort to find anything that could be taken as evidence for the literal truth of the Bible.

This quest to prove the literal truth of the Bible is itself a highly selective literalism. The late theological scholar William Sloane Coffin (Hedges, 2006) maintained that these selective literalists choose small parts of the Bible that conform to their personal theology and ideology, ignoring, misrepresenting, or fabricating all the other parts. Why, for example, if one accepts the word-by-word veracity of the Bible, many ask, would one eat prohibited shellfish? Such literalist readings are inherently flawed: if the Bible is totally true then, consequently, all of its proclamations would have to be followed to the letter. Or, if one does not accept this set of literalist assumptions, then the scriptures must be studied and interpreted in a profoundly different way—one that studies the conditions of their production, the sociopolitical factors that shaped them, and why a particular text was included as the word of God and another one was not. Theological literacy, regardless of one's beliefs or non-beliefs, becomes more and more important in a society threatened by the extremism of Dominionism and political fundamentalism and their savvy marketing skills displayed in what Shirley Steinberg and I call Christotainment (Steinberg & Kincheloe, 2008).

Thus, once again forms of theological literacy become extremely important in the contemporary sociopolitical-educational context. Moreover, in a globalized context marked by the rise of fundamentalism, the study of comparative religion becomes more and more important in this era if we are not to be misled by religious fear and hate mongers who attack other religious traditions in the effort to build up their own and to justify the exclusion of anything in the school curriculum that could be deemed non-Christian. Contrary to the charge of political fundamentalists with their distortion of court rulings about teaching religion in public schools over the last 5 decades, religion should be addressed in schools in ways that raise theological literacy. Such teaching should not promote a particular faith over others; the Lemon test coming out of the Supreme Court case *Lemon v. Kurtzman* in 1971 ruled that a theology course in public schools should not advance or inhibit religion. Such a goal becomes, of course, in the complexity of the twenty-first-century political and educational landscape extremely hard to accomplish, as political fundamentalists frame a fair analysis of different religious traditions as being intrinsically anti-Christian. Such fundamentalist advocates want nothing less than full religious indoctrination of their beliefs in public schools.

In this bizarre anti-intellectual context, political fundamentalists and Dominionists work to insulate believers from the influences of the secular world. Such insulation creates circumstances where the faithful can live in a fundamentalist community, go to a fundamentalist tax accountant, get fundamentalist marriage counseling, watch fundamentalist television and movies, go to fundamentalist theme parks, vacation at fundamentalist resorts, and send their children to private or public fundamentalist-dominated schools. By carefully staying within such an hermetically sealed educational environment, individuals can go for years without hearing, watching, or reading anything that would challenge their belief structures (Smiga, 2006; Miles, 2006; Taylor, 2006; McKenna, 2006; Chancey, 2007). Thus, a vicious and harmful anti-intellectualism in the world of political fundamentalism is allowed to flourish. Without some moderating contact with diverse viewpoints and insights, the vilification of those who do not accept political fundamentalist doctrine and the education they promote continues to intensify.

2.6 Education as a Politically Contested Space: The Recovery Movement's Deficit Model of Teaching

As numerous critical scholars have written elsewhere, a critical pedagogy appreciates that every aspect of education and every form of educational practice are politically contested spaces (Steinberg, 2001; Kincheloe, 2008). The previous discussion of the political forces constructing contemporary education illustrates the poignancy of this point at the end of the first decade of the twenty-first century.

Shaped by history and challenged by a wide range of interest groups, educational practice is a fuzzy concept as it takes place in numerous settings, is shaped by a plethora of often invisible forces, and can operate even in the name of democracy and justice to be totalitarian and oppressive. Many teacher education students often have trouble with this political dimension and the basic notion that schooling can be hurtful to particular students.

Such students often embrace the institution of education as "good" because in their own experience it has been good to them. Thus, the recognition of these political complications of schooling that often work to produce a "rational irrational education" is a first step for critical pedagogy-influenced educators and advocates of developing a rigorously intellectual, social activist teacher persona. As teachers gain these insights, they understand that cultural, race, class, gender, sexual, and religious forces have shaped all elements of the acts of teaching and learning. They also discover that a central aspect of a just and democratic education involves addressing these dynamics as they systematically manifest themselves (Kincheloe, 2001; Noone & Cartwright, 1996).

These critical political concerns play themselves out quite clearly in deficit representations of students from economically poor and nonwhite backgrounds. In work that comes from recovery movement-influenced educational, social, and psychological research and diverse forms of cultural politics, prospective teachers are taught that not all students can learn. This is the omnipresent deficit model of psychology and pedagogy that undermines so many young lives. The academic and social failure that results from such oppressive assumptions is turned inside out and represented as a *personal* failing. This regressive pedagogical personalization of failure is viewed outside of any larger social or cultural context and then is used to construct a crisis of youth. In this context, Herr (2006) describes the growth industry of "kid fixing" with its emphasis on different types of intervention for different categories of young people. For middle-class children/youth with health insurance, therapy is offered; for poor and minority young people prison is increasingly the solution of choice.

Advocates of a critical pedagogy insist that teacher educators, politicians, and educational leaders must avoid framing the problems of education and its most marginalized students as only psychological (individual) in nature and not socially constructed. Such a form of psychologization works simply to blame the victims of larger cultural problems for their sticky and disempowering predicaments. Such approaches illustrate yet again the decontextualizing tendencies of the various sociopolitical and academic ways of seeing the world analyzed in this chapter, as they substitute individual remedies for larger social problems. Evans and Prilleltensky (2006) maintain that educators and psychologists must learn how social violence is manifested in the lives of individual young people. Such a task is difficult, however, in school systems that are obsessed with testing, labeling, and categorizing children and young people. In such a context, advocates of a critical pedagogy maintain that many teacher educators and school leaders simply ignore the way that categories of child and youth pathology and "risk" are shaped by ideological dynamics in the larger society—e.g., the recovery movement.

In the pathologizing and victim-blaming deficit model of contemporary "recovered" education, the hurtful practices of such an approach can be seen in crystal clarity. Indeed, the reasons many students fail, critical pedagogy asserts, rest more in the social, philosophical/epistemological, cultural, economic, and political configurations of the society than in these attributions of individual deficiencies. How is failure defined? How is aptitude constructed? What is the process by which success gains its meaning in diverse cultures? As critical pedagogues operating as multidisciplinary scholars attempt to answer these questions, we begin to understand the complex ways that such meanings gain widespread acceptance.

In the right-wing political climate of the twenty-first century, many people believe that the only way to deal with these deficit-inscribed students is to "make them shape up" through mindless discipline, regulation, order, and low-level rote memorization of basic academic skills. While not denying that many young people need stability and predictability in their lives, such a call is ultimately an affirmation of "deficitism." This order paradigm gives educators an excuse not to present students marginalized by race or class with a challenging curriculum or to expect more from them academically. Teachers implementing a critical pedagogy avoid such assumptions, as they understand the social and psychological forces that undermine their students' achievement. Such teachers transcend the signifiers of racial or class difference as otherness, danger, chaos, and violence—representations that contribute to the marginalization of economically poor students of color by way of fear (Henke, 2000).

Anderson and Summerfield (2004) tie deficitism and the fear of otherness to the macro-context of contemporary American life. Such representations work to counter attempts to understand that contemporary American society is entering a globalized, multicultural, multi-racial, multi-religious, and multi-classed domain. Racial otherness and often urban inscriptions of diversity in America stand as the gateway to this multilogical emergent society and, as such, must be resisted. The multiplicity of the other is inferior to the monologicality of traditional Americana. Carry me back to Disney's Celebration community in Florida where even the rats are white and all children score above average on standardized tests. In this rightwing, monoculturalist, recovery representation, diversity is not recognized as the emergent American culture but one that must be destroyed before it destroys "us."

2.7 Critical Pedagogy and the Transcendence of Deficitism and Representations of the Marginalized

This chapter's effort to understand the origins of this deficitism and its influence in twenty-first-century teacher education and schooling is central to any effort to implement a rigorous, just, contextually sensitive, empowering critical pedagogy. There are no easy paths, no magic bullets, no one miraculous method that will eliminate the hard work such a process entails. Until such complex understandings of the sociocultural and political economic forces at work in contemporary education are widely cultivated in professional education, students in high-poverty schools will continue to find little opportunity to experience rigorous schoolwork with savvy teachers. Without such insights the term, racial and class diversity, itself will continue to be used as a dirty concept, deployed to denote dangerous and objectionable conditions characterized by trashy people, drugs, violence, dysfunctional families, and filth (NWREL, 1999). Implicit in the representation is that individuals through their own human inadequacy have chosen to live in such conditions. Their dilemma is their own fault—no matter how young they may be—and there is nothing we can do about it. What a horrible burden to place on young people.

Critical pedagogy constructs its philosophical foundation on notions of empowered, professionalized teachers working to cultivate the intellect and enhance the socioeconomic mobility of students by larger sociocultural and political impulses. Teachers in a critical pedagogy conduct research into these social and educational dynamics, design curricula around multiple macro-knowledges of education and the contexts in which it operates and the micro-situations in which their students find themselves in their communities and their schools.

Such teachers build coalitions of scholars in critical pedagogy and related disciplinary areas, teachers, parents, students, community members, professional social service providers and sociopolitical organizations. In this context, teachers who enact a critical pedagogy are serious students of education who apply their insights to promote new educational psychologies/learning theories, new cultural studies of the communities that surround schools and the young people who live in them, and subjugated knowledge derived from organic intellectuals who live and operate in these communities. Such teachers are motivated by the power of ideas to reshape the world in which we operate, the notion that human beings can become far more than they presently are, and the belief that ultimately the fate of humanity is related to these ideas.

This, of course, is no easy feat, and the madness around issues of knowledge, power, and pedagogy discussed here makes it no easier. In order for critical pedagogues to make substantive change, as many Americans as possible will have to understand the recovery movement and its political economic, cultural, religious, and cultural dimensions. The discourse of American life keeps moving to the right long after many predicted that a counterreaction would shift the pendulum back. The right wing has established a radically new "commonsense" in the United States over the last 30 years, a commonsense that is oppressive, bellicose, and exclusive. We have no choice—as critical pedagogues and critical teacher educators we must be able to frame the social reality educators now face in order to change it.

References

Anderson, P., & Summerfield, J. (2004). Why is urban education different than rural and suburban education? In S. Steinberg & J. Kincheloe (Eds.), *19 urban questions: Teaching in the city.* New York: Peter Lang.

Chancey, M. (2007). A textbook example of the Christian right: The national council on Bible curriculum in public schools. *Journal of the American Academy of Religion, 75*, 3, 554–581.

Coles, G. (2003). Learning to read and the "W principle." Rethinking Schools Online http://www.rethinkingschools.org/archive/17_04/wpri174.shtml. Accessed 26 September 2008.

Eisenhart, M., & Towne, L. (2003). Contestation and change in national policy on "scientifically based" education research. *Educational Researcher, 32*, 7, 31–38.

Evans, S., & Prilleltensky, I. (2006). Literacy for wellness, oppression, and liberation. In J. Kincheloe & R. Horn (Eds.), *Educational psychology: An encyclopedia.* Westport, CT: Praeger.

Fleischman, S., Kohlmoos, J., & Rotherham, A. (2003). From research to practice: Moving beyond the buzzwords. Ed Week. http://www.nekia.org/pdf/ed_week_commentary.pdf. Accessed 26 September 2008.

Foley, A., & Voithofer, R. (2003). Bridging the gap? Reading the No Child Left Behind Act against educational technology discourses. Ohio State University. http://www.coe.ohio-state.edu/rvoithofer/papers/nclb.pdf. Accessed 17 October 2008.

Fox, T. (1999). *Defending access: A critique of standards in higher education.* Portsmouth, NH: Boynton.

Garan, E. (2004). *In defense of our children: When politics, profit, and education collide.* Portsmouth, NH: Heinemann.

Gresson, A. (1995). *The recovery of race in America.* Minneapolis, MN: University of Minnesota Press.

Gresson, A. (2004). *America's atonement.* New York: Peter Lang.

Hartman, A. (2002). Envisioning schools beyond liberal and Market ideologies. Z Magazine. http://www.zmag.org/amag/articles/julang02hartman.html. Accessed 27 September 2008.

Hedges, C. (2006). American fascists: The Christian right and the war on America. New York: Free Press.

Henke, S. (2000). *Representations of secondary urban education: Infusing cultural studies into teacher education.* Unpublished doctoral dissertation, Miami University, Oxford, Ohio.

Herr, K. (2006). Problematizing the 'problem' teen: Reconceptualizing adolescent development. In J. Kincheloe & R. Horn (Eds.), *The Praeger encyclopedia of education and psychology.* Westport, CT: Praeger.

Herrnstein, R., & Murray, C. (1994). *The bell curve: Intelligence and class structure in America.* New York: The Free Press.

Horn, R., & Kincheloe, J. (Eds.). (2001). *American standards: Quality education in a complex world—the Texas case.* NY: Peter Lang.

Karp, S. (2002). Let them eat tests. Rethinking Schools Online. http://www.rethinkingschools.org/special_reports/bushplan/eat164.shtml. Accessed 22 September 2008.

Kincheloe, J. (1983). *Understanding the new right and its impact on education.* Bloomington, IN: Phi Delta Kappa.

Kincheloe, J. (1993). *Toward a critical politics of teacher thinking: Mapping the postmodern.* Westport, CT: Bergin & Garvey.

Kincheloe, J. (2001). *Getting beyond the facts: Teaching social studies/social sciences in the twenty-first century.* (2nd ed.). New York: Peter Lang.

Kincheloe, J. (2008). *Critical pedagogy.* (2nd ed.), New York: Peter Lang.

Kincheloe, J., Steinberg, S., & Gresson, A. (Eds.). (1996). *Measured lies: The bell curve examined.* NY: St. Martin's.

Kincheloe, J., Steinberg, S., Rodriguez, N., & Chennault, R. (Eds.). (1998). *White reign: Deploying whiteness in America.* New York: St. Martin's Press.

Lather, P. (2003). This IS your father's paradigm: Government intrusion and the case of qualitative research in education. Ohio State University. http://www.coe.ohio-state.edu/plather/. Accessed 22 September 2008.

McKenna, B. (2006). The prophet motive: U.S. faithful form rich market. The Globe and Mail. http://www.thegolbeandmail.com/servelet/sotry/lac.20060925.rfaith25/tpstory/business. Accessed 22 September 2008.

McNeil, L. (2000). *Contradictions of school reform: Educational costs of standardized testing.* New York: Routledge.

Metcalf, S. (2002). Reading between the Lines. The Nation. http://www.lindahoyt.com/title%20I. htm. Accessed 1 October 2008.

Miles, J. (2006). *The art of The Passion.* In T. Beal & T. Linafelt (Eds.), *Mel Gibson's Bible: Religion, popular culture, and the passion of the Christ.* Chicago, IL: University of Chicago Press.

Murray, A. (2002). Reading's new rules: ESEA demands a scientific approach. Education Update. http://www.ascd.org/publication/ed_update/200208/murray.html. Access 22 September 2008.

Noone, L., & Cartwright, P. (1996). Transforming teachers: Doing a critical literacy pedagogy in a teacher education course. Paper presented at the Australian Teacher Education Association Conference. Launceston, Tasmania. http://www.atea.schools.net.au/ATEA/96conf/noone. html. Accessed 17 October 2008.

North West Regional Educational Laboratory. (NWREL) (1999). Lessons from the cities, Part 2: The strengths of city kids. http://www.nwrel.org/nwedu/winter99/lessons2.html. Accessed 22 September 2008.

Prothero, S. (2003). American Jesus: How the son of God became a national icon. New York: Farrar, Straus, and Giroux.

Rodriguez, N., & Villaverde, L. (2000). *Dismantling white privilege.* New York: Peter Lang.

Rycenga, J. (2001). Dropping in for the holidays: Christmas as commercial ritual at the Precious Moments Chapel. In M. Mazur & K. McCarthy (Eds.), *God in the details: American religion in popular culture.* New York: Routledge.

Scripted Learning: A Slap in the Face? (2002). California Educator. http://ww.cta.org/californiae-ducator/v6:7feature_4.htm. Accessed September 26, 2008.

Sheler, J. (2006). *Believers: A journey into evangelical America.* New York: Penguin.

Smiga, G. (2006). The good news of Mel Gibson's Passion. In T. Beal & T. Linafelt (Eds.), *Mel Gibson's Bible: Religion, popular culture, and the passion of the Christ.* Chicago, IL: University of Chicago Press.

Steinberg, S. (2001). *Multi/intercultural conversations: A reader.* New York: Peter Lang.

Steinberg, S., & Kincheloe, J. (2008). *Christotainment: Selling Jesus through popular culture.* Boulder, CO: Westview.

Taylor, M. (2006). The offense of flesh. In T. Beal & T. Linafelt (Eds.), *Mel Gibson's Bible: Religion, popular culture, and the passion of the Christ.* Chicago, IL: University of Chicago Press.

Trelease, J. (2003). All in the family. http://www.trelease-on-reading.com/whatsnu-bush-mcgraw. html. Accessed 17 October 2008.

Wisconsin Education Association Council. (WEAC) (2004). The American board and fast track certification: An attack on the teaching profession. http://ww.weac.org/pdfs/2003–2004/certi-fication_research.pdf. Accessed 22 September 2008.

Chapter 3
Standards Talk: Considering Discourse in Teacher Education Standards

Nikola Hobbel

3.1 Introduction

My interest in understanding the discursive meanings of national standards in teacher education comes from my early experiences as a high school English teacher and member of our school district's K–12 English/Language Arts standards committee in the early 1990s. Standards-based teaching, at the time, involved collaboration with other teachers on the committee, as we negotiated agreement about what our students should know, and what we would consequently teach. Teachers' voices were integral to the process, and we used our knowledge of our students and the local community's resources to consider appropriate grade-level standards for our students. The process was not perfect: as Bourdieu (1974) suggests, teachers often act as if the language of standards is natural, "full of allusions and shared understandings," and assume that "academic judgments which in fact perpetuate cultural privilege" are "fair" (pp. 39–40). To us, standards-setting seemed a professional, rational exercise concluding in consensus, and we never asked whose standards we were promoting. It seemed we were promoting our own.

Standards today no longer emerge from conversations among colleagues, but instead, from state and national entities that impose narrow conceptions of good teaching on programs and people. Whether teachers and teacher educators are aligning praxis with K–12 content standards (with their associated high-stakes tests), beginning teacher standards, professional teaching standards, or teacher education accreditation standards, we find top-down regulation influencing our efforts. Politicians and policymakers often use the banner of high expectations in order to create public consensus around standards that work more as political maneuvers than as critical, equity-minded reforms.

Perhaps now more than ever, then, it is important for teachers and teacher educators to pay attention to the "language" of standards. Bourdieu (1974) points out the

N. Hobbel
Humboldt State University

S.L. Groenke and J.A. Hatch (eds.), *Critical Pedagogy and Teacher*   37
Education in the Neoliberal Era: Small Openings,
DOI 10.1007/978-1-4020-9588-7_3, © Springer Science+Business Media B.V. 2009

naturalization of a privileged language in teaching, and standards are rapidly becoming a naturalized language about teaching and teacher education. It seems that many policymakers, teachers, and teacher educators in the United States are taking up the notion of standards uncritically. But standards represent a nexus of language, knowledge, and power relationships that needs to be interrogated to fully understand what is at stake in public education in the neoliberal era.

As Ladson-Billings (1998) suggests, national teacher standards discourses are evidence of complex social and political processes that both enable and constrain teachers and teacher educators, especially in terms of preparing teachers for effective, culturally relevant practices. The national governing, professional teacher standards-setting bodies like the National Council for Accreditation of Teacher Education (NCATE) and the Teacher Education Accreditation Council (TEAC) do much to ignore increasing racial segregation in schools and intensifying poverty, and display racial, class, and gender tensions as easily conquerable through the construction of discourses of rationality, professionalism, and egalitarianism.

Ladson-Billings (1998) describes a "political symbolism" that occurs through these discourses—whereas the standards make it look as though structural reform is taking place and true educational equity is a goal, more often than not, nothing changes, especially for historically underserved students and their teachers (p. 257). Understanding the political symbolism of national teacher standards can lead us to envisioning much-needed alternatives that take educational equity-minded reform and the preparation of critically minded, multicultural teachers more seriously.

In this chapter, after a brief overview of NCATE and TEAC, I discuss the standards proposed by NCATE and TEAC with the purpose of explicating the kinds of discursive themes that are present within them, in order to gain a more detailed view of the standards' assumptions and logics. The questions I take up in this chapter include: What political and symbolic purposes do the NCATE and TEAC standards serve? How do NCATE and TEAC standards create rules and ways of reasoning that create a specific kind of common sense? What are the constraints and possibilities inherent in this common sense understanding of teacher preparation?

Instead of arguing for or against teacher education standards, per se, I want to explore the frames of reasoning that act as the NCATE and TEAC standards' underlying assumptions, what I am terming *common sense* in this discussion, and the primary discourses of professionalism, rationality, and egalitarianism that emerge from national teacher education accreditation standards.

3.2   A Brief Overview of NCATE and TEAC

Both NCATE and TEAC offer independent accreditation of programs that prepare educators (teachers, specialists, and administrators). NCATE, founded in 1954, is the more prominent of the two organizations, accrediting over 652 colleges of education and boasting the support of the National Education Association (NEA), the American Association of Colleges of Teacher Education (AACTE), and the

Association for Supervision and Curriculum Development (ASCD), to name three of 33 member organizations (NCATE, 2008). Relatively a newcomer, TEAC was founded in 1997 and currently accredits 59 programs (TEAC, 2008). Both NCATE and TEAC use program standards as gauges to determine whether a program deserves accreditation. In 2008, NCATE and TEAC created a joint "design team" to coordinate their efforts (TEAC, 2008). In fact, this unifying effort reflects an aspect of my argument: that these bodies are not in competition, but are, rather, part of a larger consensus about the efficacy of standards implementation as an effective reform policy.

In an analysis of national education standards in Canada, Portelli and Vibert (1997) indicate that discourses of nationalistic nostalgia and curricular homogenization figure largely into the impetus for promoting standards. These authors argue that in Canada, it seems practical to promote standards as a way to counter educational expectations that are "slipping in comparison to the 'good old days'" (p. 69). It seems that Canada imagines a golden past of rigor in schools, as well as a curriculum agreed to by all. Moreover, it seems that the shadow of the "Other" is present in this discourse, as historically, the notion of slipping standards has emerged during times when the population in schools and universities has become more diverse, indicating a rationalized reaction to an influx of people who are understood as poorer, nonwhite, or non-English-speaking than the established population perceives itself.

In the United States, standards promoted by NCATE and TEAC represent a compromise. This compromise is a negotiation between national ideals and, in the case of schools of education, local definitions of what constitutes good teaching. As Nóvoa (2000) puts it, this is a tension between the needs of "integration and independence" (p. 50). Local entities need integration with state and national ideals in order to symbolically legitimate their activities—to indicate the quality of their programs and communities of practice beyond their immediate regions. Integration offers programs and people an important association with the power of more prominent (i.e., state and national) ideas about what educating teachers means—in other words, integration is the stage on which actions of accountability are played out. On the other hand, independence from these same state and national policies returns legitimacy to the local arenas, symbolically imbuing programs and communities with the power of choice.

Standards offer an interesting attempt at balance between public feelings about what education should do and educators' needs to maintain control over their programs and prestige. As the state increases its control over the curricula of schools of education, integrating its political needs through bureaucratic measures of accreditation and licensing, schools of education vie for their own independence by building national organizations such as NCATE and TEAC in order to stave off the state's influence on their own institutions while simultaneously strengthening a regime of external governance. This tension is negotiated at a time of perceived crisis in education (constructed in similar ways as the Canadian crisis noted above), a time when national discourses center around "accountability" and "choice," and schools of education come under closer administration by the state more than ever.

To better understand the negotiation of tensions and perceived crises that under-gird the NCATE and TEAC standards, a bit of history is necessary.

The major "crisis" noted in histories of teacher education is the publication of *A Nation at Risk* (National Commission on Excellence in Education, 1983), in part because it caused many teacher education institutions and researchers to circle their wagons and take a defensive posture. *A Nation at Risk* characterized public educa-tion in the United States as steadily declining in quality, especially in comparison to European nations and Japan. This report revivified the discourses of the 1950s Cold War era by invoking the race for space and the launching of Sputnik as *the* impetus for earlier educational improvement. Winning an imagined international competition became the impetus for educational improvement.

The end of the Cold War was marked by the fall of the wall in Berlin, and "[a]dvocates of market-driven school reforms sometimes noted that communism's implosion demonstrated the superiority of 'free markets' to organize social activity, including education" (Weiner, 2000, p. 374). Through the late 1970s and 1980s, then, education became viewed as a global financial market (Weiner, 2000), and standards became linked to the notion of market competition in their most popular reforms. Education markets, in turn, were ideologically linked to globalization, within which the logics of competition and exceptionalism reigned. Consequently, "[c]orporate executives were often instrumental in guiding reforms of [public] school systems, which used the language and structure of private enterprise" (Weiner, 2000, p. 375).

This corporate orientation continued to underline the multifaceted support for the standards movement. Thus, the emphasis on higher expectations for students' learning and expectations for "world class" standards that began in the 1950s, as well as an emphasis on "finished products" that continued through the 1980s (Cornbleth & Waugh, 1995) produced a broad-based support for all kinds of national standards in the 1990s: teacher education standards (NCATE and TEAC), curriculum standards (e.g., National Council of Teachers of English (NCTE), National Council of Teachers of Mathematics (NCTM), and National Council for the Social Studies (NCSS)), and professional performance standards (National Board for Professional Teaching Standards (NBPTS)).

My project here is to discuss the standards proposed by NCATE and TEAC with the purpose of explicating the kinds of discursive themes that are present within them, in order to gain a more detailed view of the standards' assumptions and logics. These discursive themes illuminate the tension between integration and indepen-dence, as well as, importantly, the ways in which teacher educators imagine critical and multi-cultural pedagogy. By drawing on a broadly Foucauldian notion of discourse (Foucault, 1972; Groden & Kreiswirth, Szeman, 1994), I hope to make these themes explicit because much is taken for granted in the language of the standards.

The discourses I identify relate to each other intersubjectively; that is, they are interdependent and make a system of reasoning together. In order to discuss them in detail, however, I find it necessary to artificially separate them here. The primary discourses that emerge from national teacher education accreditation standards are those of professionalism, rationality, and egalitarianism.

3.3 The Language Behind the Standards

3.3.1 The Discourse of Professionalism

It seems to have become quite important recently for teachers to be understood as "professionals," regardless of the classed weight of the concept (Metz, 1990), and the racialized interpretations of this term in national teaching standards (Hobbel, 2001). But to understand the value of the discourse of professionalism, we have to understand its uses. This discourse is used across the political spectrum, from both the right and the left wing, for varying purposes:

> The professional teacher seems to cross ideological positions. That image is found in liberal and neoliberal reforms to decentralized school decision-making through teachers who have more autonomy and relation to local community "cultures." From the left, the professionalization of teachers is to promote the emancipatory, empowering potential of education for a democracy. The professional teacher participates with the community and the child in order to reconstruct society. (Popkewitz, 2000, p. 12)

As those on the right employ the professionalism discourse, they also push for the devolution of decision making and responsibility to more and more local spheres. The result is more responsibility for teachers without necessarily more power and resources to implement changes (Whitty et al., 1998). In this aspect of the discourse, the blame for the failure of schools can then be exported from the state to teachers themselves because their classrooms, their lives, and their students represent the end of the line.

On the left, professionalism is rhetorically leveraged as a means to empower teachers, to lay claims for the value of pedagogical content knowledge and the importance of local community contexts. Whether used by the right or the left, this discourse makes it more difficult to understand how else the teacher can be understood and constructed, if not as a professional. Any other construction or possibility becomes obscured. Either way, this is a discourse built from historically raced, classed, and gendered origins which do not allow other national conceptions of the teacher and her work to develop or be raised. Specifically, teachers in the twentieth and twenty-first centuries are seen as monolingual, white, middle-class women who have little or no communal relationships with people of color, people who speak languages other than English, and people who live in poverty. In other words, the discourse of professionalism creates a system of reasoning, a kind of normality, which ultimately sets boundaries around what being a teacher can mean.

The discourse of professionalism is repeated and reconstructed in the NCATE and TEAC standards. Both sets of standards use the term "professional" liberally, with only slight differences in nuance. NCATE aligns its definition of "professional" with the National Board for Professional Teaching Standards (NBPTS), with its emphasis on "commitment to students and their learning" (NBPTS, 2008), community membership, and responsibility. TEAC emphasizes competence, caring, and qualifications in creating the professional teacher (TEAC, 2008, p. 1).

From this, it is evident that the meaning of "professional" is fairly well taken for granted in teacher education standards. The professional is a person with advanced technical training, as in this example from the NCATE standards:

> Candidates include persons preparing to teach, teachers who are continuing their professional development, and persons preparing for other professional roles in schools such as principals, school psychologists, and school library media specialists. (NCATE, 2008, p. 12, footnote 4)

In addition to the formalized and technical training required, the definition of professional extends to actions, sensibilities, and dispositions. NBPTS (an NCATE member organization) provides the foundational discourse of the professional teacher to NCATE, a discourse which

> is centered on professional dispositions, including such actions that will take teachers' work beyond the limits of their paid day: how else will a teacher "communicate regularly with parents and guardians, ... informing them of their child's accomplishments and successes, and educating them about school programs"? How, but outside the regular school day, will a teacher spend time "observing the city council in action; collecting oral histories from senior citizens; studying the ecology of the local environment; visiting a nearby planetarium; drawing the local architecture"? (Hobbel, 2001, p. 6)

In other words, the professional teacher is recognized not only through the use of bureaucratic instruments such as certification and licensure, but also by the actions she takes as a citizen: someone actively involved with the government, environment, science, and the arts. The professional is fairly autonomous, needing little direction or surveillance from and by administrative forces. Beyond this, the professional teacher is also someone who is personable and charismatic, whose care and commitment extend beyond the classroom.

The nature of commitment to students and their learning as well as the notion of caring seem obvious, but their meanings shift according to their use in particular cultural, political, and economic spheres. As McSorley (2000) warns, the notion of caring carries cultural weight, signifying a range of meanings to teachers and their students. The connotations of caring can cause disruptions between the intentions of the caregiver and the function of this caring in the lives of students. To the point, "caring" and "commitment" can be unintentionally expressed in a way that revivifies racial and class hierarchies when this notion is taken up uncritically. Caring can mean, and often does, changing someone for her or his own good, a kind of paternalism. Since there is no call in the standards to reexamine public language, the interpretation of these terms can further oppress schooling practices while simultaneously meeting the demands of professionalism.

Instead of ensuring the egalitarianism to which they seem committed, the arbiters of standards might consequently prove complicit in a sleight of hand, recentering white, middle-class dispositions, sensibilities, and language. The teacher produced by the teacher education standards is a professional who operates logically in the best interests (as she perceives them) of her students, thereby binding herself to the discourse of rationality.

3.3.2   The Discourse of Rationality

This discourse is fashioned from western notions of science and efficiency. The discourse of rationality serves to homogenize teacher education curriculum, to weld unacknowledged political concerns to the supposed neutrality of science, and to promote quality by obscuring material realities. The following TEAC and NCATE standards show us how rationality is built as an argument from an emphasis on attending to research and evidence:

> After institutions have met certain eligibility standards, the Council requires that the program faculty prepares a research monograph, the *Inquiry Brief* [original emphasis], in which it demonstrates and documents that its programs satisfy three principles of quality:
>
> 1) evidence of student learning; 2) evidence that the assessment of student learning is valid; and 3) evidence of the program's own continuous improvement and quality control. (TEAC, 2003)

While TEAC requires an Inquiry Brief of the institutions it accredits, NCATE requires a conceptual framework: both documents require research, argument, and evidence of proof and progress. The conceptual framework(s) provides the following structural elements:

- The mission of the institution and unit
- The unit's philosophy, purposes, professional commitments, and dispositions
- Knowledge bases including theories, research, the wisdom of practice, and education policies
- Performance expectations for candidates, aligning them with professional, state, and institutional standards
- The system by which candidate performance is regularly assessed (NCATE, 2001)

Under the discourse of rationality, science is the primary logic to make sense of teacher education. Theory, evidence, and research provide costuming to teacher education institutions to show, on a national stage, that they are legitimate. Science, as a facet of rationality, allows us to think in a positivistic way about teacher education: that its whole can be divided into parts, that its parts can be accurately measured, and that these measurements can be used to logically develop reforms.

In this sense, rationality obscures those things for which measurements do not suffice—particularly the cultural and political weights of pedagogy, curriculum, and field experiences in teacher education. Rationality in teacher education standards makes the rubbled field of school resources and social, linguistic, racial, and economically heterogeneous students appear even and smooth.

Performances and dispositions, learning and assessment, quality and commitment are all examples of rational terms that can be understood in vastly differing ways. In writing about the rhetoric of educational standards, Portelli and Vibert contend: "This kind of rhetorical language gives the impression of universality or homogeneity and hides the possibility of differences" (1997, p. 71). The notion of progress, taken from regular assessment and "continuous improvement," is also bound up in the discourse of rationality, for if evidence can be gathered and measured, improvement is assumed to follow. Progress becomes problematic as it elides the complexities of historical processes that have become normalized in schools: institutionalized racism; hierarchically valued norms of behavior, learning, and speech; discipline policies, curricular content, pedagogy, and the like. The element of progress in the discourse of rationality provides an opportunity to leverage responsibility for complex events onto teachers and institutions without recognizing larger, systemic and historical influences. Progress and rationality provide policies with blankets that cover inequities.

3.3.3   The Discourse of Egalitarianism

> Set in this context, equality does not seem to be the ideal toward which we should strive; in fact, it leaves previous inequalities intact while at the same time frustrating any attempts to alter those inequalties by characterizing them as attacks on the ideal of equality. (Shannon, 1995, p. 230)

In the quote above, Shannon discusses his reasons for doubting "the value of standards [in this case national reading standards] in attempts to defeat biased schooling" (1995, p. 230). However, the teacher education standards take for granted that it *is* possible to defeat biased schooling through accreditation policies. Throughout their documents, NCATE and TEAC use multiculturalist language and orientation as if material and historical conditions such as funding, geography, quality of field experiences for preservice teachers, and calcified divides in university/school relationships did not exist. By ignoring history and institutional structures, teacher education standards do nothing to dismantle the biased and segregated nature of schools and universities. If they offer little and further act as though anti-oppressive education were merely a matter of exposure to difference, teacher education standards may in fact hide from our view possibilities for our preservice teachers and us.

Let us examine how the discourse of egalitarianism constructs schools of teacher education and the people within them. The NCATE (2007) Unit Standards use inclusion and exposure to difference as ways to meet multicultural concerns, while the TEAC goals invoke rationality and liberal education as cures for racism and ignorance.

In the NCATE (2008) Unit Standards, inclusion is constructed through the repetition and definition of the phrase "all students," as in

> [c]andidates preparing to work in schools as teachers or other school professionals know and demonstrate the content knowledge, pedagogical content knowledge and skills, pedagogical and professional knowledge and skills, and professional dispositions necessary to help all students learn. (NCATE, 2008, p. 12)

What is meant by "all students" is elaborated in a footnote:

> "All students" includes students with exceptionalities and of different ethnic, racial, gender, sexual orientation, language, religious, socioeconomic, and regional/geographic origins. (NCATE, 2008, p. 12)

Interestingly, this list of all conceivable types of difference begs the question, "Different from whom?" As Popkewitz and Lindblad (2000) point out in their description of what they term the "equity problematic," inclusion and exclusion are bound together, even though they are constructed in policy discourses as separate problems. In other words, by including exceptional students and students who differ in their description, the NCATE (2008) Unit Standards continue to underline the segregated nature of education.

In conjunction with the inclusion of all students, exposure to the Other[1] is highlighted in the NCATE Unit Standards, which call for a variety of field experiences and collaboration with families and communities. These families and communities must offer a full range of cultural, linguistic, and socioeconomic markers, in order to legitimate the unit's teacher education activities. The absent presencein this discourse is the assumption that preservice teachers, teacher educators, and programs are not *understood* as sites of diversity; indeed, the subtext is one that presumes whiteness (perhaps rightly) as the norm. Oddly enough, by noticing that teacher education is populated by preservice teachers who are overwhelmingly white and female (Darling-Hammond & Sclan, 1996), the standards envision teacher education in a way that reinscribes difference.

Simultaneously, the standards promote the possibility of progress through the rationalized activities of data collection, research, critique, and improvement plans. By making exposure to those marked as having exceptionalities and those carrying difference a matter of course, a natural activity, the standards ignore material realities such as racially segregated geographies and discursive realities such as Eurocentric ways of knowing (Ladson-Billings, 2000).

Here, the standards create a system of reasoning which draws on progress, rationality, and egalitarianism to establish an arena for teacher education. By arguing for inclusion, the NCATE standards underline exclusion. The TEAC standards execute a similar order:

> Included in the liberal arts is the knowledge of other cultural perspectives, practices, and traditions. TEAC requires evidence that candidates for the degree understand the implications of confirmed scholarship on gender, race, individual differences, and ethnic and cultural perspectives for educational practice. For all persons, but especially for prospective teachers, the program must yield an accurate and sound understanding of the educational significance of race, gender, individual differences, and ethnic and cultural perspectives. (TEAC, 2008)

Additionally, TEAC bolsters the importance of regimes of truth established by universities in calling for liberal education, even though the following paragraph has since been deleted from its program quality principles, its discourse remains:

> While the teacher may not directly teach much of the content of a general and liberal education, the content is vital to teaching all the same. It provides the teacher with a framework for distinguishing, for example, the trivial from the worthwhile, the ugly from the

---

[1] I use the term "the Other" in order to illustrate that the preservice and faculty populations are understood to be white and middle-class—the absent presences that stand in contrast to descriptors as "different" and "exceptional."

beautiful, the unjust from the just, and so on. The heart of the teacher's work, after all, is
to lead students to matters of enduring importance and away from matters of time-wasting
insignificance. (TEAC, 2003)

Historically, those things we understand as worthwhile, beautiful, and just are
laden with racial and sociocultural meanings. TEAC guidelines ignore these
implications and proceed as though these "matters of enduring importance" were
universal. In discussing the contentions surrounding varying epistemologies,
Ladson-Billings (2000) gives the following example: "[L]iterary scholars have
created distinctions between literary genres such that some works are called *literature* whereas other works are termed *folklore* [original emphasis]" (p. 257).
Which genre carries with it the "enduring importance" promoted by TEAC? To
answer "both" may be fair, but it ignores the leveraging of political power through
the hierarchically constructed status of knowledges. To assume the ideological
neutrality of the knowledge proffered by a liberal education is to perpetuate a
paradox of egalitarianism. It cannot be truly established within frameworks and
foundations that have developed over time to benefit and perpetuate themselves.
The discourse of egalitarianism shifts through this lens of inclusion and exclusion, seeming clear at first, but becoming milky and increasingly opaque with
prolonged viewing.

3.4 Concluding Thoughts

Current policy reforms such as teacher education standards complicate the task of
preparing teachers for the practice of teaching that is critical and multicultural
(Grant, 1994). By setting standards, these governing and policy bodies do much to
ignore increasing racial segregation and intensifying poverty in these times by
framing a narrow field of reasoning, thereby narrowing the field of possible debate.
This recenters regimes of truth that naturalize the governance of dispositions of
preservice teachers. Standards also display racial, class, and gender tensions that
exist as easily conquerable through the construction of discourses of rationality,
professionalism, and egalitarianism.

   If the problem of preparing and retaining teachers for the excluded were merely
a problem of having the proper formula of planning, neutral, objective distance,
exposure to difference, and a self-renewing professionalism, the equity problem
might already be solved. And yet, by offering these standards as ways to effectively
measure the actions and content of institutions, the accrediting bodies limit the field
of view, obscuring voice and possibility under the banner of high expectations.
To return to Bourdieu, the standards of teacher education offer a new form of naturalized language, "full of allusions and shared understanding," which looks, more
than ever, as though it begins to dismantle inclusion and exclusion in education.
And yet, through its very attempts and because of its political constraints, the standards
movement narrows what is possible in terms of critically disrupting these allusions
and shared understandings.

Consequently, the crisis that teacher education standards attempt to address seems to spring from a perception of the preservice teacher as the object of change. Teacher education standards seek to create programs that effectively shape prospective teachers who arrive unprepared and unaware into professional, egalitarian, rational creatures. The institution of teacher education is treated, by contrast, as a kind of tabula rasa that carries no institutionalized hierarchies of knowledge and power relationships.

Teacher education standards promote the possibility of easy reform and change without addressing geography (in terms of proximity to more diverse populations than are typically represented in teacher education programs), history (institutional history, for example, or faculty hiring and retention procedures), and material resources (to provide greater access and support to participants). Standards make sense in part because they give a nod toward the high expectations we have for teachers; however, without a more careful consideration of their discursive functions, well-intentioned standards nonetheless may do little to change unjust schooling practices. Indeed, through their language, standards may offer us a false sense that change is occurring. As we continue our work to ensure educational equity for all students, it is important to remain critically aware that we ourselves as teacher educators are part of a system that has yet to provide an adequate answer to structural inequality in the United States.

References

Bourdieu, P. (1974). The school as a conservative force: Scholastic and cultural inequalities. In J. Eggleston (Ed.), *Contemporary research in the sociology of education* (pp. 32–46). Cambridge: Methuen.

Cornbleth, C. & Waugh, D. (1995). *The great speckled bird: Multicultural policies and education policymaking*. New York: Lawrence Erlbaum.

Darling-Hammond, L., & Sclan, E. M. (1996). Who teaches and why: Dilemmas of building a profession for twenty-first century schools. In J. Sikula, T. J. Buttery, & E. Guyton (Eds.), *Handbook of research on teacher education* (2nd ed.) (pp. 67–101). New York: Macmillan.

Foucault, M. (1972). *The archaeology of knowledge & the discourse on language*. New York: Pantheon.

Grant, C. A. (1994). Best practices in teacher preparation for urban schools: Lessons from the multicultural teacher education literature. *Action in Teacher Education, 16*(3), 1–18.

Groden, M., Kreiswirth, M. & Szeman, I. (Eds.) (1994). Discourse. *The Johns Hopkins guide to literary theory & criticism*. Baltimore, MD: Johns Hopkins University Press.

Hobbel, N. (2001). Access, equity, and performance-based assessment: Reviewing the NBPTS. Paper presented at the American Association of Colleges for Teacher Education Annual Meeting, Dallas, TX.

Ladson-Billings, G. (1998). Teaching in dangerous times: Culturally relevant approaches to teacher assessment. *The Journal of Negro Education, 67*(3), 255–267.

Ladson-Billings, G. (2000). Racialized discourses and ethnic epistemologies. In N. Denzin & Y. Lincoln (Eds.), *The handbook of qualitative research* (2nd ed.) (pp. 257–277). Thousand Oaks, CA: Sage.

McSorley, K. (2000). Moving from oppression to democracy: Reframing the preparation of special education teachers. *Educators for Urban Minorities, 1*(2), 27–38.

Metz, M. H. (1990). How social class differences shape teachers' work. In M. McLaughlin, J. Talbert, & N. Bascia (Eds.), *The contexts of teaching in secondary schools: Teachers' realities* (pp. 40–107). New York: Teachers College Press.

National Board for Professional Teaching Standards (NBPTS). (2008). The Standards. http://www.nbpts.org/the_standards. Accessed 17 October 2008.

National Commission on Excellence in Education. (1983). *A nation at risk: The imperative for educational reform*. Washington, DC: National Commission on Excellence in Education.

National Council for the Accreditation of Teacher Education (NCATE). (2001–2008). *NCATE 2008 Unit Standards*. http://www.ncate.org. Accessed 22 September 2008.

Nóvoa, A. (2000). The teaching profession in Europe: Historical and sociological analysis. In E. S. Swing, J. Schriewer, & F. Orivel (Eds.), *Problems and prospects in European education*. Westport, CT: Praeger.

Popkewitz, T. S. (2000). Globalization/regionalization, knowledge, and the educational practices: Some notes on comparative strategies for educational research. In T. S. Popkewitz (Ed.), *Educational knowledge: Changing relationships between the state, civil society, and the educational community* (pp. 3–27). Albany, NY: State University of New York Press.

Popkewitz, T. S., & Lindblad, S. (2000). Educational governance and social inclusion and exclusion: Some conceptual difficulties and problematics in policy and research. *Discourse, 21*(1), 5–54.

Portelli, J., & Vibert, A. (1997). Dare we criticize common educational standards? *McGill Journal of Education, 32*, 69–79.

Shannon, P. (1995). Can reading standards really help? *The Clearing House, 68*(4), 229–232.

Teacher Education Accreditation Council. (2003-2008). *Brief overview of the Teacher Education Accreditation Council*. http://www.teac.org. Accessed 6 August 2008.

Weiner, L. (2000). Research in the 90s: Implications for urban teacher preparation. *Review of Educational Research, 70*(3), 369–406.

Whitty, G., Power, S., & Halpin, D. (1998). *Devolution & choice in education: The school, the state, and the market*. Buckingham, UK: Open University Press.

Chapter 4
Policy Failures: *No Child Left Behind* and English Language Learners

Kate Menken

4.1 Introduction

Federal education legislation has had a major impact on US public schooling in recent years. In 2001, US Congress passed No Child Left Behind (NCLB)into law, generating in its wake a large number of both intended and unintended consequences. Although the law is slated for reauthorization within the next few years, it is unclear at present if it would change substantially or not and, regardless, it is likely to have lasting effects on teaching and learning for many years to come. Thus, all educators and stakeholders in public education need to be informed about how NCLB translates into classroom practice, so that they can better understand how it affects students and teachers, and so that they might play a role in informing future education policy decisions.

This chapter begins by offering a description of the NCLB mandates in the areas of annual testing, academic progress, and teacher quality, and the controversies surrounding them. As one example of how NCLB affects US schooling, this chapter then focuses on the impact of NCLB on the instruction and educational experiences of English language learners (ELLs)—students who speak a language other than English at home, and who are in need of language support services in school because their level of proficiency in English is insufficient for them to succeed in an English-only curriculum. The chapter ends with discussion about the challenges for teacher educators and teachers, and how to better serve ELLs in the age of NCLB.

4.2 Overview of NCLB

NCLB is the most recent reauthorization of the *Elementary and Secondary Education Act* (ESEA), the main federal law funding K–12 public education in the United States. The ESEA was first passed in 1965 as part of President Johnson's

K. Menken
City University of New York, Queens College & Graduate Center

S.L. Groenke and J.A. Hatch (eds.), *Critical Pedagogy and Teacher Education in the Neoliberal Era: Small Openings*, DOI 10.1007/978-1-4020-9588-7_4, © Springer Science + Business Media B.V. 2009

"War on Poverty," with the goal of ensuring funding for the neediest students, and has been reauthorized eight times since then. Prior to NCLB, the law was reauthorized approximately every 5 or 6 years, most recently in 1994. The No Child Left Behind Act of 2001 was proposed by President (George W.) Bush shortly after his inauguration, and signed into law in January 2002.

At the core of recent reauthorizations of the ESEA has been the desire of policymakers and politicians for accountability—to see evidence that federal investments in education yield tangible, quantifiable results in terms of student achievement (Ohio Education Agency, 2007). This demand for accountability is based on a deep-seated belief that US public schools are failing, particularly after the 1983 landmark publication of *A Nation at Risk* in which the National Commission on Excellence in Education found an overall poor quality of teaching and learning. The report, in combination with a need for trained and skilled workers in a service economy that is increasingly reliant on technology and literacy, galvanized wide-scale education reform efforts across the country.

NCLB emphasizes several broad areas for school improvement, including the following: (a) annual testing, (b) academic progress, and (c) teacher quality. The law places greater emphasis on accountability than ever before in federal education legislation, and the accountability system is based primarily on student assessment. For the annual testing requirement of NCLB, each student is required to be tested each year in reading and math. Because the United States has a decentralized education system, whereby a good deal of power over schooling is allocated to state departments of education, each state has its own assessment system. Most states use standardized tests to fulfill the testing requirements of NCLB rather than more holistic forms of assessment (such as portfolios, which evaluate a wide range of samples of student work gathered over time, to provide a more complete picture of what a student knows and is able to do).

In terms of academic progress, NCLB requires that all students in US schools achieve a level of "proficient" on the tests being used in all states by 2014. Each school must meet "adequate yearly progress" goals, which are determined by their state using an extremely complicated formula based on the school's overall student population as well as certain demographic "subgroups" (such as English language learners or special education students). If a school fails to make adequate yearly progress goals, either because students fail the tests or simply do not progress in the ways they are required to do, then the school risks sanctions such as closure or a reduction in federal funding.

Thus NCLB has galvanized a national fixation on testing. We have arrived at a point in the United States where a single test score has incredibly high stakes, used in certain states to make major decisions about an individual student, including grade promotion, high school graduation, and placement into tracked programs (Heubert & Hauser, 1999). In addition, in order to meet the demand for accountability under NCLB, student performance on a single test is used to evaluate a teacher, school, school district, and state. Due to the accountability requirements, NCLB is the most invasive federal education policy ever in US history (Hill, 2000).

The scope of NCLB is broad, and in addition to the testing and progress require-ments, the law mandates that teachers be "highly qualified" and offers a measurable definition of the term. In specific, NCLB defines highly qualified teachers as those who hold at least a bachelor's degree, are certified or licensed to teach by their state, and have proven their proficiency in the content area they teach. Teachers can prove their content area competency in several ways, such as by having taken a certain number of courses in their area, by having majored in their area as an undergraduate, and/or by passing a state teaching certification exam. Much like assessment for students, under NCLB teacher certification testing has also become prevalent as a gatekeeper for entering the teaching profession (Michelli, 2005; Selwyn, 2007).

4.3   Controversy Surrounding NCLB

NCLB has been extremely controversial from the start, and the law is about to be hotly debated as it is scheduled to go up for reauthorization soon. The law has also created strange bedfellows, with supporters and opponents on both sides of the political fence. As Gándara and Baca (2008) explain:

> Conservatives have argued that the law is too prescriptive and infringes on states' rights; they assert that the federal government has no business meddling in state education poli-cies. Progressives argue that the law hurts those students most that it ostensibly sought to help because of unreasonable demands, inadequate resources to meet those demands, and sanctions that demoralize school personnel who are working hard to improve outcomes for students. (p. 6)

The legislation had strong bipartisan support when it was created, meaning that politicians from the two major political parties in the United States are deeply invested in its success. So, even if there is a change in party power in the United States before the law is reauthorized, NCLB may remain fundamentally intact.

The rationale for NCLB is that setting outcomes for student performance will require schools to put the necessary structures into place to achieve those outcomes. In addition, supporters argue that highlighting the achievement gap has generated greater attention for high needs students, who previously were overlooked. Critics, on the other hand, argue that this new attention is mostly negative and that the law is primarily punitive in its results—particularly for high needs students. For instance, recent research has found that the law may disproportionately penalize schools serving diverse student populations due to its subgroup requirements for adequate yearly progress (Policy Analysis for California Education, 2003 as cited in Editorial Projects in Education Research Center, 2004).

The emphasis on high-stakes testing promulgated by NCLB has been particu-larly controversial. High-stakes testing has been found associated with:

- Increased dropout rates, decreased graduation rates, and higher rates of younger individuals taking the Graduate Equivalency Diploma exams to avoid required graduation tests

- Low-performing students being retained in grade before pivotal testing years to ensure their preparedness, as well as suspension and expulsion of low-performing students before testing days
- Decreased focus on subjects that are not tested such as art, music, and science, and
- "Teaching to the test," where instruction is limited to only those things that are sure to be tested, and rote memorization, drills, and test-taking strategies are emphasized (Amrein & Berliner, 2002, pp. 2–3)

The higher the stakes of the tests, the more likely teachers are to report effects on teaching and learning. In spite of claims by the federal government that NCLB is closing the achievement gap, "Texas-style accountability," the model upon which NCLB is based, has been found to reduce the overall quality of schooling and has had the most harmful effects on poor and minority youth (Valenzuela, 2005).

Not only has NCLB contributed to a more challenging environment in which to teach, the teacher quality requirements have received criticism for defining high-quality teaching in an extremely narrow way. Among other issues, the law has been criticized for emphasizing expertise in content with little attention paid to pedagogy or a deeper understanding of what it means to be an effective teacher. The law's efforts to quantify teaching has come under fire for its focus on "best practices" based on "scientifically based research," which assumes the following:

> Quality teaching is a college-educated person with high verbal ability who transmits knowledge; learning is a compliant student who received information and demonstrates it on a standardized test; and, education is a set of structural arrangements that make these effective and cost-efficient. (Cochran-Smith, 2002 as cited in Nieto, 2003, p. 387)

As Nieto (2003) points out, the law is overly simplistic for failing to fully define teaching excellence.

The requirement in many states that teachers pass a certification exam has also been viewed unfavorably for barring potential teachers from receiving a state license based on their performance on a single test, even when they have successfully met all of the requirements of the higher education institution preparing them, particularly as there is little agreement on the correlation between teacher testing and success in the classroom (Selwyn, 2007). In addition, the pressure to staff schools with highly qualified teachers, in combination with the national shortage of teachers in urban and rural areas which preceded NCLB, has led, many states to lower standards and create alternative routes to certification (Michelli, 2005). Federal policy overlooked the tension between quantity and quality, made all the more complicated by the government's failure to actually come through with the funding originally promised for NCLB (Selwyn, 2007).

4.4   English Language Learners: The Fastest Growing Population in US Schools

While NCLB has proven to be controversial and may negatively impact students, teachers, and teacher preparation, perhaps no group is more negatively impacted than ELLs. More immigrants arrived in the United States in the past decade than ever before. According to the 2000 US Census, approximately 47 million people or 18% of the population in the United States speak a language other than English at home, and this number is predicted to increase to about 40% by 2030 if current immigration patterns continue (Shin, 2003; National Council of Teachers of English, 2008). ELLs are thus the fastest growing population in US schools—in 1990, 1 in 20 public school students in grades K–12 was an English language learner, while today the figure is 1 in 9; demographers estimate that in 20 years this figure could be 1 in 4 (Goldenberg, 2008). Approximately 5,119,561 ELLs were enrolled in US public schools during the 2004/05 school year. As shown in Fig. 4.1, this reflects an increase of 60.8% over the reported 1994/95 enrollment; the overall student enrollment remained relatively static during that same period, increasing by only 2.6%.

ELLs in the United States speak at least 400 languages, though Spanish is by far the most widely spoken language after English, spoken by approximately 77% of all ELLs (National Clearinghouse for English Language Acquisition, 2007). What is striking about recent demographic changes is that states that have traditionally not received large numbers of immigrants now report the greatest growth; for instance, states such as Kentucky, Georgia, and Nebraska have experienced a growth of the ELL population in the past decade that is greater than 200% (National Clearinghouse for English language Acquisition, 2007). Thus all teachers in the United States should expect to teach English language learners at least at some point in their career.

4.5   NCLB Mandates for ELLs

Within a context of rapid demographic change, NCLB was passed into law (see Menken, 2008, for more on the history of NCLB). NCLB requires that ELLs participate in all aspects of the law, including the annual testing and academic progress

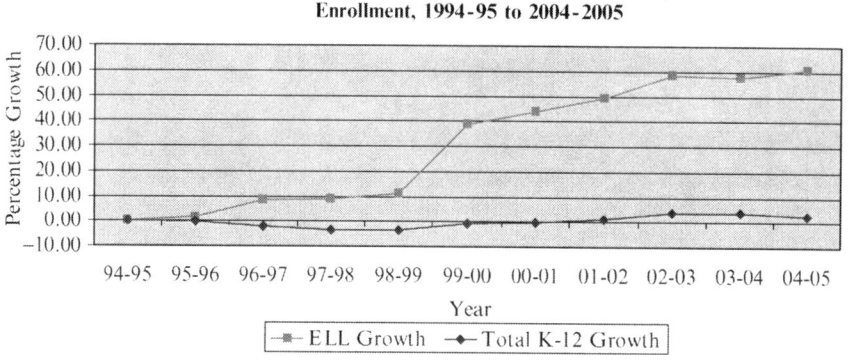

Fig. 4.1 Growth of ELL population in US public schools

components. Thus, ELLs must be included within the law's accountability system and corresponding "adequate yearly progress" goals and, like all students, ELLs must achieve a level of "proficient" on state assessments by the 2013/14 school year (US Department of Education, 2001). NCLB mandates a 95% participation rate of all students in state assessment systems, which ensures that ELLs will also be tested. Inclusion in state assessment systems must begin immediately, even if an ELL has been in the United States less than 3 years—no exemptions are permitted based on time for receiving instruction in English (US Department of Education, 2003).

The law demands two types of assessments for students who are ELLs, tests of English language proficiency and academic content. English proficiency assessments are intended to measure an English learner's progress in learning English, and must be taken at least once a year (these tests are only taken by ELLs, so these students have the burden of extra testing in comparison with other students). Students need to prove they are making progress each year toward becoming proficient in English. NCLB also requires that ELLs make progress in all of their content-area subjects such as math, science, and social studies. The law demands that ELLs participate in the same academic content assessments as those taken by native-English speakers. This includes tests of English language arts, as the federal government has since 2007 required that ELLs take the same English language arts exams as those intended for, and taken by, native English speakers.

In order to meet the law's requirement that ELLs be tested in all academic content subjects, states simply began including English learners in the exact same standardized tests—in English—as those that were already being taken by native English speakers. Thus, these tests were not intended for ELLs, nor were they originally developed with this student population in mind. Though test accommodations such as extended time and the use of bilingual dictionaries are permitted in certain states, these are as yet insufficient to make ELLs' test scores equivalent to those of native-English speakers on tests taken without accommodations (Abedi et al., 2004; Pennock-Roman & Rivera, 2006).

4.6   Impact of NCLB on the Instruction and Educational Experiences of ELLs

The enactment of NCLB in schools across the United States has resulted in a wide range of effects on teaching and learning, as well as on ELL students and the educators who serve them. This section first describes the impact of NCLB on students—particularly in terms of their future opportunities—and on the schools they attend, and then explores how the law is currently shaping instruction for ELLs and the preparation of teachers to work with these students. Much of the impact of NCLB has resulted from its testing and accountability mandates. The vast majority of states offer academic content exams in English only, so it is not too surprising that English language learners typically do not do well on the statewide tests being used.

According to national data, ELLs perform anywhere from 20 to 50 percentage points below other students on statewide assessments (Abedi & Dietal, 2004; Sullivan et al., 2005).

This is because content-area exams administered in English are first and foremost language proficiency exams, rather than assessments of content knowledge, since the student's performance is likely to be greatly influenced by his or her English language proficiency (Menken, 2000, 2008). It is important to note that when an ELL fails an academic content test that is administered in English, this does not necessarily mean that the student is failing to progress in the ways that she or he should; instead, the student's test performance may simply affirm that she or he is indeed an English language learner.

4.6.1 Impact on Students: ELLs Left Behind

What is deeply concerning for ELLs are the high-stakes attached to tests, as these students are disproportionately penalized and the schools they attend run a far greater risk of being labeled "failing." High school exit exams offer a case in point. California is 1 of 19 states requiring that all students pass high school exit exams in order to graduate. In that state, ELLs are more likely than other students to fail the high school exit exams, as 40% of ELLs failed both the English and math components of the test. Even more students failed only the English or the math component, which would likewise prevent them from being able to graduate. Thus, at least 40% of ELLs in 2006 were not eligible to graduate with their class, and this figure is likely low (Rogers et al., 2006).

New York also requires high school exit exams. As found elsewhere, ELLs in New York typically do not perform well on high-stakes tests. For instance, the ELL passing rate in New York City is typically 47 percentage points below native-English speakers on the statewide English exit exam, and on the Math exit exam the ELL passing rate is an average of 25 percentage points below that of other students (Menken, 2008). This creates a difficult situation for ELLs who have met all of the course requirements to graduate from high school, only to be barred from graduation by a single test score. When comparing states that require high school exit exams to states without them, rates of high school completion are lower and dropout rates are higher in states with exit exams (Dee & Jacob, 2006).

In New York City, ELLs currently have the highest dropout rate of all students, and the dropout rate has increased in the years since the passage of NCLB. In a given year, approximately a third of all ELLs in high school will successfully graduate, a third will dropout, and a third will continue on for a fifth year of high school (New York City Department of Education, 2008). The ELL dropout rates are provided in the table and figure below (see Fig. 4.2).

As indicated in the preceding figure (Fig. 4.1), the ELL dropout rate was 21% in 1999, as compared to a dropout rate of 16% for non-ELLs in that year. In the years since, the dropout rate for ELLs has been on average 29%, while the dropout rate for

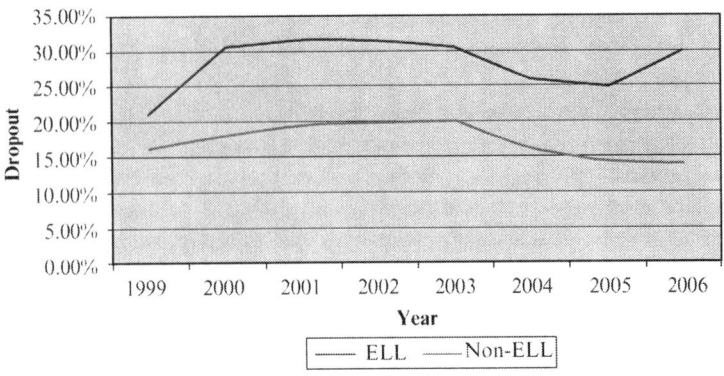

Fig. 4.2 New York City dropout rates post testing mandates, 1999–2006

non-ELLs has averaged 17%. In other words, the ELL dropout rate has increased by about 9 percentage points since 1999, which is the year when ELLs were first included in the state's high school exit exam requirement; the decision to require ELLs also to participate in exit exams was made as officials in New York realized that new federal legislation would emphasize test-based accountability for all students (Menken, 2008). One of the side effects of NCLB is that students may become more likely to dropout when they are unable to meet high-stakes testing requirements. In Fig. 4.2, it is possible to see that the achievement gap between ELLs and other students has not decreased, in spite of claims in the rhetoric about no child being 'left behind.' If anything, this gap appears to have widened.

4.6.2 Impact on Schools: High Risk for Failure

Due to its reliance on test scores to determine success or failure, NCLB is not only punitive of ELLs but also of the schools they attend. Because ELLs are more likely than other students to fail the high-stakes tests, and because calculations of 'adequate yearly progress' for ELLs are primarily based on these test scores, schools serving large numbers of ELLs are at great risk of failing to meet the requirements of NCLB. The recent listing of 'failing schools' in New York City offers a clear example of this. In March 2007, 35 schools in New York City were placed on the list of schools failing to meet annual progress goals. ELLs are overrepresented at the majority of schools on that list, because ELL enrollment at each of these schools exceeds the citywide average of approximately 13% (New York City Department of Education, 2006). According to state policy, when a school is placed on this list, it is given 3 years to demonstrate improvement, or it runs the risk of closure (Viteritti & Kosar, 2001). In the vast majority of states across the United States, the subgroup of ELLs are failing to achieve a score of 'proficient' on state language arts and math tests and meet yearly progress goals (Government Accountability

Office, 2006). This places the schools that serve large numbers of ELLs at higher risk of 'failing' than other schools.

The likelihood that ELLs will fail to make 'adequate yearly progress' creates a disincentive for schools to serve ELL students; this is a further side effect of NCLB's test-based accountability mandates. In New York City, certain schools do not admit ELLs because these students create a downward drag on schoolwide test scores. School officials also report that they will encourage secondary ELLs to leave school if they seem unlikely to pass the high-stakes tests (Menken, 2008).

4.6.3   Impact on Instruction: Teaching to the Test

In addition to affecting ELL students and the schools they attend, NCLB is also causing many changes to curriculum and instruction for ELLs. Because ELLs are more likely than their English-speaking peers to fail the tests being used in accordance with NCLB, it is even more likely that educators working with ELLs will "teach to the test." When schools and teachers focus their limited time on test preparation, this, by definition, means that other things cannot be covered. As elsewhere, schools that ELLs attend are focusing on math and English instruction at the expense of other subjects such as science, social studies, art, and music in order to carry out the accountability requirements of NCLB.

Not only are some subjects emphasized at the expense of others, in many places English as a second language (ESL) instruction is being overtaken by English language arts test preparation. Since it was required that ELLs also participate in statewide English language arts exams, many schools have called upon their ESL teachers to prepare their ELL students to take—and pass—these tests. This is mainly a futile exercise. The majority of ELLs will, by definition, fail an English language arts test simply because they are ELLs, even if they are rapidly acquiring English. Regardless, the pressure for ELLs to pass the tests has resulted in changes to ESL programming.

In the past, ESL classes focused on teaching the four language skills of reading, writing, listening, and speaking, in both an academic register as well as for social purposes, with the goal of teaching students sufficient English to succeed in an English-medium classroom and in their lives outside of school. Thus, beginning ESL classes were crucial for offering new arrivals a foundation in the language. However, secondary ESL teachers are now responsible for teaching ELLs, including beginners, topics such as literary terminology, how to write formulaic exam essays, fiction reading, and literary response and expression. Though this is not problematic in its own right, it occurs at the expense of helping ELLs learn other aspects of the English language. In many classrooms in New York, an English language arts test preparation guide is now used as the primary course textbook, in-class assessments are simply test items taken from past statewide exams, and students spend a tremendous amount of time in class using past test items in a 'drill and kill' approach to test preparation (Menken, 2008).

'Teaching to the test' in classrooms with ELLs necessarily involves language, and has galvanized widespread changes to language of instruction. Nationally, large numbers of bilingual education programs have been lost since the passage of NCLB; for instance, bilingual programs in New York have rapidly been replaced by English-only programs in the years of NCLB's implementation (Menken, 2008). This is because the pressures to pass tests in English lead to English-only instruction, in spite of tremendous support in research and practice for the argument that ELL students who have the opportunity to develop and maintain their native languages in school are likely to outperform their counterparts in English-only programming and experience academic success (Baker, 2006; Crawford, 2004; Evans & Hornberger 2005; Krashen & McField, 2005; Menken, 2008; Wiley & Wright, 2004). The typical pattern is that ELL students in well-implemented bilingual programs will not perform as well as their peers in English-only programs within the first few years of instruction, but with time they will have superior educational outcomes (Goldenberg, 2008). However, as Gándara and Baca (2008) explain, English-only testing jeopardizes bilingual programs because students are not initially able to compete in English with their peers in English-only programs. Lower scores in the first few years of instruction lead to sanctions for not making sufficient annual progress, even though the data show that this is a normal growth pattern and that scores will improve significantly with time. NCLB does not permit the time required.

4.6.4 Impact on Teacher Quality: Teachers of ELLs Left Behind

Beyond the testing and accountability mandates, which have received more attention in research about ELLs, the teacher quality component of NCLB is also having significant impact on the instruction of ELLs. Although NCLB requires that all teachers be "highly qualified," there is no mention in the law of what it means to be a "highly qualified" teacher of ELLs; the law is noticeably silent about the qualifications necessary to teach English learners. As Harper et al. (2008) note:

> This failure to acknowledge ESL as a subject in which teachers must be highly qualified effectively denies its value and status as curriculum "content" and reinforces the common assumption that teaching ELLs requires little more than a set of pedagogical modifications applied to other content areas.

As these authors note, NCLB implies that teaching ELLs is simply good teaching and requires no specialized expertise.

The teacher quality mandates of NCLB have been found associated with a de-professionalization of teachers of ELLs and an undermining of effective pedagogy and curricula for this student population. Harper et al. (2008) argue that NCLB's failure to recognize the profession of ESL teaching as an academic discipline displaces and negatively impacts ESL teachers. This problem has been compounded by NCLB's literacy program called "Reading First," which they find in Florida has resulted in ESL teachers essentially becoming reading teachers, employing pedagogy mismatched to the needs of ELLs, and sacrificing other aspects of language learning beyond reading.

In addition, there is a dearth of teachers prepared to actually teach ELLs, and this situation has only been compounded by the demands for teacher quality built into NCLB and its silence on ELL teacher preparation. Nationally there has been a shortage of ESL and bilingual teachers at least since the 1980s. Many states do not even offer teacher certification in this area, in that 16% of states do not offer ESL certification and 50% do not offer bilingual certification (National Clearinghouse for English Language Acquisition, 2006). In states that do offer certification in these areas, teacher certification exams have been found to disproportionately bar bilingual teachers from entering classrooms even when they have met all of the other degree requirements, and in spite of research support for the benefits of minority teachers working with minority students (García & Trubek, 1999).

Schools of education have also historically done a poor job of preparing teachers of ELLs in that only a minority offer ESL and/or bilingual teacher preparation, and fewer than one sixth of institutions require preparation for mainstream teachers concerning the education of ELLs (Menken & Antunez, 2001). In the absence of federal funding to support the teacher quality requirements of NCLB, many states have turned to alternative certification options in order to staff classrooms with ELLs (Michelli, 2005). New York City offers a case in point, where in recent years hundreds of teachers with the least preparation have been placed in schools with the greatest staffing needs, particularly those labeled 'failing' under NCLB; these teachers begin teaching ESL or bilingual education with just a 6-week summer program as prior preparation, while pursuing an alternative route to certification. Not only has NCLB missed the opportunity to improve the quality of ELL teachers by failing to acknowledge English language learning as a specialized discipline, it seems it may be making matters worse.

4.7   Discussion

No Child Left Behind is shaping many aspects of US public schooling today, and has come to play a central role in the daily lives of students, teachers, and teacher educators. This is particularly due to the law's accountability system, which requires annual testing of students to offer proof of their academic progress, and due to the law's teacher quality requirements. Though the law was passed with the stated goal of improving public education, it seems that some of the measures it employs have created a set of negative consequences, in spite of its intentions.

This is particularly the case for English language learners; within the NCLB context, language has become a liability for these students, whose participation in NCLB has more often led to punishment and a restriction of their future opportunities than to an improvement in the quality of education they receive. The reality is that NCLB was passed into law with little consideration of the specialized needs of English language learners, who have been included as an afterthought into statewide testing regimens—often with deleterious consequences. For many new arrivals, the task of passing a standardized test in English is too great a challenge, and they fail in large numbers because they have not yet acquired sufficient English to pass. Because a single test score is now used to determine a wide range of high-stakes decisions, the ELL dropout rate has increased and the graduation rate has decreased in recent years, and the schools that serve large ELL populations are disproportionately being sanctioned. In addition, the quality of education ELL students receive is being threatened by an emphasis on test preparation during instruction, which has led to a loss of bilingual programs and an undermining of research and practices proven effective in the education of this student population.

Teacher educators are finding it extremely difficult to maintain high standards in the face of these challenges. In schools driven by high-stakes testing, it is not easy to find teachers who put into practice the pedagogies that student teachers have read about in their theory classes. Moreover, schools of education have compromised too much in their efforts to comply with state and federal demands to staff classrooms with certified teachers; in the case of ELLs, few future teachers are being prepared to work with this student population, and many enter classrooms through alternative routes to certification with limited preparation.

All stakeholders in public education play a key role in determining and implementing educational policy. NCLB was developed with very little of this communication between policymakers and practitioners, and thus slipped into schools without contestation or public debate. Although politicians set the course for NCLB, teachers and teacher educators play an essential role in ensuring a high-quality education for ELLs, and therefore have a responsibility to advocate for ELLs by informing policymakers of the impact of NCLB on schooling.

Teacher educators also have a responsibility to inform teachers that they have the final say in how policy is enacted in their classrooms, and that they may do so in ways that are consistent with effective practices. For instance, teachers can emphasize in their instruction the skills needed to pass high-stakes tests, instead of directly teaching to the test through a reliance on testing 'drill and kill' and rote memorization. Additionally, native language development for ELLs, particularly in literacy, yields positive outcomes in the long run for the students' performance on tests in English. Moreover, schools of education must make good on their promises to prepare teachers by offering degree programs in ESL and bilingual education, and by infusing a focus on ELLs into coursework for mainstream teachers. There is every practical possibility of improving federal policy for English language learners, what remains to be seen is whether we can turn this into a period of possibility for these students.

References

Abedi, J., & Dietal, R. (2004). Challenges in the No Child Left Behind Act for English Language Learners. CRESST Policy Brief 7. Los Angeles: National Center for Research on Evaluation, Standards, and Student Testing.

Abedi, J., Hofstetter, C., & Lord, C. (2004). Assessment accommodations for English language learners: Implications for policy-based empirical research. *Review of Educational Research*, *74*(1), 1–28.

Amrein, A. & Berliner, D. (2002). An analysis of some unintended and negative consequences of high-stakes testing. Education Policy Research Unit, Arizona State University. http://www.asu. edu/educ/epsl/EPRU/epru_2002_Research_Writing.htm. Accessed Retrieved 15 March 15 2003.

Baker, C. (2006). *Foundations of bilingual education and bilingualism* (4th ed.). Clevedon, Avon: Multilingual Matters.

Crawford, J. (2004). No child left behind: Misguided approach to school accountability for English language learners. Paper presented at the Forum on Ideas to Improve the NCLB Accountability Provisions for Students with Disabilities and English Language Learners, Washington, DC.

Dee, T. & Jacob, B. (2006). Do high school exit exams influence educational attainment or labor market performance? NBER Working Paper, No. W12199. http://ssrn.com/abstract=900985. Accessed 11 July 2006.

Editorial Projects in Education Research Center. No child left behind. (2004).http://www.edweek. org/rc/issues/no-child-left-behind /levelId = 1000&. Accessed 8 July 2008.

Evans, B. & Hornberger, N. (2005). No child left behind: Repealing and unpeeling federal language education policy in the United States. *Language Policy, 4*, 87–106.

Gándara, P. & Baca, G. (2008). NCLB and California's English language learners: The perfect storm. *Language Policy, 7*(3), 1–16.

García, O. & Trubek, J. (1999). Where have all the minority educators gone and when will they ever learn? *Educators for Urban Minorities, 1*, 1–8.

Goldenberg, C. (2008). Teaching English language learners: What the research does—and does not—say. American Educator. http://www.aft.org/ pubs- reports/american_educator /issues / summer08/goldenberg.pdf. Accessed 18 July 2008.

Government Accountability Office. (2006). No child left behind act: Assistance from education could help states better measure progress of students with limited English proficiency. Washington, DC: Government Accountability Office.

Harper, C.A., de Jong, E.J., & Platt, E.J. (2008). Marginalizing English as a Second Language Teacher Expertise: The exclusionary consequence of No Child Left Behind. *Language Policy* 7(3), 267–284.

Heubert, J., & Hauser, R. (Eds.). (1999). *High stakes testing for tracking, promotion, and graduation.* Washington, DC: National Academy Press.

Hill, P. (2000). The federal role in education. In D. Ravitch (Ed.), *Brookings papers on education policy 2000* (pp. 11–40). Washington, DC: Brookings Institution Press.

Krashen, S. & McField, G. (2005). What works? Reviewing the latest evidence on bilingual education. *Language Learner, 1*(2), 7–10.

Menken, K. (2000). What are the critical issues in wide-scale assessment of English language learners? NCBE Issue Brief No. 6. Washington, DC: National Clearinghouse for Bilingual Education. http://www.ncbe.gwu.edu/ncbepubs/issuebriefs/ib6.pdf. Accessed 2 May 2002.

Menken, K. (2008). *English learners left behind: Standardized testing as language policy.* Clevedon, Avon: Multilingual Matters.

Menken, K. & Antunez, B. (2001). An overview of the preparation and certification of teachers working with limited English proficient (LEP) students. Washington, DC: National Clearinghouse for Bilingual Education.

Michelli, N. (2005). The politics of teacher education: Lessons from New York City. *Journal of Teacher Education, 56*(3), 235–241.

National Clearinghouse for English Language Acquisition. (2006). Which states offer certification or endorsement in bilingual education or ESL? Washington, DC. http://www.ncela.gwu.edu/ expert/faq/09certif.html. Accessed 18 September 2008.

National Clearinghouse for English Language Acquisition. (2007). The growing number of limited English proficient students, 1995/96–2005/06.Washington, DC. http://www.ncela.gwu. edu/policy/states/reports/statedata/2005LEP/GrowingLEP_0506.pdf. Accessed 12 June 2008.

National Council of Teachers of English. (2008). English language Learners. <http://www.ncte. org/edpolicy/ell. Accessed 3 August 2008>.

New York City Department of Education (2006). http://schools.nyc.gov/default.aspx

New York City Department of Education, Office of English Language Learners. (2008). New York City's English language learners: Demographics and performance. Draft Report. New York.

Nieto, S. (2003). Challenging current notions of "highly qualified teachers" through work in a teachers' inquiry group. *Journal of Teacher Education, 54*(5), 386–398.

Ohio Education Agency (2007). The Elementary and secondary education act of 1965: From the war on poverty to no child left behind. http://www.ohea.org/GD/Templates/Pages/OEA/OEADetail.aspx?page=3&TopicRelationID=170&Content=8038. Accessed 1 August 2008.

Pennock-Roman, M. & Rivera, C. (2006, April). A review of test accommodations for ELLs: Effect sizes in reducing the mean achievement gap. Paper presented at the Annual Meeting of the American Educational Research Association, San Francisco, CA.

Rogers, J., Holme, J., & Silver, D. (2006). More questions than answers: CAHSEE results, opportunity to learn, & the class of 2006. UCLA/IDEA Publications. http://www.idea.gseis.ucla.edu/resources/exitexam/pdfs/IDEA-CAHSEEff.pdf. Accessed 10 August 2008.

Selwyn, D. (2007). Highly quantified teachers: NCLB and teacher education. *Journal of Teacher Education, 58*(2), 124–137.

Shin, H. (with Bruno, R) (2003). Language use and English speaking ability, 2000: Census 2000 Brief. U.S. Census Bureau. http://www.census.gov/prod/2003pubs/c2kbr-29.pdf. Accessed 30 July 2008

Sullivan, P., Yeager, M., Chudowsky, N., Kober, N., O'Brien, E., & Gayler, K. (2005). *State high school exit exams: States try harder, but gaps persist.* Washington, DC: Center on Education Policy.

US Department of Education. (2001). *The No Child Left Behind Act of 2001. P.L. 107–110.* Washington, DC: US Department of Education.

U.S. Department of Education, Office of English Language Acquisition, Language Enhancement, and Academic Achievement for Limited English Proficient Students (2003, February). *DRAFT Non- regulatory guidance on the Title III state formula grant program. Part II: Standards, assessments, and accountability.* Washington, DC: US Department of Education.

Valenzuela, A. (Ed.) (2005). *Leaving children behind: How Texas-style accountability fails Latino youth.* New York: State University of New York Press.

Viteritti, J., & Kosar, K. (2001). *The tip of the iceberg: SURR schools and academic failure in New York City* (Civic Report No. 16). New York: Manhattan Institute for Policy Research.

Wiley, T., & Wright, W. (2004). Against the undertow: Language- minority education policy and politics in the "age of accountability." *Educational Policy, 18*(1), 142–168.

Chapter 5
Issues in Critical Teacher Education: Insights from the Field

J. Amos Hatch and Susan L. Groenke

5.1   Introduction

As we began organizing our ideas for this book, we looked for an opportunity to include some contextual information about the current state of affairs in critical teacher education. We were in the process of identifying individuals we knew were doing critical pedagogical work in their teacher education programs and inviting them to submit abstracts for possible chapters in our book. But we realized that, to our knowledge, no one had undertaken a systematic effort to try and capture a sense of what issues confront teacher educators trying to utilize critical approaches in their work, or what those critical educators are doing in response to those issues. We decided to create and distribute an open-ended questionnaire designed to collect some information about their efforts from critical teacher educators. This chapter summarizes our findings from an analysis of responses to that questionnaire.

The questionnaire was simple in design, consisting of four open-ended prompts (called "Questions" in this report): (1) The major issues I confront as I "do" critical pedagogy at my institution are...; (2) Some ways I deal with these issues are...; (3) Some ways I encourage the development of critical pedagogical attitudes and skills in my teacher education students are...; and (4) The main critical texts (books, articles, chapters, other) that I have found useful with my teacher education students are.... We set up a Web-based data collection port that allowed us to distribute our questions via e-mail to everyone we could identify who had written or presented on topics related to critical pedagogy in teacher education and to post the questionnaire on the Listservs of organizations that include scholars doing critical work in education settings. In order to avoid institutional review board requirements for getting informed consent from each participant, data collection was anonymous. All responses were electronically submitted to a university-run server, and the data we received from server administrators were stripped of any identifying information.

In total, 65 participants submitted responses. We did a straightforward typological analysis (Hatch, 2002), parsing data by prompt for the first three questions,

J.A. Hatch and S.L. Groenke
University of Tennessee

S.L. Groenke and J.A. Hatch (eds.), *Critical Pedagogy and Teacher Education in the Neoliberal Era: Small Openings*,
DOI 10.1007/978-1-4020-9588-7_5, © Springer Science + Business Media B.V. 2009

searching for patterns and themes within each set of responses, hypothesizing generalizations that reflected patterns and themes, and then deductively checking to be sure generalizations were supported by the data. In this chapter, we report analyses of data from Questions 1 and 2 (issues and how they are addressed). Because of space limitations, we elected to leave Question 3 data for another day. We conclude the chapter with a bibliography generated from responses to the fourth question. Analytic generalizations are organized under Questions 1 and 2 in the following sections, and data excerpts are used to bring our participants' voices to the descriptions. Many of the excerpts displayed were selected because they support more than one of the generalizations presented across the chapter.

We believe the issues identified by our respondents, the approaches they use to encourage critical pedagogy development in the face of those issues, and the texts they recommend are instructive. As we completed and wrote up our analysis from the questionnaire and edited the chapters submitted for inclusion in this book, we saw close connections between our findings and the contextual influences described in Part I, and the stories of "small openings" in Part II. Knowing something about what those in the field are facing and doing is important, and hearing the voices of critical teacher educators on the front lines provides a contextualized backdrop for considering the ideas in this book.

5.2   Issues Confronting Teacher Educators Trying to "Do" Critical Pedagogy

5.2.1   Issues Related to Students

Our analysis revealed issues identified by critical teacher educators in three domains—issues related to students, colleagues, and expectations. In this section, we present analytic generalizations based on data generated in response to Question 1 that fell under the theme of "issues related to students." Our teacher educator respondents reported that their students often: (a) resisted the critical pedagogy their instructors were utilizing and trying to encourage; and (b) lacked experiential and background knowledge on which to scaffold critical understandings. Sub-generalizations within these organizers are presented below.

5.2.1.1   Teacher Education Students Often Resist Critical Pedagogical Approaches

Although it was not universally mentioned, a large majority of the critical teacher educators reported that their undergraduate teacher education students were reluctant to accept the premises of critical pedagogy and sometimes resisted (actively and/or passively) the critical pedagogical theories and methods their instructors were trying to introduce. It is worth noting that several respondents said that their graduate students were more open to critical pedagogy than undergraduates, and some explained this phenomenon based on undergraduate students' lack of back-ground knowledge and experience, and their desire for the "practical skills of teaching." The words of one respondent reflect the sentiments of many:

> I don't have any real difficulty doing critical pedagogy with graduate students. I struggle, though, using these approaches with my undergraduate preservice teachers—they are not inclined to engage deeply with challenging content, they shy away from discussion of issues of race, class, and power, and they couch their resistance in terms of a pressing need for "practical" information.

5.2.1.2 Students Resist Challenges to Their Own Beliefs and Values

Critical teacher educators believe that one of the roadblocks that limit their students' understanding and acceptance of critical perspectives is that the development of a critical consciousness involves a careful critique of one's own life story in order to seek meaning and critically reflect on connections to others (Pongratz, 2005). Engaging in such a critique is problematic for many students, as one respondent explained:

> When it comes to working with students, the major issues are getting them to acknowledge their own privilege. [They] are convinced of the existence of individual and institutional racisms but are mostly skeptical of a systemic racism. All view issues of class from a lens that accepts capitalism as a natural political economy without alternatives. All readily agree that a student-centered pedagogy is important, but very few show enthusiasm for the radical edge that comes from Freire's problem-posing.

5.2.1.3 Students Demonstrate "Willful Ignorance" About Social Inequalities and Their Place in Perpetuating Injustice

Teacher educators in our study reported that their students had difficulty acknowl-edging patterns of social injustice, even when confronted with clear evidence. One respondent characterized preservice teachers as "willfully ignorant" because, even in the face of direct experience, they "deny oppression in the community and even the pattern of oppression in the college." Others noted that students resist questioning "current inequalities in education and how educators may unknowingly or unintentionally contribute," and they seem to operate on a "series of stereotypical assumptions: critical pedagogy is anti-American; critical pedagogy is anti-practice; etc." Sentiments like these illuminate the widespread belief among those respond-ing to our questions that passive and active resistance from their students is a major issue for critical teacher educators.

5.2.1.4 Teacher Education Students Often Lack the Background Knowledge and Experience to Understand Critical Pedagogical Approaches

Another strong pattern under the theme of issues related to students was teacher educators' perceptions that their students come to them with backgrounds that make it hard for the students to deal with the complexity of understanding critical pedagogies. Teacher educators used the following descriptors to characterize their students: mostly white, female, conservative, churchgoing, middle-class, Anglo, privileged, and status quo in their perspectives. The literature confirms that the cadre of preservice teachers and the current teaching force are dominated by white, Anglo, middle-class females, while the students in schools are increasingly children of color who do not speak English as a first language and who do not come from backgrounds similar to their teachers (Chizhik, 2003; Hollins & Guzman, 2005; National Center for Children in Poverty, 2006). These demographics are problematic for teacher educators across the board, but a lack of background knowledge and experience in diverse settings poses particular challenges for those attempting to introduce critical theory and critical pedagogy to their students. Some sub-generalizations from the data related to these perceived gaps are presented below.

5.2.1.5 Students Lack Foundational Knowledge on Which to Build Critical Understandings

Some of our participants pointed to their students' limited understanding of what the teacher educators believed to be basic knowledge of educational history, theory, methods, and social foundations as roadblocks to exploring critical perspectives. The logic seems to be that teacher educators cannot expect their students to critique contemporary practices in education when those students do not have a grasp of the understandings upon which those practices are based. For example, as one respondent noted:

> The level of understanding that the students have of the basics of education is limited. It is difficult to expose them to controversies and critiques of pedagogy until they understand the principles behind some of the conflicts found within educational *pedagogy*.

5.2.1.6 Students Have Never Learned to Think Critically

Another gap in preservice teachers' learning identified by respondents had to do with the inability of the future teachers to do the mental processing necessary to engage in critical thought. As will be seen below, some explained this inability as a developmental problem related to youth and inexperience, while others saw it as more of a gap in student learning—that is, no one ever taught them to think critically. Our respondents complained that their students focused on single dimensions of schooling and were cognitively unable to pull back and consider other, more critical, points of view. One teacher educator explained:

> I work with a white student population that does not know how to look critically at the way schools work and the power that teachers have to transform lives through curriculum and instruction and self-reflection. They think multicultural education is solely content integration and distracts from goals of fairness and colorblindness.

5.2.1.7   Students Avoid Complexity, Expecting Single "Right" Answers

Another common complaint was students' expectation that the world be broken down into yes/no, black/white, and right/wrong binaries. Many of our respondents believed that the avoidance of complexity in favor of simple answers that applied directly to a narrow view of teaching was an important issue they faced as critical teacher educators. As one university instructor complained,

> My students get frustrated that there isn't one "right" answer. They also are frustrated that I ask them to question everything. Some feel that they are given no "practical experience" for teaching.

5.2.1.8   Students Are Afraid to Openly Discuss Issues of Race and Social Justice

The data show that critical teacher educators rely on discussions to help their students learn about critical pedagogical approaches. This becomes problematic when those students are uncomfortable and avoid talking openly in group discussions. Respondents acknowledge the difficulty of discussing sensitive subjects (for them and their students), but they are frustrated by some of their students' avoidance of open dialog. Examples from two participants follow:

> Students resist discussing critical issues and engaging in the difficult conversations around socially constructed categories of gender, race, ethnicity, class, sexual orientation, ability, etc.

> Some think that the way to stop racism is to stop talking about it. They think it does not exist and that talking about it brings it into existence

When we asked critical teacher educators about the major issues they faced in doing their work, issues connected to students centered around the related phenomena of student resistance and student background or knowledge deficits. From the perspectives of participants in this study, many of the preservice teachers with whom they work, at some level, lack the will and the ability to engage with the complexities and politically charged content of critical pedagogy. We will describe ways they deal with student issues below; but next is a description of issues related to working with colleagues.

5.2.2   Issues Related to Colleagues

Data supported several generalizations about critical teacher educators' perspectives on issues related to working with university colleagues. Overall, our respondents found their colleagues to be lacking in understanding of critical pedagogical approaches and unsupportive of efforts to move in critical directions. Their perceptions related to issues with colleagues are outlined below.

5.2.2.1 Teacher Education Colleagues Often Neither Understand nor Support Critical Pedagogical Approaches

Respondents had mixed views on institutional support where they work, and sometimes administrators at department, college, and university levels were more supportive of their critical endeavors than their immediate teacher education colleagues. Several noted difficulties negotiating relationships with senior colleagues when those colleagues had a hand in promotion and tenure and faculty evaluation procedures. As one junior faculty commented:

> There are no major issues at the administrative level. My department embraces critical pedagogy and encourages faculty to use it in the classroom. [I do have issues with] faculty evaluation procedures that don't take into account the long processes that critical consciousness raising engender.

Similar issues related to "expectations" from institutions and other sources are taken up in a later section. Next, sub-generalizations that characterize issues directly tied to colleagues are presented.

5.2.2.2 Colleagues Misunderstand or Misinterpret Critical Pedagogical Purposes and Practices

Many of our participants noted that some of their colleagues had shallow or distorted views of critical pedagogy. The issues in this domain do not come from colleagues who are opposed to critical approaches for theoretical or political reasons; they result from a lack of understanding. As the quotes below demonstrate, this lack of understanding can make connecting with some colleagues difficult:

> Other professors who just don't know what "it" is [are an issue].

> Even though my institution is supportive of critical pedagogy, many of my colleagues are living within the hegemony of "nice" and "solution-oriented" so we have some odd conversations.

5.2.2.3 Colleagues Feel Threatened by Critical Pedagogy

Other teacher educators in our study noted collegial issues around dealing with those who do understand, but basically disagree with, or feel threatened by, critical approaches. Some reported that their faculty colleagues complained that students were not getting a balanced view of what it means to be a teacher from critical educators, arguing that the critical teacher educators were emphasizing social critique at the expense of teaching prospective teachers how to teach. Others, like the respondent below, noted that colleagues felt as though they were personally under attack when issues of inequality and injustice were brought to the table:

> Much of the critical pedagogy I do centers around issues of power and privilege in regards to diversity. Many of my colleagues (mostly white, well-educated people) seem to feel

threatened by anything that smacks of "diversity." They don't want to deal with it in their teacher education classes.

5.2.2.4 Colleagues Are Unwilling or Unable to Invest the Time and Effort Necessary to Implement Critical Pedagogical Approaches

Even colleagues who seem to understand and at least tacitly support critical pedagogy still generate issues for critical educators because of the time and energy it takes to include critical approaches in already packed teacher education programs. Many respondents feel disconnected and frustrated because their colleagues see critical work as low on the list of what needs to be addressed in the preparation of new teachers. For example, one participant reported:

> Lack of collegial support [is an issue]. There seems like so much that we need to cover with our undergraduate students to prepare them to teach in our state and to prepare them for the Praxis exams that the critical part seems to wait until the end or get pushed aside. Others are just trying to get everything in, and we don't even have the time to talk collectively how to infuse critical pedagogy more.

5.2.2.5 Colleagues Do Not Believe Students Are Ready for Critical Pedagogy

That critical theoretical principles and critical pedagogical approaches are too complex for teacher preparation students to handle is a theme woven across the data. Here it takes form in colleagues' perceptions that introducing critical concepts is either inappropriate or a waste of time because typical teacher education students are not cognitively or experientially sophisticated enough to get it. Critical teacher educators who disagree see this as an issue in their colleagues and not their students, for example:

> One [issue] is misunderstanding what critical pedagogy can be. People at my institution have a very narrow (and outdated) frame of reference for critical pedagogy. Also, most don't think students are developmentally ready for critical work.

While not everyone responding to our survey noted that issues around colleagues were salient to their work as critical educators, most did include references to relationships and attitudes of colleagues as "issues" as they responded to Question 1. As the quotes in this section reveal, critical teacher educators' colleagues frequently did not offer support for their critical coworkers because of a lack of understanding, opposition to critical approaches, inadequate time and energy, and differing conceptions of student capabilities.

5.2.3 Issues Related to Expectations

The third theme in our analysis of responses to Question 1 addressed respondents' identification of issues related to expectations associated with their work. These expectations emanated from many places, both inside and outside their institutions. They were identified as issues because teacher educators in our study saw these expectations as roadblocks in the way of their critical efforts.

Expectations from students, accrediting bodies, state governments, and education systems in general were mentioned as impediments to the utilization of critical approaches and the encouragement of critical development within students. Overlapping with many of the issues in the first two sections above, the sub-generalizations in this section show some of the perceived difficulties of doing critical pedagogy in contemporary teacher education contexts.

5.2.3.1 Teacher Educators Believe Their Students Expect to Be Trained to Teach, Not to Learn to Think Critically

Many questionnaire respondents noted that a major issue for them was their teacher education students' expectation that they be taught how to teach. For the students, learning how to teach meant acquiring a set of skills that would enable them to manage their classrooms and efficiently convey curriculum content. It appears that many teacher education students see the activities associated with developing critical perspectives in themselves and their future students as not just unnecessary, but as getting in the way of learning the techniques they believe they will need to be successful in their future classrooms. In one teacher educator's words:

> Many students are more concerned with classroom management and lesson plans than discussing social justice and how to challenge existing policies and curriculum. It is difficult for many to think that critiquing texts or the educational system is what a "good" teacher does.

5.2.3.2 Teacher Educators Believe the Focus on NCATE Expectations and State Standards Constrains Their Teaching of Critical Pedagogy

Part of the reason future teachers are so obsessed with the "technocratic rationality"(Giroux, 1983) at the base of their resistance to critical pedagogies is the pervasive influence of that rationality on the expectations imposed on teacher education institutions by external forces such as NCATE, INTASC, state departments of education, and other standards-setting bodies. Teacher education students are expected to demonstrate technical competencies, and their instructors are expected to ensure that those competencies are mastered. Along with the teacher educator below, our respondents identified the influence of these external expectations as a deterrent to implementing critical approaches:

> [I experience] resistance from students and colleagues who want to focus on preparation for teaching to standards. NCATE and associated professional associations do not value critical approaches to teaching and learning—and so shape and constrain what many think of as possible.

5.2.3.3   Teacher Educators Believe Education Systems at All Levels Promote Technologies of Teaching and Discourage Critical Pedagogical Approaches

Participants in our study saw expectations to produce higher test scores via the application of a narrow set of teaching "technologies" at all levels of the current educational landscape as being an impediment to promoting critical pedagogy. The influence of standards-based accountability and associated scientifically based teaching materials and methods has had, our respondents believe, a profound effect on teaching at all levels and limited the space for, and perceived efficacy of, critical approaches. The following quote summarizes the negative impact of expectations of students, standards-setting organizations, and the field at large on critical educators' efforts to introduce critical perspectives to their students:

> Another issue I confront is the broader push of educational "systems" (including the university) that encourage technicism in our profession. This push creates the expectation in some students that they are being "trained" to be a teacher, which sometimes manifests itself in a resistance to thinking critically about teaching and learning, curriculum, and social issues related to equity.

5.3   Ways Teacher Educators Deal with the Issues

5.3.1   Issues Related to Students

Even though respondents noted an array of issues related to students, colleagues, and expectations, no one said we should give up on efforts to bring critical pedagogy to teacher education. When they wrote about how they deal with the issues they face at their individual institutions, they used phrases like the following to signal their commitment to working through and around the impediments they perceived: "don't give up," "slowly but surely," "step by step," "it takes time," "keep on regardless," "do it anyway," "forge on, chip away." This spirit is expressed in their descriptions of how they handled issues related to students.

5.3.1.1   Critical Teacher Educators Employ a Variety of Strategies to Deal with Student Resistance and Lack of Background Knowledge

The data analysis related to ways critical educators respond to challenges posed by their preservice teacher education students revealed the set of sub-generalizations reported next. Some of their approaches are closely tied to the affective side of dealing with difficult concepts and anxious feelings; others are more about ways to structure and implement instructional experiences. Even though the sub-generalizations are reported as distinct categories, it was clear in the data that teacher educators were trying complex combinations of approaches in their work. An excerpt from data in this domain shows some of this complexity:

> People who are initially resistant to this process, often become quite engaged. It works best when I have a forum that can meet regularly. People need to trust that what they say is interesting and worth discussion. People also need to really learn how to listen and how to ask questions that help people articulate their thoughts rather than shutting them off. It takes time.

5.3.1.2 Critical Teacher Educators Avoid Confrontations and Build Relationships with Students

As the quote above captures, developing trusting relationships between students and their instructors and among the students themselves is seen a vital to facilitating the development of critical perspectives. Respondents in our study made many references to taking time to connect with students and creating safe settings in which difficult conversations can take place. Many explicitly said they avoid confrontations with students because they are counterproductive to the teacher educators' critical aims. For example,

> [w]e have found that direct confrontation (stirring up white guilt with white privilege lectures, etc.) can be counterproductive and have tried to present data and analytic techniques so they can draw conclusions that they then own more strongly (a constructivist approach). We also have come to aim less at Halleluiah Choruses (students are good at giving you what you want, at least until they get the final grade) and more at "haunting" them after they get into their own classrooms and see clear examples of what we told them back in preservice teacher ed.

5.3.1.3 Critical Teacher Educators Infuse Critical Pedagogy with More Traditional Teaching Approaches

Several respondents stressed the need to integrate critical pedagogical approaches with the other content and instruction of their teacher education programs. They believed that isolating critical perspectives from other content and separating critical teaching approaches from other pedagogies encouraged students to see critical pedagogies as unrelated to "real" curriculum and instruction. Like the teacher educator described below, they try to stress the interrelatedness and applicability of critical approaches to what good teachers do:

> I integrate critical perspectives into the course content, using critical pedagogies to teach the courses, positioning critical perspectives as knowledge needed to be effective teachers, to meet the kids' needs, etc.

5.3.1.4 Critical Teacher Educators Use Salient Examples to Demonstrate How Critical Pedagogy Can Benefit Preservice Teachers and the Students They Will Teach

Another theme under ways to respond to student resistance and lack of knowledge was to teach with concrete examples—rather than abstract theoretical constructs. Understanding critical theory is considered tough intellectual territory by many of the participants in this study, and developing critical pedagogies can be a daunting conceptual challenge for many students. A solution suggested by our respondents was to bring the critical concepts to life by pointing out examples of injustice and identifying opportunities to challenge the hegemony of the status quo in the immediate surroundings. As a critical pedagogue in the field of reading education explained:

> I stress that the experiences of the people I am teaching about are those of a marginalized, oppressed community in this country and that education is political. I bring examples of this oppression into class and present examples of resistance. I attempt to help them see how critical literacy benefits not only the students, but also themselves and society.

5.3.1.5 Critical Teacher Educators Build Awareness Using Readings and Discussion

Space would not allow us to report analyses of data from Question 3 here, but readings and discussions were the two most frequently mentioned ways to develop critical pedagogical attitudes and skills in teacher education students. These instructional approaches also emerged in this part of the analysis as ways to deal with issues related to students. Examples follow:

> We read texts that are very explicit in how to question the educational system and what they might do within their own classroom with their students. They need concrete examples to bridge the theory and practice.

> [We do] LOTS of discussion, helping students (preservice teachers) see how critical pedagogy could be relevant to their lives as teachers, parents, members of society.

5.3.1.6 Critical Teacher Educators Teach Analytic Skills and Let Their Students Identify Their Own Issues

In response to their perceptions that students lack the capacities and willingness to confront the challenges of critical pedagogy, some of our respondents noted a concerted effort to provide experiences that promote the development of students' critical and reflexive capabilities. A common strategy was to set up course experiences in ways that encourage students to identify for themselves the areas in which they want to concentrate and decide for themselves how they want to enrich their understandings and take action. As one critical teacher educator explains:

I present conceptual frameworks, background information, investigation processes, etc., but a lot of what we do comes from the students. Most students love that and dig into it.

The teacher educators in our study used several approaches to deal with the issues they see as blocking their attempts to "do" critical pedagogy. Our analysis revealed an array of approaches, but most included attention to both the affective and cognitive aspects of developing a critical perspective. Many teacher educators explicitly avoided entering confrontational situations with their students and worked hard to implement instructional activities that were grounded in real-world experience and to which students could develop personal connections. The following excerpt captures many of the sentiments expressed in this part of the data set:

I have them generate areas of concern in schools/schooling and use those to frame the course. I have them do the work—presentations etc—on the theorists so that they own the ideas as presenters and as the peers of the presenters. They make the connections for each other. I can give input too—teachable moments. I make sure we have lots of opportunity and support for the difficult discussions.

5.3.2 Issues Related to Colleagues

The data on respondents' ways to deal with issues related to colleagues are not as rich as those supporting other domains in the analysis. Like all of the themes and generalizations reported in this chapter, there is considerable overlap. We have tried to reduce some of that overlap in this report, for example, by leaving descriptions of connecting with like-minded colleagues for the next section on issues related to dealing with expectations.

5.3.2.1 Critical Teacher Educators Address Issues Related to Colleagues Who Don't Understand or Don't Agree with Critical Approaches by Trying to Educate Colleagues and Working to Develop Relationships with Them

Helping colleagues understand critical pedagogies and trying to develop relationships with colleagues are responses to issues that applied to dealing with both those colleagues who lacked information or had misunderstandings about critical approaches and those who seemed to understand but disagreed with the appropriateness of teaching preservice teachers about critical theory and critical pedagogy. Sub-generalizations in each area follow.

5.3.2.2 Critical Teacher Educators Try to Educate Their Colleagues Who Don't Understand or Support Critical Perspectives

Most respondents characterized their relations with colleagues who didn't "get" or "buy into" principles of critical perspectives as nonconfrontational. They were more likely to try to educate their colleagues by offering indirect information and modeling how to implement critical approaches than to lecture or get into arguments. For example,

> I suggest books for them to read (I do not participate in conversion).

> I work at educating the faculty and trying tactfully to demonstrate to them what critical pedagogy (and all the forms of critical theory) are all about.

5.3.2.3 Critical Teacher Educators Try to Develop Relationships with Colleagues Who Don't Understand or Support Critical Perspectives

Critical educators in our study used relationship building as a strategy for attempting to influence teacher education colleagues who didn't understand or support their efforts to do critical pedagogy. As will be seen in the section on dealing with issues related to expectations, keeping a low profile and not rocking the boat are strategies that often seem necessary in settings where colleagues and students may not understand or may resist critical theoretical work. The example shows a common frame of mind in dealing with colleagues:

> [I work at] developing relationships with my peers, in order to show that I am not mean-spirited. I also make sure I am very well informed on the latest research/theories.

5.3.3 Issues Related to Expectations

Although we did not have information about respondents' identities, roles, or institutional affiliations, the data include enough imbedded information to make us confident that our study participants are at various stages of their careers and working at a variety of institutions. As is evident above, participants experienced constraints based on expectations emanating from sources ranging from students to policymakers. In some cases, expectation issues were annoyances to be overcome; in others, they involved making decisions that had a direct impact on careers. The excerpt below gives a feel for the risk that some teacher educators face when they adopt critical stances in their teaching:

> As a junior faculty member, there is not much that I can do to complicate both how critical pedagogy is understood and how evaluations of teaching are conducted. Ironically, the hierarchical structures are overly prohibitive for these conversations and this work.

5.3.3.1 Critical Teacher Educators Utilize a Variety of Strategies for Dealing with Issues Related to Expectations from Inside and Beyond Their Institutions

When we asked respondents to identify issues they faced in their efforts to "do" critical pedagogy (in Question 1), they had a lot to say about expectations from sources close to them (students and colleagues) and sources from a distance (accreditation systems and standards). The analysis reported here focuses on strategies those responding to our questionnaire used to deal with expectation issues at all levels.

5.3.3.2   Critical Teacher Educators Go Underground

Many of those responding made references to being subversive rather than openly resistant to dealing with expectations issues in their individual contexts. While not all of these responses were explicitly tied to the vulnerabilities associated with promotion and tenure requirements, there were indications across the data that tenure-seeking faculty sometimes felt they needed to be more circumspect in their efforts to do critical pedagogy. Some sample comments serve as examples:

> I quietly (sometimes) subvert the dominant discourse.

> I use my imagination to see where I can fit critical pedagogy into my work while flying under the radar.

> I just keep going ahead and not "advertising" what I do.

5.3.3.3   Critical Teacher Educators Seek and Maintain Support from Inside and Outside Their Institutions

Finding others who share a critical orientation and actively seeking to build and maintain connections with them is a common strategy among our respondents. Sometimes these supportive connections come from within their institutions; sometimes critical teacher educators reach out across institutional and disciplinary boundaries to find understanding and support:

> I work collaboratively with like-minded colleagues, some of whom share some of the same students. When students hear similar things across courses, it is harder to pass critical pedagogy off as my personal quirk.

> I share information in appropriate venues, share readings as individuals are open, challenge my graduate students to insist on those types of discussions in their other classes, ignore the ignorance and network with others outside the institution for support.

5.3.3.4   Critical Teacher Educators Connect Their Critical Perspectives to Their Scholarship

It is interesting to us that making their critical pedagogical approaches an important part of their scholarship was the most widely cited element in this part of the analysis. In some ways, satisfying hierarchically imposed expectations for tenure and promotion by generating scholarly productivity around critical theoretical interests seems a bit subversive in and of itself. In any case, like the participant below, many critical teacher educators saw their scholarship as a way to connect their interests in promoting social justice to institutional expectations.

I try to do my research on the topic of these collaborations so that there is overlap for me in my work. I try to make my work and its positive effects visible at the university. I also try not to see tenure as validation for my work; rather I find the validation in the work itself and its influence on my students and their future teaching. I try to look for funding to support this type of work.

5.3.3.5   Critical Teacher Educators Are Proactive in Promoting Their Critical Agendas

Just as there are teacher educators who feel the need to "lay low" as they do their critical work, so there are those who are in settings where they feel safe openly promoting their critical agendas. A number of respondents were vocal in their proactive stance in relation to dealing with expectations issues at their institutions. Some appeared to act alone, while others described group efforts to advance critical issues. Two examples follow:

I serve on committees in my school in order to work for change. I strive to continue to get diversity issues and issues of power and privilege into the curriculum across our College of Ed by working with department heads and instructors.

We do work on action plans that can be enacted within our respective environments. Although, there is often retaliation from administration for such action, and we are labeled as "trouble makers," having a group of mentors who try to enact critical pedagogy and utilize the theoretical underpinnings for support helps our causes.

The data show a range of patterns in response to expectations that our participants see as problematic for implementing critical pedagogy in teacher education programs. It seems understandable that many teacher education faculty adopt a stance that keeps them "under the radar" as they do their critical work, while others are more proactive in their own settings. We see these varied responses as necessary adaptations to complex conditions that include the institutional constraints, where scholars are in their careers, and what personal and professional resources are available for support. This section demonstrates that critical teacher educators face expectations from many sources with strategies suited to a wide range of circumstances.

5.4   Summary

We set out to generate contextual information about the current state of affairs in critical teacher education. We designed an online survey to gather perspectives of higher education instructors who do critical pedagogy in their workplaces. In this chapter, we reported results of a typological analysis of responses from 65 anonymous critical teacher educators to questions about what they see as issues that impact their work and what they do in response to those issues. In addition, a bibliography was generated from a question that asked respondents to identify the major critical texts they have found to be useful with teacher education students. We see the bibliography (included at the conclusion of this chapter) as particularly valuable because it highlights texts that critical teacher educators nominated as appropriate, not only for their own enlightenment, but for guiding the critical development of *teacher education students.*

To summarize the findings, our respondents named issues with students, colleagues, and expectations as impediments to their critical pedagogical efforts. They saw many of their teacher education students resisting critical theory and critical pedagogy, that is, unwilling to critique their own beliefs, values, and roles in perpetuating social inequality. The teacher educators in the study also believed that many students lack the experiential and foundational knowledge necessary to understand critical pedagogical approaches, that students do not have the capacity to think critically, that they avoid complexity in favor of "right answers," and that they are afraid to discuss issues of social justice. In terms of issues related to colleagues, respondents complained that their colleagues frequently neither understood nor supported their efforts to implement critical approaches. Some colleagues who seemed to understand critical pedagogy felt threatened by it; others were unwilling to put in the time necessary to do critical work or believed that it would be a waste of effort because students were not ready for critical approaches. Expectations-related issues identified in the study were teacher educators' perspectives that students expected to be trained to teach, not to think critically. Respondents also believed that expectations emanating from standards promulgated at all levels of the education system constrained their efforts to teach critical pedagogy and their students' efforts to implement critical approaches in the schools.

Our participants' responses to the issues blocking their critical efforts were also organized by students, colleagues, and expectations. For dealing with student resistance and lack of preparation, critical teacher educators used a variety of affective and cognitive strategies, including avoiding confrontations and building relationships, infusing critical approaches with more traditional pedagogies, using salient examples, building awareness through readings and discussion, teaching analytic skills, and giving students responsibility for identifying and addressing their own issues. When colleagues did not understand or did not agree, our respondents worked to educate them about critical pedagogies and to seek relationships with them on which understandings could be built. For dealing with expectations from inside and outside their institutions, many study participants kept a low profile, preferring to be quietly subversive rather than confrontational in their critical efforts. Others were more proactive in promoting their critical agendas. Across the board, respondents dealt with expectations that constrained their critical work by seeking support from inside and outside their home institutions and by finding ways to connect their critical perspectives to their scholarly endeavors.

We have reported the findings just summarized as descriptions of what our respondents had to say about what it's like to do critical pedagogy where they live and work. At this point, we have opted not to offer a nuanced interpretation or critique of the themes and generalizations reported. As we reflect on all the elements of the book in our concluding chapter, we will return to the findings in this study and connect them to elements revealed in both the "contexts" and the "stories of small openings" chapters of this book. For now, critical teacher educators' perspectives on issues they confront in relation to students, colleagues, and expectations and what they do in response to those issues serve as a practical backdrop for considering the contexts described above and the stories of practice to follow. We believe the voices of our study's participants ring true in response to the contextual influences that impact contemporary efforts to encourage critical pedagogies in teacher education programs and echo many of the successes and failures embedded in the narratives of practice that follow.

References

Chizhik, E. W. (2003). Reflecting on the challenges of preparing suburban teachers for urban schools. *Education and Urban Society, 35*(4), 443–461.

Giroux, H. A. (1983). Rationality, reproduction, and resistance: Toward a critical theory of schooling. *Current Perspectives in Social Theory, 4,* 85–117.

Hatch, J. A. (2002). *Doing qualitative research in education settings.* Albany, NY: State University of New York Press.

Hollins, E., & Guzman, M. T. (2005). *Research on preparing teachers for diverse populations.* In M. Cochran-Smith & K. M. Zeichner (Eds.), *Studying teacher education: The report of the AERA Panel on Research and Teacher Education* (pp. 477–548). Mahwah, NJ: Erlbaum.

National Center for Children in Poverty. (2006). Basic facts about low-income children: Birth to age 6. http://ncep.org/pub_ycp06b.html. Accessed 12 January 2007.

Pongratz, L. (2005). *Critical theory and pedagogy: Theodore W. Adorno and Max Horkheimer's contemporary significance for a critical pedagogy.* In G. E. Fischman, P. McLaren, H. Sunker, & C. Lankshear (Eds.), *Critical theories, radical pedagogies, and global conflicts* (pp. 154–163). Lanham, MA: Rowman & Littlefield.

Bibliography

Adams, M., Blumenfeld, W. J., Castaneda, R., Hackman, H. W., Peters, M. L., & Zuniga, X. (Eds.). (2000). *Readings for diversity and social justice.* New York: Routledge.

Adams, M., Bell, L. A., & Griffin, P. (Eds.). (2007). *Teaching for diversity and social justice.* New York: Routledge.

Adams, N. G., Shea, C. M., Liston, D. D., & Deever, B. (1998). *Learning to teach: A critical approach to field experiences.* Mahwah, NJ: Erlbaum.

Allen, J. (2007). *Creating welcoming schools: A practical guide to home-school partnerships with diverse families.* New York: Teachers College Press.

Anyon, J. (2005). *Radical possibilities: Public policy, urban education, and a new social movement.* New York: Routledge.

Apple, M. W., & Beane, J. A. (Eds.). *Democratic schools.* Alexandria, VA: Association for Supervision and Curriculum Development.

Ayers, W., Hunt, J. A., & Quinn, T. (Eds.). (1998). *Teaching for social justice: A democracy and education reader.* New York: Teachers College Press.

Banathy, B. H. (1996). *Designing social systems in a changing world.* New York: Plenum.

Banks, J. A. (1997). *Educating citizens in a multicultural society.* New York: Teachers College Press.

Banks, J. A., & Banks, C. A. M. (Eds.). (2007). *Multicultural education: Issues and perspectives.* Hoboken, NJ: Wiley.

Bigelow, B., Christensen, L., Karp, S., Miner, B. & Peterson, B. (Eds.). (1994). *Rethinking our classrooms: Teaching for equity and justice.* Milwaukee, WI: Rethinking Schools.

Blaise, M. (2005). *Playing it straight: Uncovering gender discourse in early childhood education.* New York: Routledge.

Bomer, R., & Bomer, K. (2001). *For a better world: Reading and writing for social action.* Portsmouth, NH: Heinemann.

Buhrow, B., & Garcia, A. U. (2006). *Ladybugs, tornadoes, and swirling galaxies: English language learners discover their world through inquiry.* Portland, ME: Stenhouse.

Chaudhry, L. N. (2000). "You should know what's right for me!" A hybrid's struggle to define empowerment for critical feminist research in education. In B. Merchant & A. I. Willis (Eds.), *Multiple intersecting identities in qualitative research* (pp. 33–42). Hillsdale, NJ: Erlbaum.

Cochran-Smith, M. (2004). *Walking the road: Race, diversity, and social justice in teacher education.* New York: Teachers College Press.

Coles, R. (1986). *The political life of children.* Boston, MA: Atlantic Monthly Press.

Cowhey, M. (2006). *Black ants and Buddhists: Thinking critically and teaching differently in the primary grades.* Portland, ME: Stenhouse.

Darder, A., Torres, R. D., & Baltodano, M. (Eds.). (2003). *The critical pedagogy reader.* New York: Routledge.

Davis, B., Sumara, D. J., & Luce-Kapler, R. (2000). *Engaging minds: Learning and teaching in a complex world.* Hillsdale, NJ: Erlbaum.

Delpit, L. (1995). *Other people's children: Cultural conflict in the classroom.* New York: New Press.

Dewey, J. (1929). *My pedagogic creed.* Washington, DC: Progressive Education Association.

Dewey, J. (1938). *Experience and education.* New York, Macmillan.

Dozier, C., Johnston, P., & Rogers, R. (2006). *Critical literacy/critical teaching: Tools for preparing responsive teachers.* New York: Teachers College Press.

Finn, P. J. (1999). *Literacy with an attitude: Educating working-class children in their own self-interest.* Albany, NY: State University of New York Press.

Finn, P. J., & Finn, M. E. (Eds.). (2007). *Teacher education with an attitude: Preparing teachers to educate working-class students in their collective self-interest.* Albany, NY: State University of New York Press.

Freire, P. (1970/2000). *Pedagogy of the oppressed.* (30th anniversary edition). New York: Continuum.

Freire, P. (1973/2005). *Education for critical consciousness.* New York: Continuum.

Freire, P. (2004). *Pedagogy of indignation.* Boulder, CO: Paradigm.

Gale, T., & Densmore, K. (2000). *Just schooling: Explorations in the cultural politics of teaching.* Philadelphia, PA: Open University Press.

Gay, G. (Ed.). (2003). *Becoming multicultural educators: Personal journey toward professional agency.* San Francisco, CA: Jossey-Bass.

Giroux, H. A. (1988). *Teachers as intellectuals: Toward a critical pedagogy of learning.* Granby, MA: Bergin & Garvey.

Greene, M. (1988). *The dialectic of freedom.* New York: Teachers College Press.

Harste, J. C. (2003). What do we mean by literacy now? *Voices from the Middle,* 10(3), 8–12.

hooks, b. (1994). *Teaching to transgress: Education as the practice of freedom.* New York: Routledge.

hooks, b. (2003). *Teaching community: A pedagogy of hope.* New York: Routledge.

Hultqvist, K., & Dahlberg, G. (Eds.). (2001). *Governing the child in the new millennium.* New York: Routledge/Falmer.

Jones, S. (2006). *Girls, social class and literacy: What teachers can do to make a difference.* Portsmouth, NH: Heinemann.

Kincheloe, J. L. (1993). *Toward a critical politics of teacher thinking: Mapping the postmodern.* Westport, CT: Bergin & Garvey.

Kincheloe, J. L. (2004). *Critical pedagogy primer.* New York: Peter Lang.

Kozol, J. (1991). *Savage inequalities: Children in America's schools.* New York: Crown.

Kumashiro, K. K. (2004). *Against common sense: Teaching and learning toward social justice.* New York: Routledge/Falmer.

Ladson-Billings, G. (1997). *The dreamkeepers.* San Francisco, CA: Jossey-Bass.

Ladson-Billings, G. (2001). *Crossing over Canaan: The journey of new teachers in diverse classrooms.* San Francisco, CA: Jossey-Bass.

Latham, G., Blaise, M., Dole, S., Faulkner, J., Lang, J., & Malone, K. (2006). *Learning to teach: New times, new practices.* Oxford: Oxford University Press.

Lee, E. (Ed.). (2002). *Beyond heroes and holidays: A practical guide to k-12 anti-racist, multicultural education and staff development.* Washington, DC: Teaching for Change.

Leistyna, P., Woodrum, A., & Sherblom, S. A. (1996). *Breaking free: The transformative power of critical pedagogy.* Cambridge, MA: Harvard Educational Review.

Levstik, L. S., & Barton, K. C. (2005). *Doing history: Investigating with children in elementary and middle schools.* Mahwah, NJ: Erlbaum.

Lindsey, R. B., Roberts, L. M., & Jones, F. C. (2005). *The culturally proficient school: An implementation guide for school leaders.* Thousand Oaks, CA: Corwin.

Macedo, D. P. (2006). *Literacies of power: What Americans are not allowed to know.* Boulder, CO: Westview.

MacNaughton, G. (2005). *Doing Foucault in early childhood studies: Applying poststructural ideas.* London: Routledge.

Marshall, C., & Oliva, M. (2006). *Leadership for social justice: Making revolutions in education.* Boston, MA: Pearson/Allyn & Bacon.

McLaren, P. (2002). *Life in schools: An introduction to critical pedagogy in the foundations of education.* Boston, MA: Allyn & Bacon.

McLaren, P., & Kincheloe, J. L. (Eds.). (2007). *Critical pedagogy: Where are we now?* New York: Peter Lang.

Morrell, E., & Rogers, J. (2006). Becoming critical public historians: Students study diversity and access in post-"Brown v. Board." *Social Education, 70,* 366–369.

Nieto, S. (1999). *The light in their eyes: Creating multicultural learning communities.* New York: Teachers College Press.

Nieto, S. (2004). *Affirming diversity: The sociopolitical context of multicultural education.* Boston, MA: Allyn & Bacon.

Norton, B., & Toohey, K. (Eds.). *Critical pedagogies and language learning.* New York: Cambridge University Press.

Oakes, J., & Lipton, M. (2007). *Teaching to change the world.* Boston, MA: McGraw Hill.

Oakes, J., & Rogers, J. (2006). *Learning power: Organizing for education and justice.* New York: Teachers College Press.

Ore, T. E. (Ed.). (2003). *The social construction of difference and inequality: Race, class, gender, and sexuality.* Boston, MA: McGraw-Hill.

Paley, V. (1979). *White teacher.* Cambridge, MA: Harvard University Press.

Parker, W. C. (2002). *Teaching democracy: Unity and diversity in public life.* New York: Teachers College Press.

Paul, R.W., & Elder, L. (2002). *Critical thinking: Tools for taking charge of your professional and personal life.* Upper Saddle River, NJ: Prentice Hall.

Rothenberg, P. S. (Ed.). (2001). *Race, class, and gender in the United States:* An integrated study. New York: Worth.

Schneider, B. (Ed.). (1997). Race: *An anthology in the first person.* New York: Crown.

Shor, I. (1980). *Critical teaching and everyday life.* Boston, MA: South End Press.

Shor, I. (1992). *Empowering education: Critical teaching for social change.* Chicago, IL: The University of Chicago Press.

Shor, I. (1996). *When students have power: Negotiating authority in a critical pedagogy.* Chicago, IL: The University of Chicago Press.

Sleeter, C. E. (2005). *Un-standardizing curriculum: Multicultural teaching in the standards-based classroom.* New York: Teacher College Press.

Soto, L. D. (Ed). (2000). *The politics of early childhood education*. New York: Peter Lang.

Soto, L. D., & Swadener, B. B. (2002). Toward liberatory early childhood theory, research, and praxis: Decolonizing a field. *Contemporary Issues in Early Childhood*, 3, 38–66.

Steiner, S. F., Krank, H. M., McLaren, P., &. Bahruth, R. E. (Eds.). (2000). *Freirean pedagogy, praxis, and possibilities: Projects for the new millennium*. New York: Falmer.

Stock, P. L. (1995) *The dialogic curriculum: Teaching and learning in a multicultural society*. Portsmouth, NH: Boynton/Cook.

Sylvester, P. S. (1994). Elementary school curricula and urban transformation. *Harvard Educational Review*, 64, 309–331.

Takaki, R. T. (1993). *A different mirror: A history of multicultural America*. Boston, MA: Little, Brown & Company.

Vasquez, V. M. (2004). *Negotiating critical literacies with young children*. Mahwah, NJ: Erlbaum.

Wink, J. (2005). *Critical pedagogy: Notes from the real world*. Boston, MA: Pearson Education.

Yelland, N. (Ed.). (2005). *Critical issues in early childhood education*. London: Open University Press.

Zinn, H. (1980). *A people's history of the United States*. New York: Harper & Row.

Zurita, M. (2000). La mojada y el coyote: Experiences of a wetback researcher. In B. Merchant & A. I. Willis (Eds.), *Multiple intersecting identities in qualitative research* (pp. 19–32). Hillsdale, NJ: Erlbaum.

Part II
Enacting Critical Pedagogies
in Teacher Education

Chapter 6
A Critical Pedagogy of Race in Teacher Education: Response and Responsibility

Jill Ewing Flynn, Timothy J. Lensmire, and Cynthia Lewis

6.1 Introduction

We teach in a land-grant university located in an urban setting, but it is not an urban university. Rather than reflecting the cultural and linguistic diversity of the metropolitan area and schools, students who attend the university and enroll in our courses for preservice teachers are predominantly white. This context creates a specific set of challenges related to our work as critical educators. We have found that a critical pedagogy of race with white preservice teachers needs to position them as "responsible" without necessarily positioning them to feel "guilty." While the challenges of doing this work are complex, in this chapter we share texts and pedagogies we have used to constructively address them.

Our chapter focuses on issues that locate the lived and constructed nature of race at the center of any enactment of critical pedagogy. We have been tested in our efforts to help students understand and work to counteract the institutional, systemic nature of white privilege. Some of our preservice teachers rely on color-blind discourse, often for complex reasons. Others see race as a problem to be solved rather than something they themselves are implicated in or embody. And still other preservice teachers struggle to translate their intellectual knowledge of racism into concrete classroom practices.

Tim is an associate professor of Culture and Teaching and Literacy Education, teaching classes of preservice as well as practicing elementary and secondary teachers. Cynthia is a professor of Literacy Education, teaching classes in the post-baccalaureate English Education program that prepares students for secondary English teaching. When we began this chapter, Jill, a Ph.D. student, served as the student teaching coordinator for English Education and taught several courses in the program as well.

J.E. Flynn, T.J. Lensmire, and C. Lewis
University of Minnesota

S.L. Groenke and J.A. Hatch (eds.), *Critical Pedagogy and Teacher*
Education in the Neoliberal Era: Small Openings,
DOI 10.1007/978-1-4020-9588-7_6, © Springer Science + Business Media B.V. 2009

In this chapter, Cynthia and Jill examine the complex dilemmas that arose—for them and for their students—when they attempted to enact a critical pedagogy of race with white preservice teachers. Next, Tim shares a narrative account of how one class took up issues of race and white privilege in a meaningful way. We end by considering how the pedagogy enacted by Tim and his students may provide ideas and inspiration for other teacher educators to address race and privilege productively with white teachers.

6.2 Difficult Discussions and Transitions

It is often hard for white people to talk about race and whiteness. Research has documented the difficulty people have talking about race, especially people from white, middle-class backgrounds like most of our preservice teachers. The literature on teacher education students' examination of their own cultural privilege (Florio-Ruane, 2001; Gaine, 2001; Huerta & Flemmer, 2005; Cross, 2005; LeCompte & McCray, 2002; Solomon et al., 2005; Allard & Santoro, 2006; Gay & Kirkland, 2003; Milner, 2006) shows that white preservice teachers frequently use the discourses of color blindness, meritocracy, and individualism to defend their views and avoid acknowledging white privilege. LeCompte and McCray (2002) observe that "white teachers are unable to 'see' themselves as raced or as having a culture. Subsequently, they may struggle with the notion that their Whiteness affords them privilege and power and threatens oppression for their students of color" (p. 26). Socialized into the normalization of whiteness, white students "resist seeing White as a race or the relevance of race to teaching or to their own lives" (Greene & Abt-Perkins, 2003, p. 20).

It is important to recognize that this phenomenon is not due simply to the individual and privileged resistance of white people. It is admittedly difficult for white preservice teachers to recognize the racism inherent in institutions such as schools when they have enjoyed invisible privileges and not been invited to question institutional racismthemselves (LeCompte & McCray, 2002). Instead, many whites see racism as a series of individual acts or choices (McIntosh, 1990; Greene & Abt-Perkins, 2003). Unfortunately, though, defining racism "as an individual, ethical act shuts down discussions about racism—especially among White people or in mixed-race groups—because people do not want to be put in the position of being judged. White researchers/teachers then avoid this work" (Greene & Abt-Perkins, 2003, p. 7). This avoidance occurs across settings, such as K–12 classrooms (Beach et al., 2008), preservice teacher education (LeCompte & McCray, 2002), and professional learning communities (Lewis et al., 2001).

One of Cynthia's experiences teaching a methods course for preservice teachers helped her to understand how her pedagogy may have been implicated in some of her students' resistance to critical discussions about race.

6.2.1   Cynthia's Story

One of my English Education students, Sarah (all student names are pseudonyms), objected to an assignment that asked her to describe the demographics of the students she would be student teaching in order to plan lessons with them in mind. I wanted my teacher education students to carefully consider the context of the classroom they would be entering—including race, ethnicity, social class, and gender—as they selected texts and planned lessons. Sarah expressed discomfort that the only way she would be able to determine the ethnic or cultural background of several students would be by asking them directly and, perhaps due to her anxiety, misinterpreted the assignment to be requiring this level of imposition.

Beyond not wanting to talk to students about their racial identities, Sarah believed that noting students' races would signal to them that she cared about this socially determined descriptor rather than their worth as individuals. She claimed that she wanted the students to know that she saw them as more than just their race, and she even cited course readings over several semesters—Thandeka (1999), Heath (1982), and Delpit (1995)—to justify her color-blind approach.

Many students like Sarah, a white, middle-class woman, have little practice talking about race—so little that she seeks to avoid any mention of it with her future students. As critical teacher educators, we must be careful how we engage with students like Sarah. Sarah's objection had come via e-mail, and I now believe that my reply shut down further communication. I responded by letting Sarah know she had misinterpreted the readings if she thought these articles argued that she should not talk about race with her students, and I offered to sit with Sarah to further discuss the readings. However, the tone of my e-mail perhaps communicated another message—one that attempted to regulate Sarah's discourse and beliefs, trying to patrol her response, rather than creating a truly dialogical space to talk about the construct of race. For even as Sarah seemed to want to avoid explicit talk about race, she also expressed a belief that should be affirmed and that could be built upon in future explorations of race—that our students are deserving of our respect as individuals.

In a way, Sarah's objection to the assignment might have been a way of rejecting white privilege. Her anxiety over acknowledging race may well have been rooted in discomfort with the act of Othering that she saw in my request to describe the racial/ethnic makeup of the class, an act that from her perspective white people are unjustly allowed to perform from their normalized position. By *not* acknowledging race, her message to me made clear, she saw herself as connecting to the humanity of her students. This is the seduction of white privilege and the complicated web of relations it sets up.

As is often the case in our busy lives in universities, the semester was soon over and Sarah and I did not engage in conversation about this assignment and the issues it raised for them. Instead, Sarah's next e-mail reply thanked me and confirmed that she now understood the assignment.

Sometimes, our preservice teachers imagine that they themselves do not embody white privilege, that race and racial injustice are simple problems to be solved in order to help others. Some of Jill's students struggled to see the complexity of racial injustice. Here she discusses two students who experienced this struggle in different ways.

6.2.2   Jill's Story

During one of my methods courses, Amanda frequently verbalized her commitment to urban teaching. Having volunteered in New Orleans after Hurricane Katrina, having done international community service work, and having substitute taught in city schools, Amanda imagined herself in a diverse classroom in the future and seemed to embrace the role of the white savior teacher so often portrayed in popular media. Given her work with and for people of color, she believed that she already knew what there was to know about race and difference. She insisted that all she needed to do was to listen, to be helpful, to care. As Beach et al. (2008) point out, attitudes such as these sometimes function to negate "any implication that Whites are directly or indirectly responsible for economic inequality related to institutional racism" and instead focus on the idea "that everyone is the same, assuming that racial conflicts and inequality would be solved if everyone just got along better" (p. 11). Amanda thus embodied a different version of color-blind philosophy.

Other preservice teachers embrace open, frank discussions of race and racism in their methods courses, perhaps imagining their future teaching selves enacting liberatory pedagogy. For many students like these, however, thoughtful consideration of course materials is not enough; translating their intellectual knowledge of white privilege and institutional racism—and the need to critically interrogate issues of social injustice—into classroom teaching practices proves daunting. Nicholas, for example, student taught at an urban middle school with a predominantly African-American student body. As someone who engaged thoughtfully in class discussions of race throughout the English Education program, he seemed to be a strong candidate for teaching a racially diverse student population. In addition, his mother taught in a city school, he had previously worked for a nonprofit organization that advocated for American Indian students, and, as a gay man, he understood firsthand some of the effects of marginalization.

Issues of race were salient right from the start of Nicholas' student teaching experience. Even before assuming responsibility for classes, he participated in a team meeting in which the sixth-grade teachers reviewed the list of failing students: who was failing multiple subjects, who would need to repeat sixth grade as a result. Virtually the entire list (and it was tragically long) were black boys. (It was not clear what the team meant to do with this information, though at least they had made note of the racial disparity.)

His students' low achievement was of concern to Nicholas. Although I was not a constant presence in his classroom, from my observations as well as his own reports on his students, there were at least three or four boys in each class who appeared to be actively resisting Nicholas, his lessons, and school in general. He had made some attempts to connect personally with these students, but his success proved limited.

I suspect that some students perceived Nicholas as something of an intruder, after taking many months to build a trusting relationship with their talented and caring regular teacher, who then gave over the class to her student teacher. Still, even as Nicholas was intellectually aware of the need for culturally relevant pedagogy and of some of the ways he embodied white privilege, he was not able to connect what he knew about institutional racism or larger societal forces to what he viewed as the defiant, inappropriate behavior of these boys. Many times he expressed frustration over his students' "lack of respect." He remarked that he suspected most of them "can do whatever they want at home," and then have trouble adjusting to school as a result. Unfortunately, Nicholas seemed to move fairly quickly to a stereotyped, default interpretation of the actions of these young black boys. In other words, even someone with intellectual knowledge of racism and the desire to work for social justice needs help and direction in making sense of classroom experiences and translating these experiences into meaningful work with students in school.

These are some of the challenges we face as critical teacher educators. As Lewis et al. (2001) point out, "if teachers and students do not learn to interrogate white privilege and power, then there is little hope for educational reform" (p. 319), reform that is vital for addressing the needs of our students and our society. For white teachers, examining their own racial identity and coming to understand the institutional racism in American society are paramount. We take this challenge seriously, and we are striving to find productive ways to do this work with our preservice teachers.

6.3   Conversations About Difference

In the next section, Tim narrates an account of an ongoing event in one of his language arts methods courses. Like all descriptions and stories, there is much to discuss, and much that we will not be able to take up in detail here. We share this account as an example of how we might help students feel *responsible* for addressing institutional racism and for confronting white privilege, without disabling this work by positioning them as *guilty*. The texts used—and the ways students took ownership of learning about and from them—helped preservice teachers start sorting through the relevance of race, racism, and whiteness to their work in schools.

6.3.1   Tim's Story

In the first session of my language arts methods course for preservice elementary education teachers, I asked them to talk with me about what they had learned in relation to schooling and diversity, in relation to how race, gender, sexuality, and social class play out in classrooms. What topics and issues had they taken up in foundations and other courses? What did they feel they had had the chance to explore in some depth? What had not been addressed well?

Perhaps because I approached it in terms of opportunities to learn, rather than asking them about their own competency/knowledge or lack of it, they talked with me in what seemed to be fairly direct and open ways. They felt that they hadn't learned much; that at best, they were introduced to the notion of cultural differences or mismatches in classrooms. And even this introduction to the idea of cultural differences was cursory, with a few examples given and not much else. As we talked, the students expressed some frustration with not having the chance to learn more. They were worried about their ability to succeed in the practicum placements that accompanied this class, worried about what would happen in their student teaching the following semester. They knew that they would be working in schools and classrooms with highly diverse student populations.

I was somewhat taken aback by what they told me. I hadn't had tremendous confidence in our teacher education program's success at supporting our future teachers in thinking and working through questions of difference, but the dearth of opportunities and the fact that these students seemed quite aware of, and worried about, this lack jolted me. I hadn't planned on making changes in my class on the basis of this conversation—I had thought of it more in terms of knowing my students better and making subtle shifts in emphasis at different points in the semester. But now this didn't seem enough.

I felt stuck. I had plenty to teach in this methods course, which was the primary opportunity for them to learn about teaching language arts, as well as a significant part of their education in children's literature. To be sure, my course was already driven by progressive and critical approaches to literacy instruction, but it felt like what I was trying to do would be undermined by my students' lack of opportunities to explore identity and difference.

In the time between the first and second class, I decided that in each class session throughout the rest of the semester we would have "conversations about difference." The following are my notes for introducing these conversations to my students:

- Too often in this country, difference (cultural, racial, social class, sexuality, etc.) is imagined and defined as deficit or inferiority—this plays itself out in myriad sorts of ways, including what happens in schools and classrooms.
- If we are truly to be committed to teaching the children in front of us, we need to get smarter about how difference plays out and the consequences of difference for us and our students.
- From here on out, for each session, we are going to take 20–30 minutes to have a conversation about difference—of course, our conversations about writing and literature should be permeated by this, but we will set aside some time each session to do this.
- The conversation will be started by two of you each session—as a pair, you'll read an article or chapter, and then write a one-page single-spaced text for us (bring enough copies for yourselves and everyone else, including Tim).

- About two thirds of the page will be a close tracing/summary of the argument, along with discussion of key concepts and ideas.
- About one third of the page will be your response to this piece, which could include what you found most interesting/compelling, questions you had about the piece that you would like to discuss with classmates, ways that ideas in the piece might play out in your own teaching, etc.
- We'll experiment with how best to start and engage in the conversation—next time, we'll begin with having everyone read the one-page text first, and then begin asking questions about the piece and going from there.
- Start with chapter from Lisa Delpit's (1995) *Other Peoples' Children.*
- Need two volunteers—you will do this writing in place of assigned writing everyone else does (but the reading is extra).

In launching these "conversations about difference," a major concern was how to do (add) something serious without being unfair to the students—they already had a heavy workload in the class. These conversations added reading, but only for the people who volunteered for any given session (often, the writing they did as volunteers substituted for other assigned writing).

The readings that became the focus of the conversations included fairly popular pieces (e.g., McIntosh [1990] and Sleeter [1993]), but I also wanted to give students access to work that might help them understand race and whiteness in society and schools from historical perspectives (including Lipsitz's [1995] writing on the "possessive investment in whiteness"and Grande's [2004] historical account of Indian education); from anthropological and feminist perspectives (including excerpts from John Langston Gwaltney's [1980] *Drylongso* and Goodman and Kelly's [1988] article on issues confronting profeminst male teachers in elementary schools); and psychoanalytic perspectives (Thandeka's [1999] account of white racial identity development as involving, in family and society, the abuse by white authority of its own white children and youth).

Students took up their reading and summarizing of arguments seriously. In any given conversation, two students were positioned as "temporary experts" on their article or chapter. This expert status was signaled both in the routine of the conversations (their one-page text was read, first, in silence by the rest of the class, and then they called on classmates and responded to questions about their text) and signaled by room arrangement (the pair was seated together at a table in front of the class). The pairs were usually anxious that their written text captured the argument and explained key concepts (they would often ask me to read and respond to their texts before the session, even though I had not suggested this or made it a requirement) and they clearly wanted to be able to answer their classmates' questions. One of the effects of this was that they seemed to become invested in the argument of a particular piece in a way that they might not in a traditional student role. I tended to stand back, observe, but would occasionally participate in the conversation to ask questions or to try to help explain difficult concepts or ideas.

I know that other professors sometimes ask students to lead discussions of articles and chapters, so I think it important to note a few differences here that might help us understand the particular energy and seriousness with which my students pursued this work. First, these conversations about difference resulted from a discussion in which the students themselves identified a lack in their own education—these conversations were my attempt to respond to a problem they identified. Second, only the students leading the discussion, the temporary experts, had read, had access to, the article or chapter under discussion. This happened because I didn't want to overload students with extra reading, but one of the effects of this was that students could only get access to certain arguments and concepts through the students leading the discussion. That is, the rest of the class was dependent on the one-page texts and responses to questions provided by the temporary experts. Third, none of this work was graded by me, except in the most abstract sense that I made it an ungraded requirement that everyone act as a temporary expert at least once during the course. My sense is that their work on this was driven by their own interests in learning about difference, as well as by their desires to look smart and competent in front of their peers and me and to be helpful to others.

At least two stories in relation to these conversations are worth relating. The first happened during the conversation on Peter Murrell's (1993) piece on Afrocentric immersion schools, which includes the claim that white teachers fear black male students. Some students agreed with this claim; others disagreed. The class was doing a good job of sorting through various perceptions and emotions they associated with working with students of color. Then Phyllis told the class that she didn't know what to do. She had been attacked by a black man, and now she panicked and began shaking whenever she was physically close to a black male. She explained that she understood that her response involved stereotyping—she understood that there was no logic, no justice, in her body responding the way that it did. But despite the work she was doing to overcome her fears, this is how she responded. She was crying and the class was quiet.

There was a stillness in the room that seemed, to me, to be born of thoughtfulness, contemplation. Eventually, I thanked Phyllis for her courage in sharing her experiences with us and reminded the class that race and racism were not just intellectual/cognitive or historical or institutional. They are also inside our bodies, organize our insides, are part of our hearts.

The second story happened right at the end of the semester, and while it didn't occur during one of our conversations on difference, I know that the conversations played a role.

In this course, in addition to readings I assigned, I also had small groups pick books that they wanted to read in order to extend, fill in gaps, talk back to, my official curriculum. One small group chose to read Gary Howard's (1999) book on white racial identity and teaching. Their work included identifying an excerpt from the book for all of us to read, leading an hour-long session in the class about the book, and writing a group paper about what they learned.

When this group finished their hour-long session with us, I complimented their work and said that they had represented well Howard's ideas about what sort of action white people need to take in response to our white supremacist society. I also noted that other writers and activists had different ideas. I mentioned two.

First, the Reverend Thandeka (1999), who suggests that white people need to start their work engaging in some sort of individual or group therapy to uncover and work through the shame that is at the core of white racial identity. And second, the Race Traitors (e.g., see Ignatiev & Garvey, 1996), who think that at any and every moment white people need to deny and contest white privilege (and their classification as white), especially in relation to authority figures—with the classic example being that when a police officer pulls you over (if you are a white person) and is about to let you off with a warning, you say something like, "You must think I'm white."

It is the final day of the course and we have just finished. One of my students, JB, comes up to me and says that her final paper will be late. As I begin to say that that's all right, that we can negotiate a new due date, she asks me if she can tell me why it will be late. I say sure.

She says that she didn't finish it because she was feeling a little unsettled, and that she was feeling a little unsettled because yesterday, after her work in her practicum, she was driving home in her car when she was pulled over by a police officer. He told her that one of her signal lights was out, that she should get it fixed, and that he'd let her off with a warning. JB told me that she was feeling good—her semester was ending well and she had had a good day with her practicum students. She told the police officer, "You must think that I'm white."

He pulled her out of the car, gave her two sobriety tests, and then gave her two tickets (I don't know what violation he made up for the second one). I looked at JB in wonder and asked her if she would like to tell the class her story. She did, and as she finished, half the class looked at her (as I did) with wonder, trying to figure out how she had the guts to do that, and the other half was already whooping and hollering, fists in the air, yelling, "We'll help you pay for your tickets!" And they did.

6.4   Dialogic Discourse to Responsible Action

As Kress (1993) has argued, signs are not arbitrary but motivated. This means, of course, that signs are produced through structures of power. And the fact that signs are motivated and produced through structures of power means that their boundaries are enforced, as Kress suggests, more or less rigidly. Given these conditions, locating the spaces in which the meaning of signs is somewhat fluid is important to understanding the ways that learning occurs through interaction (Lewis, 2004). Perhaps Tim's pedagogy worked to make the sign more fluid. When signs such as "race" and "whiteness" are not tightly patrolled or regulated (as they were with Sarah), students are able to discuss them in a dialogic way that leads to critical learning.

We are conceptualizing learning, here, as appropriating and reconstructing the discourses within one's social world. This process, as Deborah Hicks (1996) suggests, represents a rearticulation rather than a recapitulation of existing discourses. (This is, of course, a Bakhtinian notion, but Hicks nicely connects her theory of language to a theory of learning.) Fixed, stable discourses are most likely to be interrupted when more dialogic conversations occur, conversations that include multiple voices and social meanings. There was something about the readings and the way that Tim's students entered into dialogue that helped interrupt fixed discourses about race and difference. We believe that Tim's students felt comfortable enough to be tentative, exploratory, and intertextual in their conversations. If agency is "the making and remaking of selves, identities, activities, and relationships within structures of power" (Moje & Lewis, 2007), then the agency that clearly developed for JB and others in the classroom derives from their dialogism.

In the end, dialogism cannot be made or forced to happen, but we can work to create conditions in which it is more likely to occur. On the first day of his class, Tim declares that, to the extent that he can influence how the group talks together, he will use his influence to facilitate a "conversation" discourse rather than the "debate" discourse traditionally valued and practiced in schools. He lists the difference on the board (see Table 6.1).

Talking through these two ways to conceive of, and participate in, classroom talk, Tim encourages students to break out of the individualistic, competitive norms and discourses of traditional classrooms to create a more communal, critical space, where conversations serve to facilitate both enjoyment (pleasure) and learning. Productive dialogic discourse, then, is one of the essential elements of a critical pedagogy of race with white students.

In addition, it is vital that this critical pedagogy of race positions white students as responsible without necessarily positioning them to feel guilty. While white students sometimes manifest resistance to discussing race, their opposition does not always stem from negative intentions. Trainor's (2005) study of college sophomores' responses to literature points out that while white students do often rely on discourses of individualism and color blindness, at times these rationales grow from the desire to see positive change in the world. Discussing Ralph Ellison's short story "Battle Royal," Trainor's students wanted to see both themselves and the story's characters as "strong and powerful agents operating within a stable, predictable community" (p. 153). Students strove to view their social worlds as orderly and logical, expressing a "desire to get past racism" (p. 161).

Thus, Trainor (2005) points out, it is important to acknowledge that White students' reliance on particular discourses does not always reveal merely a motivation for "self-interest, power, or gain" (p. 163). She advocates that teachers "help students honor their deeply held commitments to ideals like community and strength, while simultaneously finding ways to move beyond the White talk that

Table 6.1 Conversation discourse versus debate

	Conversation	Debate
Other	Partner	Opponent
Task	Look for new understandings	Identify weaknesses
Goal	Learn/pleasure	Win

expresses them, creating new rhetorics and new way
ess" (p. 163). This is an argument against a lot of
white privilege in a way that calls out resistance.
both form and content, Tim's students' conversa
students to begin exploring their implication in a ra
ring resistance or paralysis that would shut down ta
(1995) is particularly effective in facilitating this sta

Lipsitz (1995) documents how there has been a l
policy and in more local practices, in whiteness
contributed to racial inequality. However, most Americans—and most of our pre-service teachers, including Amanda and Nicholas—are unaware of the policies and programs that created this possessive investment in whiteness, which raises important questions about the ways in which we attempt to enact antiracist pedagogy. As Lipsitz puts it:

> Because they are ignorant of even the recent history of the possessive investment in whiteness—generated by slavery and segregation but augmented by social democratic reform—Americans produce largely cultural explanations for structural societal problems. The increased possessive investment in whiteness generated by the dis-investment in American's cities, factories, and schools since the 1970s disguises the general problems posed to our society by de-industrialization, economic restructuring, and neoconservative attacks on the welfare state as *racial* problems. It fuels a discourse that demonizes people of color for being victimized by these changes, while hiding the privileges of whiteness by attributing them to family values, fatherhood, and foresight—rather than to favoritism. (p. 379)

While we seek to have preservice teachers understand the institutional aspects of racism, we need to make sure that our pedagogies and texts do not end up reverting to the personal. For example, McIntosh (1990) intends to expose the larger societal forces that are indeed invisible to whites, privileges due only to their skin color. Yet her examples often cause us to see white privilege from an individual stance, as they focus on her personal experiences as a white woman. This popular article—often treated as though it is an antidote to white privilege and taught in many teacher education courses—is effective because it personalizes structural inequity.

However, because it is about personal experiences, the personal is often what students take from the piece. In so doing, they sometimes note situations that are complicated by social class and other inequities as proof that the examples are not necessarily about white privilege, but about other forms of privilege. The article does not help students to understand specific societal investments in whiteness over time, as does Lipsitz's (1995) article.

Lipsitz (1995) reminds us that we need to consider not only the individual, and not only the cultural, but the societal. He observes that "studies of culture too far removed from studies of social structure leave us with inadequate explanations for understanding racism and inadequate remedies for combating it" (p. 371). Reading Lipsitz's article, as Tim's preservice teachers did, can educate students about and make them aware of historical events and the effects of policies that have devastating effects on communities of color. This piece serves to provide students with

storical and institutional account of racial inequality and even an
why white people might default to racial/cultural explanations for
y. Students do not have to feel guilty that policy was set up this way, but
re responsible for their understanding of it—as well as for determining what
y will do about it.

A question that remains is what we expect our preservice teachers to do with their knowledge of white privilege and institutional racism, assuming that we are able to mitigate their guilt without absolving responsibility. As a result of his student teaching experience, Nicholas questioned his commitment to urban teaching. Frustrated and disheartened, he began to wonder if teaching in a setting more congruent with his own cultural background would be more productive for him. He despaired of fully understanding the multiple racial, ethnic, cultural backgrounds of the students who would learn with him in a classroom located in our university's metropolitan area.

Jill tried to tell him that the conversation the sixth-grade team had about the racial makeup of retained students was a start. The ability to talk about race and culture with other teachers—and taking the initiative to do so—was a beginning. She shared with him some of the practices and beliefs of the culturally responsive teachers she has studied in her dissertation research. She reminded him of the work he read by Linda Christensen (2000) in his literature methods course, of examples of units and lesson plans and student writing that focused on social justice teaching in the urban English classroom. She told him that if small groups of teachers and students didn't start working together to address some of these problems, they would persist.

But was this enough? Maybe more models of this kind of work, of classroom teachers successfully embodying critical, antiracist pedagogy are needed for preservice teachers to make sense of these ideas and practice liberatory teaching in their own classrooms. And teachers need to find allies—like JB's classmates—who can support them in their work, who will tell them they did the right thing, who will help them pay the fines when they violate racial barriers.

They need, too, the kind of dialogic conversations that occurred in Tim's class. Whereas dialogic discussions are characterized in educational research as consisting of open-ended questions with teachers and students building on each others' turns, we are using dialogic in the Bakhtinian sense. Dialogic conversations involve addressing and answering previous and future utterances across time and space. There has to be an awareness of other utterances and social meanings in order for a conversation to be dialogic.

Tim allowed various forms of antiracist work to speak to, and collide with, each other, which then helped JB to situate herself within this complex array of possibilities. When teacher education students become teachers, they need to find ways to sustain dialogic conversations that challenge and inspire them to be responsible, to learn about and teach the ways that inequitable structures are historically perpetuated, and to think through the complex ways that this knowledge will affect their practice.

References

Allard, A. & Santoro, N. (2006). Troubling identities: Teacher education students' constructions of class and ethnicity. *Cambridge Journal of Education*, 36(1), 115–129.

Beach, R., Thein, A., & Parks, D. (2008). *High school students' competing social worlds: Negotiating identities and allegiances in response to multicultural literature*. Mahwah, NJ: Erlbaum.

Christensen, L. (2000). *Reading, writing, and rising up: Teaching about social justice and the power of the written word*. Milwaukee, WI: Rethinking Schools.

Cross, B. (2005). New racism, reformed teacher education, and the same ole' oppression. *Educational Studies*, 38(3), 263–274.

Delpit, L. (1995). *Other people's children: Cultural conflict in the classroom*. New York: The New Press.

Florio-Ruane, S. (2001). *Teacher education and the cultural imagination: Autobiography, conversation, and narrative*. Mahwah, NJ: Erlbaum.

Gaine, C. (2001). If it's not hurting it's not working: Teaching teachers about "race." *Research Papers in Education*, 16(1), 93–113.

Gay, G. & Kirkland, K. (2003). Developing cultural critical consciousness and self reflection in preservice teacher education. *Theory into Practice*, 42(3), 181–187.

Goodman, J. & Kelly, T. (1988). Out of the mainstream: Issues confronting the male profeminist elementary school teacher. *Interchange*, 19(2), 1–14.

Grande, S. (2004). *Red pedagogy: Native American social and political thought*. Lanham, MD: Rowman & Littlefield.

Greene, S. & Abt-Perkins, D. (2003). *Introduction: How can literacy research contribute to racial understanding?* In S. Greene & D. Abt-Perkins (Eds.), *Making race visible: Literacy research for cultural understanding* (pp. 1–31). New York: Teachers College Press.

Gwaltney, J.L. (Ed.). (1980). *Drylongso: A self-portrait of black America*. New York: Random House.

Heath, S. (1982). *Questioning at home and at school: A comparative study*. In G. Spindler (Ed.), Doing the ethnography of schooling: Educational anthropology in action. New York: Holt, Rinehart & Winston.

Hicks, D. (1996). *Contextual inquiries: A discourse-oriented study of classroom learning*. In D. Hicks (Ed.), *Discourse, learning, and schooling* (pp. 104–144). New York: Cambridge University Press.

Howard, G. (1999). *We can't teach what we don't know: White teachers, multiracial schools*. New York: Teachers College Press.

Huerta, G. & Flemmer, L. (2005, March). Identity, beliefs, and community: LDS (Mormon) pre-service secondary teacher views about diversity. *Intercultural Education*, 16(1), 1–14.

Ignatiev, N. & Garvey, J. (Eds.) (1996). *Race traitor*. New York: Routledge

Kress, G. (1993). Against arbitrariness: The social production of the sign as a foundational issue in critical discourse analysis. *Discourse & Society*, 4(2), 169–191.

LeCompte, K. & McCray, A. (2002). Complex conversations with teacher candidates: Perspectives of whiteness and culturally responsive teaching. *Curriculum and Teaching Dialogue*, 4(1), 25–35.

Lewis, C. (2004). *New directions in critical discourse analysis*. Keynote Address. CDA Language Education Conference. Indiana University, Bloomington, IN.

Lewis, C., Ketter, J., & Fabos, B. (2001). Reading race in a rural context. *International Journal of Qualitative Studies in Education*, 14(3), 317–350.

Lipsitz, G. (1995). The possessive investment in whiteness: Racialized social democracy and the "White" problem in American studies. *American Quarterly*, 47(3), 369–387.

McIntosh, P. (1990). White privilege: Unpacking the invisible knapsack. *Independent School*, 49(2), 31–36.

Milner, H.M. (2006). Preservice teachers' learning about cultural and racial diversity: Implications for urban education. *Urban Education, 41*(4), 343–375.

Moje, E.B. & Lewis, C. (2007). Examining opportunities to learn literacy: The role of critical sociocultural literacy research. In C. Lewis, P. Enciso, & E. Moje (Eds.), *Identity, agency, and power: Reframing sociocultural research on literacy.* Mahwah, NJ: Erlbaum.

Murrell, P.C., Jr., (1993). *Afrocentric immersion: Academic and personal development of African American males in public schools.* In T. Perry & J. W. Fraser (Eds.), *Freedom's plow: Teaching in the multicultural classroom* (pp. 231–260). New York: Routledge.

Sleeter, C. (1993). *How white teachers construct race.* In C. McCarthy & W. Crichlow (Eds.), *Race, identity and representation in education* (pp. 157–171). New York: Routledge.

Solomon, R.P., Portelli, J., Daniel, B., & Campbell, A. (2005, July). The discourse of denial: How white teacher candidates construct race, racism, and "white privilege." *Race, Ethnicity, and Education, 8*(2), 147–169.

Thandeka, A. (1999). *Learning to be white.* New York: Continuum.

Trainor, J. (2005). "My ancestors didn't own slaves": Understanding White talk about race. *Research in the Teaching of English, 40*(2), 140–167.

Chapter 7
Anti-Oppressive Pedagogy in Early Childhood Teacher Education: A Conversation

Beth Blue Swadener, Cristian R. Aquino-Sterling, Mark Nagasawa, and Maggie Bartlett

> What I have been proposing is a profound respect for the cultural identity of students—a respect for the language of the other, the color of the other, the gender of the other, the class of the other, the sexual orientation of the other, the intellectual capacity of the other; that implies the ability to stimulate the creativity of the other. (Paulo Freire in McLaren, 2000)

7.1 Contexts of Our Work

As advocates of critical pedagogy (CP) and anti-oppressive education, in as much as these paradigms serve as critical lenses for "learning to question" (Freire and Faundez, 1989) and for critically "reading the world" (Freire and Macedo, 1987) and our experiences in it, we understand that all forms of educational practice occur within politically contested spaces (Adams et al., 1997; Apple, 1995, 1996; Kincheloe, 2005). One of the aims and challenges of our pedagogical practice/*praxis* as critical teacher educators is to address explicitly the contested political and social dimensions of the classroom and other learning spaces we inhabit, in order to co-create a safe, democratic, and participatory teaching/learning environment conducive to identifying and examining our assumptions, values, and belief systems regarding the culture, language, race, class, gender, sexual orientation, and religion of "the other."

In various capacities, we all teach within the context of an Early Childhood Education (ECE) teacher education program in the Southwest United States. In addition, we have worked together over the past several years in early childhood professional development projects focused largely on preschool teachers working in high poverty settings and linguistically diverse communities, ranging from urban predominantly Hispanic settings to indigenous (tribal) communities in rural areas. This has provided contexts for us to work with more diverse groups of future teachers than reflect the national profile of predominantly white, middle-class teachers (Darling-Hammond and Bransford, 2005).

B.B. Swadener, C.R. Aquino-Sterling, M. Nagasawa, and M. Bartlett
University of Arizona

S.L. Groenke and J.A. Hatch (eds.), *Critical Pedagogy and Teacher Education in the Neoliberal Era: Small Openings*,
DOI 10.1007/978-1-4020-9588-7_7, © Springer Science + Business Media B.V. 2009

As we discussed issues related to critical pedagogy in early childhood teacher education and challenges in our various roles as teacher educators and critical scholars, we decided to use our dialogue as the basis of this chapter. We started with face-to-face conversations and then utilized an online dialogue, transcripts of which form the bulk of our chapter. In our various conversations, Beth typically posed questions and we all discussed those and other issues that were raised. In that regard, the chapter also represents our work in mentoring each other in the applications of critical pedagogy to our work in varied fields related to ECE, including policy studies, language and literacy, early childhood, and special education. Given the often theoretical online discussion, we frequently mentioned readings that had been particularly influential in our work in teacher education and they are included as references.

We begin with reflections on our journeys to critical pedagogy and some of the major influences on our thinking and then move into a discussion of specific challenges and promising practices in the context of our experiences (together and individually) in the borderlands of the Southwest United States. Among the topics we address are ideological and practical tensions in critical pedagogy; issues of "methods fetish" (Aronowitz, 1993; Bartolomé, 1994, 2007); and dynamics of doing critical pedagogy in the shadows of No Child Left Behind (NCLB) and related high-stakes testing, teacher-proof curricula, and neoliberal/neoconservative policies. We conclude with reflections on how critical pedagogy has impacted our lives and praxis, framed within Freire's notion of "radical love" (Freire, 1970, 1998a; Darder, 2003).

7.2 Journeys to Critical Pedagogy

Beth: As a European-American woman of lower-middle-class background, benefiting from an array of unearned privileges, I have actively interrogated ways in which my work may be reproducing colonial, exploitive, or oppressive patterns and relationships for many years. My lifelong commitment to social justice has been strengthened by my work in "unlearning oppression" and participation in multiracial alliances since the early 1980s, as well as by my activism in social justice movements from the early 1970s through the present. One of my central identities is activist–scholar. I have been doing research and volunteer work in sub-Saharan Africa since the mid-1980s, and have worked in high poverty urban school and preschool settings in the United States for the past 18 years. I have long done collaborative research with urban educators committed to reflecting social justice and inclusion in their pedagogy. My current research is an international study of children's rights and unmediated voices, and I am part of two transnational collaborative projects focusing on children's rights and social inclusion.

For many years, I have co-facilitated an "unlearning oppression" workshop for my teacher education courses, and I typically do this the second week of class, in order to be transparent regarding my critical, liberatory, and ally stances regarding working with diverse children, families, and communities. The workshop is based on a set of working assumptions regarding the dynamics of institutional oppression and strategies for interrupting oppression and being strong allies across difference. Cristian has been a frequent co-facilitator of the workshop over the years. My critical pedagogy has been informed by a range of scholars/colleagues/critical friends including Mary Smith Arnold, Carl Grant, Christine Sleeter, Mara Sapon-Shevin, bell hooks, Lourdes Diaz Soto, Kagendo Mutua, Kevin Kumashiro, Valerie Polakow, and Patti Lather.

I'd be curious to hear more about your journeys to critical pedagogy and how it informs your work in teacher education.

Cristian: My journey to critical pedagogy started when I became a graduate student in the MA program in Hispanic Literatures at Columbia University and first read *El Masacre se pasa a pie* (Prestol-Castillo, 1989), a *novela-testimonio* in which the author denounces the atrocious events which occurred in my native Dominican Republic in October 1937, when a dictator ordered the massacre of thousands of Haitian immigrants. Reading Prestol-Castillo's work led me begin to inquire into the historical roots of contemporary issues regarding the social, political, and economic conditions of Haitian immigrants and their descendants in the Dominican Republic. The book also led me to question my own schooling experiences on the island. I remember asking myself why I had not been given the opportunity to read this book and why it was not included in the Dominican school curriculum. Most importantly, I felt the need to identify how Prestol-Castillo's work informed the contemporary conditions of Haitian immigrants in the island. This experience is an instance of how I began to read the world critically and to question what appeared to be neutral and apolitical schooling practices.

My journey into critical pedagogy continued as I became familiar with Michael Apple's *Ideology and Curriculum* (2004), a book which provided the theoretical foundations for engaging in dialogue regarding the politics of education and helped me acquire a critical interpretive lens to analyze my schooling experiences, as well as to think about the relationship between society, schooling/education, and curriculum. Reflecting on these experiences provided for me a vivid example of how teaching is always a political act and never a neutral one—an example of how the official school curriculum could serve as a means to restrict what is learned at school. Without the possibility of questioning the status quo, it becomes impossible to interrupt oppression. And, without acquiring what Paulo Freire referred to as *conscientização*, which implies an understanding of oppressive conditions, it is virtually impossible to work for social change in our world.

My disposition to engage critical perspectives influenced my work with preservice teachers within the contexts of an early childhood/elementary education program at Arizona State University (ASU). While in the program, I had the opportunity to learn and to co-facilitate the "Unlearning Oppression" workshop with Beth, and to design and facilitate, among other courses, a course on Structured English Immersion Theories and Practices. Through the Unlearning Oppression workshop, preservice teachers considered the importance of deconstructing assumptions regarding "the other"; the importance of learning to question and looking deeper into social and political dynamics of public schools as to assess how we, as teachers, may be colluding (or not) with oppressive situations.

During the course, I felt compelled to provide information on the effectiveness of bilingual education programs and practices, and, although the federal government mandates required us to teach about methods for Structured English Immersion (SEI), in addition, we read works that provided information on the effectiveness of bilingual education programs in the United States and abroad. We also read works that depicted the challenges and opportunities of immigrant children in US public schools and that brought a human face to the issue of learning English as a second language. By reading about and engaging various perspectives on the effects of structured English immersion versus those of bilingual education, preservice teachers learned to critically assess what researchers in these fields suggested regarding the validity and effectiveness of two distinct approaches to educating English Language Learners. Preservice teachers also had the opportunity to debate for and against both approaches.

Critical pedagogy provided for us a *dispositivee*—a tool for creating a teaching/learning space where educational policies, curriculum, and teaching methods were not taken at face value, and for realizing that teaching is always a political and never a neutral act.

Maggie: My journey toward emancipatory education began in middle America with little exposure to visible ethnic, religious, cultural, sexual, or linguistic differences. School was never a place of great success or joy for me. However, I have traveled a path that situates me in schools, learning and teaching, and using ideas bound in a framework of freedom, equity, and inclusion.

Some of my first memories of "difference" and acceptance was a friendship that my family had with a Mennonite foster family. The family consisted of a mother and three siblings. All the children, who were all around my age of 9, functioned with multiple disabilities. Those Friday evening dinners and family get togethers still are some of my favorite childhood memories. As I continued through K–12 public education, I always remember empathizing with others who were "different," perhaps because that is where I felt most accepted. While I was not an advocate or ally at that point in my life, it was ever-present in my mind.

College was an analogous experience to high school, yet in an ever-smaller and "whiter" town, within a college that was rife with racism, sexism, homophobia, etc. Again, I was still not an advocate or ally, but I felt unsettled by the institution and culture and knew that change was needed.

Once out of college I joined the US Peace Corps and became a volunteer in rural northern Namibia, Southern Africa. This event began to tap into my advocacy and alliances with people who were marginalized. It was also at this point that I began to interrogate what it meant to be white, privileged (as it is all relative), educated, and all the trappings that go along with those identities.

This path then led me to teaching in the field of special education. This job had many similarities to my work in a postapartheid country. The power structures that were at play in the school system that regulated children with disabilities to inequitable learning situations is what I saw in Namibia, including lack of resources, different treatment, social exclusion, and negative constructions of difference.

These episodes throughout my life have situated me in a framework that is bound by Freire's notion of freedom that includes a desire of living and working in an environment that values people, treats all equitably, and encourages cultural differences and expression. This idea of a world that functions based on freedom, equity, and inclusion is supported in my work by scholars from the fields of disability studies, postcolonial, and African scholars among others. It also has transformed the way I teach and work with educators.

In my practice of critical pedagogy, I strive to allow space to interrogate current policies and practices for children with disabilities embedded in notions of deficit thinking, special educator as expert, child as recipient of knowledge and curriculum, and the powerlessness which children with disabilities and their loved ones may experience. Two ways that I am able to facilitate discussions are working with teachers in a master's program and with early childhood educators teaching in Head Start programs. Most students in the courses I teach are middle-class white women. In class, I attempt to gently prod and question to see if we can make explicit some assumptions that surround notions of power relations and privilege. Moreover, the format of the class attempts to demonstrate methods to embrace children's differences and view them as an asset. In contrast, I am working with Head Start teachers earning their bachelor's degree in early childhood education. This group of dedicated women teaches in predominately Hispanic-serving settings and are, for the most part, bilingual. At times I take on different roles with these experienced teachers. They tend to embrace culturally relevant pedagogies and understand funds of knowledge and community strengths (Gonzalez et al., 1993).

Mark: I was raised to neither ask questions nor consider my funds of knowledge. This makes sense to me as I consider where I come from. I am a yonsei or fourth-generation Japanese-American. As the grandchild of immigrant laborers to what was the Kingdom of Hawaii and the child of migrants from the Territory of Hawaii to the US mainland, I was raised to work hard in school and to conform. The unsaid-but-understood rule was that I had an obligation to be successful, for my great-grandparents and grandparents had worked hard and had humbled themselves so that we could have better lives.

My explorations of CP began with my return to graduate school in 2003. In my first seminar, Beth shared an article that she and Lourdes Diaz Soto (Soto and Swadener 2002) had recently published. They wrote of the need to decolonize early childhood education and to question the primacy of scientist practice. I really struggled with that piece. What did this have to do with teaching young children or teaching teachers of young children? Colonization happened to other people and in different times.

However there was one line in the article that I kept thinking about. Amidst all the unfamiliar theoretical references, they talked of starting with reflections on our lives and experiences. This made sense and led me to explorations of my cultural identity and relationship to (post)colonial Hawaii, altering my perspective on *shikata ga nai* (loosely: the way things are; it cannot be helped) by giving me a very personal illustration of what Freire (1970) called "limit situations"—what is actually possible when one explores what seems impossible.

More recently I have been thinking about Parker Palmer's (1998) *The Courage to Teach* and his question "Who is the self that teaches?". His is a critical question because as we investigate the self, the picture gets much more complicated and race, class, gender, sexuality, ability, culture, history, etc. become almost unavoidable things to consider.

Palmer's work serves as a reminder to me that in the heady world of critical theory, critical pedagogy is still about teaching. It is a uniquely human and potentially risky act, practice, craft, enactment, or performance. His discussions of identity, integrity, dualism, fear, and the structure/agency binary help me to make sense of the tensions that we discussed the other afternoon—can there be many ways of being a critical teacher? What of "irreconcilable" ideologies, "right" answers, and the power asymmetries that exist between students and teachers?

7.3   Tensions and Contradictions in Critical Pedagogy in ECE Teacher Education

Beth: How do you reconcile your beliefs, ideology, and commitments to social justice with what students believe, or their commitments, which may not be framed in ways we might agree are "critical" or anchored in social justice? This question, in fact, brings to mind the possibility we may tend to implicitly assume that many of our students are victims of "false consciousness" and the potential colonizing discourse that may be associated with consciousness-raising. It also brings to mind the explicit resistance we may face when teaching from critical perspectives.

Mark: I try to remind myself that I did not always have the perspective that I do now. I am particularly mindful of having had teachers who espoused critical theory but who seemed to want us to regurgitate their ideas. As a teacher I want students to be able to articulate and justify their professional beliefs and actions. My approach has been to a get at critical questions and issues while also trying to address students' pressing questions and concerns.

One of the classes I teach is an integrative curriculum class that is tied to a preschool student teaching experience. One of the key skill sets we work on is linking assessment, planning, and instruction. Many students seem to see assessment as something outside of themselves, something done to students, so to illustrate the important role teachers play in assessment I have been using ethnography as a metaphor, drawing on Harry Wolcott's (2008) distinctions between looking and seeing, to explore "objective" observation and interpretation. We work at describing still photos, children's work samples, and classroom video footage to identify specific details, what children were working on, and what teachers' instructional intentions may have been. This provides an avenue to ask questions about what they noticed about gender relations, race, language, adult/child dynamics, ability, and other underlying assumptions embedded in common activities.

Maggie: I, like Mark, encourage students to question our course content and form their own beliefs. The curriculum I have compiled has readings from multiple perspectives, some of which I do not embrace. While I do not demand they ascribe to my beliefs, I do insist on an ability to support and justify their ideas. In the class that I am currently teaching, this situation just occurred. In discussions, I ask that students try to tease out examples of possible oppression and power. In doing so, a teacher/student brought up her ability to easily address issues with her first-grade students but not with colleagues. In this dialogue, issues of power or gender surfaced, so I brought it up. To my surprise, the student responded that it was not an issue of power; she simply insists that her class is harmonious and will confront issues immediately to resolve problems. On the other hand, she doesn't want to ruffle feathers by confronting colleagues. I was surprised that no one else in class expressed that this has embedded power differentials. In turn, I had to then ask myself whether I was imposing my assumptions on her ideas.

Beth: I think some of the student resistance relates to what has been described in some feminist literature as imposition or impositional teaching—that is imposing one's views on students in a way that is limiting, restrictive, or even contradictory to the purported critical or social justice message. It also brings to mind some of the long-term feminist literature on the roles of silence, contradictions of "giving voice," and critiques of liberatory pedagogy, including those found in critical race theory. I have attempted to practice what I teach. I think "critical scholars" must do more than just write about social justice—it is a constant struggle that is very real (that problematic term not to be confused with "Truth") to countless people.

One of the projects that I have been deeply engaged with over the past 7 years is the Local to Global Justice Teach-In at Arizona State University. This acts in some ways as a bridge between critical pedagogy and strengthening connections between global struggles and local actions and organizing on a range of social justice issues. Over 500 activists from the Southwest gather for 2–3 days each year and we learn from each other and nationally known activist speakers in a range of participatory ways, functioning in many ways as a social forum. Cristian has led a team of Spanish translators for the event and we have had some powerful "speak out" panels of indigenous Mexican graduate students over the years. This year some of our doctoral students teaching in the early childhood program worked with a group of children and youth to have a Youth Teach-In as part of the event. It was interesting to see the interface of teacher education with this event and the many layers of critical pedagogy that transpired.

Mark: I wish I could have participated in the Teach-In this year, but I now have an idea about encouraging participation in the Youth Teach-In as a project option to encourage exploration of the differences between education and schooling. This also makes me think about Beth and Cristian's earlier discussions of using the Unlearning Oppression workshop in their classes. I also incorporate this into mine.

Maggie brought up something that I have encountered too. It is hard for people to talk with each other about their differences. Kwame Appiah (2006) says we live in a world of strangers, and I believe that if adults are unable to do this, then we will have a hard time teaching children how to do this.

One of our unlearning oppression activities involves perspective-taking and empathy for parents from a range of backgrounds. Each student receives a slip of paper with a general descriptor (e.g., white, Appalachian parent), a direct quote from a parent about a problematic situation they have faced, and the stem, "I feel…" In my experience, students have been very thoughtful regarding issues of gender, race, class, language, and (dis)ability but seem to have a more difficult time with things that can be seen as involving (im)morality, such as religious diversity, sexuality, and family composition. In one example, a lesbian mother discusses her daughter's troubles relating to activities at school. I have never had anyone voice empathy with the parent's perspective, with the voiced opinion consistently being that the mother's sexuality has no bearing on school. I ask if it matters to the couple's daughter and if this example speaks to how unsaid assumptions about "normal" and "abnormal" families are expressed in common activities at school, particularly in early childhood classrooms.

In other examples, parents describe their children's experiences around holidays. Interestingly these discussions have been very impassioned, with a common opinion being that people belonging to religious minority groups often unfairly exclude their children from the enjoyment of celebrations. I have tried to use this as an opportunity to discuss celebrations and holidays as "cultural icebergs" to explore the underlying values and power relationships within them. These have not been easy conversations, but my intent is to call attention to the skills or habits of mind we are practicing, such as listening, empathy, perspective-taking, integrity, and the ability to disagree while still regarding each other. In terms of "critical tasks," being explicit about this sort of interpersonal ethics, of the kind Martin Buber (1970) or Appiah (2006) discuss, seems quite important.

Cristian: I cannot help but to think about two key works in the field of education and critical pedagogy that have influenced my perspectives on the issues you have raised. The first is Elizabeth Ellsworth's (1989) article, "Why doesn't this feel empowering?" The other is Jennifer Gore's (1993) *The Struggle for Pedagogies*. What I have learned from both Ellsworth and Gore is that the hope of a critical pedagogy is to be found in dialogue. Dialogue, and the willingness to entertain various, and at times conflicting perspectives on an issue, is key to the work of teachers working for social justice.

Beth: I recall knowing some of the students in the class that Liz Ellsworth wrote about and their critiques of the article. I also appreciated Gloria Ladson-Billings (1997) essay, titled "I know why this doesn't feel empowering: A critical *race* analysis of critical pedagogy." Arguing that "one problematic and enduring aspect of critical theory/pedagogy [is] its failure to address adequately the question of race" (p. 127), Gloria challenged critical educators to recognize that education can no longer be "race neutral"or "colorblind"(p. 131) and notes that "while critical theory may be explicit about unequal power relations vis-à-vis class and culture, it tends to be mute in relation to race (as well as gender, as explained by Ellsworth)" (pp. 130–131). To me, any anti-oppressive teacher education approach must foreground critical race theory and examine parallel (and nonhierarchical) sources of oppression—including racism and white supremacy.

7.4   The "Methods Fetish" and Other Dilemmas

Mark: In some of our earlier discussions, Cristian brought up Lila Bartolomé's (1994) idea of the "methods fetish" in teacher education. I think this is a central problematic in the practice of CP. Teaching is a profession, and those drawn to the field come with a (very reasonable) expectation to be taught how to teach. Unfortunately, it seems that CP and effective teaching are often thought of as mutually exclusive.

I could project this problematic on students, attributing the "methods fetish" to some sort of deficiency on their part, but to do so is both unjust and shirks my responsibility to them as a teacher. Teachers do need to know how to plan, facilitate peace in their classrooms, teach, and balance all of the other demands placed upon them.

Beth: This respect for teachers is so critical. Thinking more about the "methods fetish," I am reminded of Macedo's (1997) description of Freire's "anti-method pedagogy," in which he argues against "reducing dialogue and problem posing to a mere method" (p. 8). He cites a number of examples of how middle-class university-based colleagues fall into a "romantic paternalism" (p. 6) that may involve the community but doesn't threaten their expert position or privilege. Macedo advocates an anti-method pedagogy that "forces us to new dialogue as a form of social praxis so that the sharing of experiences is informed by reflection and political action" (p. 8). I think this maps well on the methods fetish critique and also raises more questions about what we might do in the name of critical pedagogy that actually has contradictory, even colonizing tendencies in our work as early childhood teacher educators.

Cristian: I think you have touched on a key point, Beth. How does one then foster a teaching and learning environment where preservice teachers become critical reflective practitioners? This is indeed a key question to which Carr and Kemmis (1986) and Schon (1983) have provided some answers. In their work on becoming a critical and reflective practitioner through "Action Research," these authors suggest that it is through exposing students to the varied contradictions we find in our society that a new consciousness or way of thinking and action upon these issues may emerge in preservice teachers. They further suggest that preservice teachers could acquire these critical perspectives by conducting research on their own practices.

Maggie: Throughout this discussion, I connect with how we all question our praxis—if we are truly utilizing critical pedagogy and not employing colonizing practices. Each new course section I teach, I reevaluate the syllabus and make changes that attempt to increase the literature and space needed to interrogate and develop a critical consciousness. I have recently incorporated work by Mara Sapon-Shevin that offers a social justice-based critical view of special education and advocates for full inclusion. This view is often met with resistance from practicing general education teachers as either improbable or even impossible.

7.5   Critical Pedagogy in the Shadow of NCLB and Good Start/Grow Smart

Beth: Speaking of reading and teaching against the grain, many teachers I work with do not resist critical perspectives as much as feel that they express having too many competing pressures of high-stakes testing and other accountability measures. Indigenous educators I work with critique NCLB as pushing out language-and culture-revitalization initiatives and urban educators see it as biased against so many of the children they teach. Many of us who advocate full inclusion also note the requirements of most students to take the tests with few, if any, accommodations. They see the implicit bias in many of these standards-based movements and can begin to identity neoliberal and neoconservative discourses, but they feel captive to at least some degree of NCLB—especially if they are teaching in "underperforming" districts or those "at risk" of being taken over by the state. How have you experienced critical pedagogy in the shadow of NCLB?

Cristian: There is indeed a great body of literature in teacher education which relates to how to prepare teachers to teach under the accountability regime of NCLB. Sleeter's (2007) edited work, *Facing Accountability in Education*, comes to mind. Critiques of NCLB vary a great deal in terms of ideological standpoints. Not all critiques of NCLB critique the policy in the same way, for the same reasons, and with the same intentions. In my dissertation, I provide a typology of critiques of NCLB based on how scholars participate in the cultural assumptions (closing the achievement gap and providing equal educational opportunities) and instrumental logics (accountability, standards, and high-stakes testing) of NCLB. Although some progressive scholars may decry the injustices of NCLB's accountability system, for example, they do so in the hope that a better accountability system may be implemented. Some radical critiques move away from the discourse of accountability, standards, and testing altogether. However, I have found that the discourse in which NCLB is framed has become so dominant that many scholars are now trying to find ways to work within the system itself.

Mark: This warms my pragmatic heart because, while I think it very important to offer critiques from as many perspectives as possible, ultimately the existential question is what do we do? As we talked about before, none of us can step outside of discourse, the superstructure, culture, society, etc.

Despite all that concerns me about NCLB, in my analysis it is hybrid and multi-vocal and the spirit of the original Elementary and Secondary Education Act (ESEA) remains. I recently attended the state Reading First conference. As expected there was a heavy dose of the National Reading Panel (NRP) recommendations (NICHHD, 2000) and of the so-called big 5 of literacy in English: phonemic awareness, phonics knowledge, fluency, vocabulary, and comprehension, but there was also seemingly earnest discussion of closing achievement gaps to give children chances to succeed in school (and therefore life).

While this is problematic, I found myself thinking about Lisa Delpit's (1995) arguments that people outside of the culture of power need to be both taught the skills to survive in the dominant society while also being taught about the functioning of power. As teacher educators, our students' effectiveness and professionalism will be judged based on their ability to implement the dominant modes of teaching and to be able to perform on the measures (however misguided) being used. Are we not failing them, and their students, if we do not teach them how to operate within this system, while also equipping them to read and act against the grain? For example, one early literacy activity that I am planning for the upcoming year involves examining the NRP recommendations, reflecting upon the genres commonly found in preschool libraries, and facilitating the retelling of stories to link oral and written language. Part of this discussion will also involve thematic and interpretive analysis of text and illustrations, the "literacy wars," and the unsaid assumptions we use to make instructional decisions.

Maggie: Mark raises the important question of whether, if we do not teach students to operate successfully within the mainstream of society and understand and identify issues of power, we may not be successfully providing an "appropriate" or relevant education. I see (at least) two sides to this. I agree that we need to educate students to understand this hierarchical, power-driven society in which we live. In doing so, we acknowledge it and then share strategies about how to function within that paradigm. I see this all the time in the special education field. We are consistently "training" children with disabilities to function like "typical peers." We teach social skills, coping strategies, and academic skills that will help the child live within our communities.

In contrast, I grapple with that and wonder if it is the minority group (e.g. children with disabilities, underprivileged youth, second language learners, etc.) that we should be teaching this notion of successful border-crossing (Giroux, 2005). I think we should not place all of the burden on the minority group. I would argue that people in the "mainstream" need to take responsibility for this and be willing to learn more about inclusive communities that embrace the difference. When we begin to embrace difference, people can express their social, historically, and cultural beings and it will not be a deficit, but an advantage.

In relation to NCLB, the policy explicitly disregards children with disabilities and their needs and, in my mind, is in direct contention with the Individuals with Disabilities Education Act (IDEA). In some districts, students are expected to be taught on grade level; if a student is in fifth grade and functioning at the second-grade level it simply does not matter. The child will be taught and tested at the fifth-grade level, often without the accommodations/modifications that are used in the classroom as stipulated by the student's Individualized Education Plan (IEP). The wide range of childrens' skills and rates of learning is often overshadowed by the emphasis on grade-level testing. My point is that I hope for a day when we don't have to teach students to function analogously to dominant culture. Until then I don't know how we can *not* teach minority students to be able to adapt to mainstream norms, but my hopes are that we could embrace linguistic, ability, sexual, gender, cultural, and ethnic differences.

7.6 Critical Pedagogy and Anti-Oppressive Education: What's "Radical Love" Got to Do With It?

Beth: In closing our conversation, I wonder whether we can focus a bit more on the "specifics" of ways in which our work with critical pedagogy has impacted our practice and our lives. In particular, I wonder if we could frame our closing reflections on radical love and its role in anti-oppressive education and our work in teacher education.

Cristian: Critical pedagogy has provided another lens from which to reread my previous experience living in the Dominican Republic as a child where, more often than not, Haitian immigrants and Haitian-Dominican children were (and still are) treated as less than human beings. CP has provided me with the theoretical grounding to reflect on my experiences as an immigrant youngster at a public high school in New York City. CP has revolutionized my perspectives on the personal as well as the structural/systemic causes of persistent social, academic, and economic underachievement among so-called minorities in the United States. CP has brought me face-to-face with the various ways in which my own (conscious as well as unconscious) assumptions, values, belief systems could (and have) served as vehicles for perpetuating and the cycle of oppression. Most importantly, CP has assisted me in acquiring the habits of mind and heart, a disposition to "radical[ly] love" (Freire, 1970; Darder, 2003) and to foster democratic spaces for teaching and learning whenever I find myself in the position to do so.

I agree with Kincheloe that "all descriptions of critical pedagogy—like knowledge in general—are shaped by those who devise them and the values they hold" (2005, p. 7). Our very notions of critical pedagogy and anti-oppressive education cannot be disassociated from our histories and identities as conditioned and situated sociocultural and sociopolitical human entities. While sharing historical roots, including in The Frankfurt School of Critical Theory, critical theory has been expanded and redefined according to the "signs of the times" and the contexts in which it has been applied.

As many scholars note, it was the publication of Paulo Freire's *Pedagogy of the Oppressed* in 1967 which marked the beginning of the critical pedagogy movement in education in the Americas. Drawing on liberation theology and the critical theory of the Frankfurt School in Germany, Freire espoused the idea and praxis of *conscientização* or learning to perceive social, political, and economic contradictions which brought about and sustained the oppression of marginalized peoples in Brazil and other developing countries, and invited us to take action against the oppressive elements of such unsettling realities (Freire, 1970). By the mid-1970s, scholars in education and other disciplines began to adapt Freire's idea of critical pedagogy and to relate it to a so-called first-world context (Kincheloe, 2005). Freire's ideas and praxis was moved by what he called "radical love" for those who are oppressed and who suffer as a result of structural and systemic inequalities perpetuated at global and local levels. This "radical love" must transfer into our practice with ECE preservice teachers.

Maggie: Like Cristian, the notions of critical pedagogy and radical love are lenses I've used to understand my education and praxis. When I first came to ASU, I kept reading about teaching as a social and political act, and teachers as agents of change. That was initially unsettling to me until my realization of the ability of it to transform some aspects of education for children with disabilities. Now, I embrace this awareness and ability to be an agent of change. Using the idea of radical love allows us all to teach and live in a way that challenges existing inequities.

What I do grapple with is applying the same level of radical love when working with people that have ideas I believe to be oppressive. In my mind, radical love must be used to decrease marginalization while still having space for varying views—even views that are oppressive. While I do not condone those views, and challenge the ideas, would I not be an oppressor if I was unwilling to allow for that space in my classroom? The more I learn and the more I grow as an instructor, the more transformative critical pedagogy and radical love inform my personal life and praxis.

Mark: What comes through for me as I reflect on our conversation about praxis is that we have all discussed how critical pedagogy ideas and practices have affected our being. Each of us is motivated by a sense of justice and responsibility to be moral and ethical agents, while also recognizing the potential dangers of doing this in an anti-dialogic or formulaic way.

When thinking about Freire's notion of radical love, I am reminded of Kwame Appiah's (2006) discussion of loving humankind but not necessarily loving actual people. He argues that it is not enough to have an abstract concern for human life or well-being but it is also a sense of obligation to others and a deep concern for particular lives in all their complexity and contradictions. For me this tempers the application of critical theory, which in some instances can lend itself to views of others that leave us disconnected from them—an impediment in teaching.

Beth: In thinking about how both Freire's radical love and Appiah's cosmopolitan applied ethics and identity theories apply to our engagement with critical pedagogy, I think about how *relational* this work is. For me it goes beyond naming, interrupting, and unlearning forms of oppression and encouraging teachers to be critical intellectuals. It is certainly not about formulas or prescriptions, reflecting a methods fetish—even culturally relevant curriculum formulas, and it is more than learning to be allies across a range of different identities and complex communities, although that seems important. It is about love—a love that it filled with hope, kindness, and promise for all children and an authentic respect for and engagement with those who have chosen to teach.

References

Adams, M., Bell, L.A., & Griffin, P. (Eds.). (1997). *Teaching for diversity and social justice: A sourcebook.* New York: Routledge.
Appiah, K.A. (2006). *Cosmopolitanism: Ethics in a world of strangers.* New York: W.W. Norton.
Apple, M.W. (1995). *Education and power* (2nd ed.). New York: Routledge.

Apple, M.W. (1996). *Cultural politics and education*. New York: Teachers College Press.

Apple, M.W. (2004). *Ideology and curriculum*. (3rd ed.). New York: Routledge.

Aronowitz, S. (1993). Paulo Freire's radical democratic humanism. In P. McClaren (Ed.), *Paulo Freire: A critical encounter*. New York: Routledge.

Bartolomé, L.I. (1994). Beyond the methods fetish: Toward humanizing pedagogy. *Harvard Educational Review, 64*(7), 173–194.

Bartolomé, L.I. (2007). Critical pedagogy and teacher education: Radicalizing prospective teachers. In P. McLaren & J. Kincheloe (Eds.), *Critical pedagogy: Where are we now?* (pp. 263–286). New York: Peter Lang.

Buber, M. (1970). *I and thou*. (W. Kaufman, Trans.). New York: Free Press.

Carr, W., & Kemmis, S. (1986). *Becoming critical: Education, knowledge and action research.* London: Falmer.

Darder, A. (2003). Teaching as an act of love: Reflections on Paulo Freire and his contributions to our lives. In A. Darder, R. Torres, & M. Baltodano (Eds.), *The critical pedagogy reader* (pp. 497–511). New York: Routledge Falmer.

Darling-Hammond, L., & Bransford, J. (2005). *Preparing teachers for a changing world: What teachers should learn and be able to do*. San Francisco, CA: Jossey-Bass.

Delpit, L. (1995). *Other people's children: Cultural conflict in the classroom*. New York: The New Press.

Ellsworth, E. (1989) Why doesn't this feel empowering?: Working through the repressive myths of critical pedagogy. In C. Luke & J. Gore (Eds.), *Feminisms and critical pedagogy* (pp. 90–119). New York: Routledge.

Freire, P. (1970). *Pedagogy of the oppressed*. New York: Herder & Herder.

Freire, P. (1998). *Pedagogy of the heart*. New York: Continuum.

Freire, P. & Faundez, A. (1989). *Learning to question: A pedagogy of liberation*. New York: Continuum.

Freire, P. & Macedo, D. (1987). *Literacy: Reading the word and the world*. South Hadley, MA: Bergin & Garvey.

Giroux, H. (2005). *Border crossings: Cultural workers and the politics of education* (2nd ed.). New York: Routledge.

Gonzalez, N., Moll, L.C., Floyd-Tenery, M., Rivera, A., Rendon, P., Gonzales, R., & Amanti, C. (1993). *Teacher research on funds of knowledge: Learning from households*. Santa Cruz, CA: Center for Research on Education, Diversity & Excellence.

Gore, J. (1993). *The struggle for pedagogies: Critical and feminists discourses as regimes of truth*. New York: Routledge.

Kincheloe, J.L. (2005). *Critical pedagogy*. New York: Peter Lang.

Ladson-Billings, G. (1997). I know why this doesn't feel empowering: A critical race analysis of critical pedagogy. In P. Freire (Ed.), *Mentoring the mentor: A critical dialogue with Paulo Freire*. New York: Peter Lang.

Macedo, D. (1997). An anti-method pedagogy: A Freirian perspective. In P. Freire (Ed.), *Mentoring the mentor: A critical dialogue with Paulo Freire*. New York: Peter Lang.

McLaren, P. (2000). *Che Guevara, Paulo Freire, and the pedagogy of revolution*. Lanham, MD: Rowman & Littlefield.

National Institute of Child Health and Human Development. (2000). *Teaching children to read: An evidence-based assessment of the scientific research literature on reading and its implications for reading instruction*. Washington, DC: U.S. Government Printing Office.

Palmer, P.J. (1998). *The courage to teach: Exploring the inner landscape of a teacher's life*. San Francisco, CA: Jossey-Bass.

Prestol-Castillo, F. (1989). *El Masacre se pasa a pie*. Santo Domingo: Ediciones Taller.

Schon, D. (1983). *The reflective practitioner: How professionals think in action*. New York: Basic Books.

Sleeter, C.E. (2007). *Facing accountability in education: Democracy and equity at risk*. New York: Teachers College Press.

Soto, L.D. and Swadener, B.B. (2002). Toward liberatory early childhood, theory, research and praxis: Decolonizing a field. *Contemporary Issues in Early Childhood, 3*(1), 38–65.

Wolcott, H.F. (2008). *Ethnography: A way of seeing* (2nd ed.). Lanham, MD: AltaMira.

Chapter 8
Integrating Macro- and Micro-Level Issues in ESOL/Bilingual Teacher Education

Maria Dantas-Whitney, Karie Mize, and Eileen Dugan Waldschmidt

8.1 Challenges

Schools are greatly influenced by what happens outside of the school doors. The social environment influences policies at the federal and state level, which ultimately impact what occurs in the classroom. Inequities that are prevalent in the greater society are reflected in inequities in student achievement and school outcomes. It is important for teachers to understand the sociopolitical context and impact of the broader, societal forces that are prevalent in the twenty-first century on schools.

Students and educators are living in the post-9/11 era where the fear of "terrorists"has influenced our domestic policy about others who are "foreign." Efforts to "protect" the United States have been focused on militarizing the southern Mexican border despite the entry of more people who are undocumented from Canada (Public Broadcasting Service, 2003). This attempt to exclude people has also influenced views of language. The English Only movement and anti-bilingual initiatives have strengthened their efforts to devalue the linguistic heritage of a growing number of school-age students (Crawford, 2004; Menken, 2008).

Another broader, macro-level force that is prevalent in the twenty-first century includes neoliberalism, or the capitalist interests of the business community (Apple, 2001). Testing, textbook, and tutoring companies are posting record profits, and education has become—literally—big business. Neoliberal policies have applied a business model to education, increasing the focus on outputs—or student scores—and decreasing the focus on inputs—or educational resources. Schools have been asked to produce better results, commonly referred to as standards, and educators are being held accountable for student progress. A positive feature of the accountability and standards movement has been the increased focus on the educational attainment of underperforming groups. Schools now disaggregate and separately

M. Dantas-Whitney and K. Mize
Western Oregon University

E.D. Waldschmidt
University of New Mexico

S.L. Groenke and J.A. Hatch (eds.), *Critical Pedagogy and Teacher Education in the Neoliberal Era: Small Openings*, DOI 10.1007/978-1-4020-9588-7_8, © Springer Science + Business Media B.V. 2009

report the scores of subgroups such a low-income students, students who receive special education services, and English language learners (ELLs). On the other hand, focusing on uniform outcomes has greatly increased the reliance on scripted curricula that do not take into account the linguistic and cultural needs of English language learners.

In 2002 with the No Child Left Behind (NCLB) Act, high-stakes tests were attached to these neoliberal policies. Instead of being considered as a measure of student achievement, standardized tests are now the primary tool used to measure student learning (Neill, 2005). In the effort to have every student on grade level by 2014, predetermined goals for student test scores are measured by Adequate Yearly Progress (AYP), and schools are penalized if they fail to meet these incremental gains (Garcia et al., 2008). Even if the majority of students are making progress, the failure of one subgroup to meet AYP results in sanctions for the entire school that get progressively worse with each ensuing "failure." With such high stakes attached to the scores of marginalized and historically underperforming student groups, it is especially important to ensure that the assessments used are valid and reliable for these students. Nevertheless, standardized tests have been continuously proven to be heavily biased against students from culturally, linguistically, and socioeconomically diverse backgrounds (Menken, 2008; Neill, 2005).

Current educational practices that reduce and narrow complex ideas to measurable, decontextualized, and meaningless tasks are especially impacting students from diverse backgrounds. In addition to these student groups experiencing more drill and remediation, policies have encouraged districts to unnecessarily segregate or track students within schools according to their perceived ability levels (Garcia et al., 2008). For English language learners in particular, there is a push to have separate, grammatically based English Language Development classes in some states, like Oregon (Mize & Dantas-Whitney, 2007) and New Jersey (Zehr, 2007).

Under NCLB, a single student can be counted in multiple subgroups, such as "Latino, Limited English Proficient, and Low Income," meaning that one score on a standardized test can be counted three times. As a result, some districts are artificially distributing students to limit the percentages of certain student groups; new policies in New York and North Carolina, for example, limit the percentage of English language learners who can attend each school to reduce the likelihood that student subgroups will negatively impact the school's rating (Siegal, 2008). Paradoxically, pushing more students out of schools creates the appearance that test scores are rising and that the achievement gap is narrowing, both of which improve the school's ranking under the No Child Left Behind Act (McNeil et al., 2008). Without federal policies acknowledging the structural inequalities in our society, schools are, in essence, being held accountable for ethnic, linguistic, and socioeconomic demographics.

Despite the universally appealing notion that no child will be left behind, failing to address the structural inequalities that plague our schools perpetuates under achievement. Arroyo from the Education Trust (2007) analyzes funding trends from 1999 to 2005, and indicates that school districts with the greatest needs in terms of student demographics still receive the lowest amount of funding.

Because a great proportion of school funds stem from local property taxes, schools in higher socioeconomic areas tend to have bigger coffers, despite the extra funds that schools in lower socioeconomic areas receive from the federal government. These findings extend to districts with a high population of English language learners, who generally receive less financial support than low-ELL districts. Instead of acknowledging these material realities and the need for more educational inputs, neoliberal policymakers continue to demand higher qualifications of teachers while simultaneously decreasing their efficacy and ability to use their skills in the classroom. By keeping the focus on teacher quality and student achievement, neoliberalism makes it look as if educators alone can reverse the structural inequities that are impacting our schools. In effect, these neoliberal policies are contributing to "even more educational apartheid, not less" (Apple, 2001, p. 41).

8.2 Teacher Educators in ESOL/Bilingual Education

Those of us in teacher preparation need to encourage our teacher candidates to be critical of the status quo and conscious of how local classrooms are influenced by structural inequalities at the macro level. We borrow Bartolomé and Balderrama's (2001) definition of critical sociocultural consciousness as an understanding of "the possible linkages between macro-level political, economic, and social variables, and subordinated groups' academic performance at the micro-level classroom" (p. 48). If teachers in today's schools do not understand how the egregious underachievement and disaffiliation of students from diverse backgrounds are influenced by the broader sociopolitical context, they may infer that racial, linguistic, socioeconomic, and/or cultural backgrounds are to blame for these outcomes. For example, if preservice teachers find that the English language learners in their schools repeatedly score lower on achievement tests, they may learn to anticipate this underperformance or conclude that it is acceptable. Instead, preservice teachers need to understand the macro-level issues, such as how the process used to create standardized tests privileges test-takers who are native English speakers from the majority culture, and the need for authentic assessments that measure the growth of language as well as content. We want them to question the educational structures that impact English language learners at the micro level—in their own classroom and school—so that they help change tracking procedures and monocultural curricula in their district and state (macro) levels.

When educators question the status quo and consider alternative explanations for student underachievement in schools (Valdés, 1996), this knowledge must be linked to action and advocacy for students, their families, and their communities. Advocacy comes in many forms—standing up, speaking out, using covert practices, educating participants—and is often a difficult role for beginning teachers and experienced teachers alike. This chapter tells the story of how three teacher educators work to foster critical sociocultural consciousness so that preservice teachers are inspired to become advocates.

To contextualize our chapter, we first describe our collaboration as teacher educators and researchers of our own practice. Two of us (Maria and Eileen) are former colleagues in the English for Speakers of Other Languages (ESOL)/Bilingual teacher education program at a large public university, where we conducted a study that examined our students' written reflections as a way to assess our practice as teacher educators. The results revealed that many of our students held reductionist perspectives about their roles as teachers. They often viewed teaching as a technical, nonlocalized activity, which could be defined by a collection of strategies that are universally effective for all learners (Dantas-Whitney & Waldschmidt, 2006). As an outcome of this study, we considered curricular changes to encourage our students to critically examine the local context of their learners' lives, their classrooms, and their schools, as well as to make connections to theoretical perspectives and macro-level policies.

Since that time, Maria and Eileen moved to different universities, but continued to collaborate on research projects. Together with Karie, Maria's current colleague, we have been exploring micro- and macro-level issues related to ESOL/Bilingual teacher education. Keeping in mind the results from the previous study, we have been working to develop assignments to encourage beginning teachers to engage in critical dialogues, and examine personal beliefs, educational practices, and larger sociopolitical systems.

We follow a recent tradition in teacher education which involves teacher educators collaboratively examining their own practices (Zeichner, 1999). In this chapter, we examine students' written assignments in order to assess our goal of facilitating their development of critical sociocultural consciousness vis-à-vis their work with bilingual learners. For this purpose, we focus on one interview assignment given within Maria's introductory course in the ESOL/Bilingual endorsement program at Western Oregon University. Even though Maria was the course instructor, all three authors worked in close cooperation to examine the students' written assignments. As teacher educators, we have found this process of collaboration to be an important source of professional development and growth.

8.3   The Program, the Students, and the Course

Western Oregon University's ESOL/Bilingual Education program offers an add-on endorsement in ESOL or Bilingual/ESOL to the Oregon teaching license. The program requires completion of coursework in four key areas: (1) history, current policy and practice; (2) culture; (3) language and language acquisition; and (4) instruction and assessment, and a supervised practicum experience. Students may complete the endorsement program by itself or in conjunction with an undergraduate or graduate degree, so the program serves both preservice and in-service teachers. The majority of the students in the program are female, Caucasian, and monolingual; however, a recent bilingual teacher initiative at the university has been attracting more students who are Latino and/or bilingual. Faculty members in the program possess advanced degrees in ESOL/Bilingual Education and many years of classroom experience working with English language learners.

One of the first courses students take in the program is "Fostering Cultural and Community Connections in the ESOL/Bilingual Classroom.[1]" Course topics include the interrelatedness among language, culture, and learning; sociopolitical factors and school practices that affect the academic achievement of English language learners; and linguistically and culturally responsive practices that foster meaningful learning in the classroom and that build strong partnerships between families, schools, and communities. In addition to García's (2002) text, *Student Cultural Diversity: Understanding and Meeting the Challenge*, other course readings explore principles of multicultural education (e.g., Nieto, 2003); parent involvement in schools (e.g., Ada, 1999), research on "funds of knowledge" (e.g., González et al., 2005); issues related to language, discourse, and power (e.g., Delpit, 1992; Fillmore, 2000); and culturally relevant teaching practices (e.g., Jones et al., 2001). Course assignments include an article review, a classroom observation, an evaluation of a curriculum or textbook used in schools, and an interview with an immigrant to the United States. The course assignments attempt to build awareness of systems, in schools and society at large, which either promote or hinder educational opportunities for English language learners. This type of awareness-raising and critical thinking is the first step toward action that initiates change (Okazaki, 2005).

In this chapter, we examine in depth one particular assignment given within the introductory course — the interview assignment — and our students' reflections about it.

8.4   The Interview Assignment

The interview assignment asks students to interview an immigrant from a different cultural and linguistic background than themselves, focusing on the following themes: (1) experience with K–12 schooling (as a parent or student); (2) positive or negative experiences in learning a second language; and (3) experiences with racism, discrimination, or prejudice in the United States or another country. Since this assignment is part of an introductory course, it is one of the first assignments completed by the students in the program. Students are encouraged to describe their interviewee's experiences and to relate the content of the interview to the topics covered in class discussions and readings. In addition, they are asked to reflect on how they will use the insights gained through this interview in their role as educators. We hope that this close examination of one person's immigrant experience helps our students begin to understand and question macro-level forces that affect individuals.

We have found that many of our students have never had contact with a person who has immigrated to the United States. One of the first challenges for them is to locate an individual they can interview. This realization (e.g., lack of contact with immigrants) is often the first lesson learned through the assignment. Other than suggesting places to find potential interviewees (e.g., the university's office of Multicultural

---

[1] This course is offered in both face-to-face and online formats. For the purposes of this chapter, we focus on the online course sections taught between spring 2005 and spring 2007.

Students Services, or the English as a Second Language (ESL) programs at the local high school and community college), we do not facilitate the interviews in any way. We purposefully leave the assignment as open-ended as possible.

After the students complete their interviews, their written reports are a testimony to the fact that the immigrant experience is not a uniform phenomenon. Their descriptions show that acculturation into a new society can be very different for each person, depending on the individual's family situation, level of education, cultural background, social status, peer group, support from teachers, etc. Since the interview reports are posted online, all the students are encouraged to read and respond to each other's papers so they can learn from the collection of diverse experiences.

8.5   A Framework for Reflection

As part of the interview assignment, there is an expectation that students will engage in self-reflection, examine their own beliefs and attitudes in light of course topics, and transfer the new knowledge into instructional practices and opportunities for their learners (Gay & Kirkland, 2003). As Whipp (2003) suggests, however, teacher educators should provide students with a framework for reflection in order to scaffold their development of critical sociocultural consciousness.

To this end, we have utilized the following set of guiding questions (see Table 8.1) to make expectations for critical reflection explicit. This framework describes four phases to foster critical consciousness about social, cultural, and political issues. The first phase, *naming*, is a descriptive phase in which individuals identify problems and conflicts. The second phase, *relating*, is a personal interpretative phase, where individuals connect issues with their personal experiences and emotions. The

Table 8.1 Ada and Olave's (1986) framework for questions to guide student reflection

Phases of reflection	Questions
Descriptive phase (naming)	• What, where, when, who, why? • What is the problem? What are the conflicts?

Personal interpretative phase (relating)	• What does this have to do with me?
	  • Have I ever experienced or seen this before?
	  • How does it make me feel? How does it make others feel?

Critical analysis phase (thinking/reacting)	• Is this a valid concern/problem? Why?
	  • Does this happen here? To whom? How?
	  • What ideas do I have in creating change for others or me?
	  • How does it affect others in a greater context?
	  • What other factors are involved that may be bigger than me?

Creative or social action phase (doing)	• What can I/we do to solve the problem?
	  • How do I/we start?
	  • What have I learned about this process that has an impact on me?
	  • What will I do with it? When?
	  • Who will participate with me? How?

third phase, *thinking/reacting*, is a critical analysis phase. During this phase, individuals evaluate the problem, consider possibilities for change, and analyze larger, macro-level factors. Finally, *doing* is the creative or social action phase. Here individuals consider actions to solve the problem, think about steps in the change process, and strategize ways of mobilizing others to work toward solutions. We have successfully used this framework to structure students' reflections and class discussions.

Without this framework, we have found that most of our students stay at the level of naming (describing the topics and relating them to class readings), and relating (making connections with self). While each phase is important, most students need scaffolding (e.g., guiding questions) to engage in the critical analysis and social action phases. In the next section, we share excerpts from students' reflections, as structured by Ada and Olave's (1986) framework.

8.6   Students' Reflections

8.6.1   Naming: Descriptive Phase

By far the most common type of reflection the students engaged in was to relate topics from the interview to the themes we were exploring in class. Four themes were prevalent in their reflections: language learning, language loss, cultural conflict, and the role of schooling. As the students explored these themes, they consistently made use of the literature to aid understanding about their interviewees' experiences.

8.6.1.1   Language Learning

Almost all the students reflected on their interviewees' difficult experiences learning English. These experiences were described as "frustrating," "embarrassing," and "humbling," and were often combined with feelings of isolation and oppression:

> He was a bit embarrassed that he couldn't read in his own language very well. Not being literate in Spanish made it that much more difficult to learn English.

> She said that people here ask her again and again to repeat herself. ... She hears "huh, or what?" a lot. She feels that people do not listen to her speech, but look at her as an Asian person who cannot speak English.

8.6.1.2   Language Loss

Another theme present in many of the interview reflections was regret about losing a native language. "While virtually all children who attend American schools learn English, most of them are at risk of losing their primary languages as they do so.

... In the case of most present-day immigrant children, the learning of English is a subtractive process ... with English quickly displacing and replacing the primary language" (Fillmore, 2000, p. 203).

Invariably, loss of the mother tongue was associated with feelings of disconnect from family and culture:

> *Once he went to school, he picked up English very quickly. That was the only language spoken to him at school. By first grade he was speaking fairly fluently, and by 5th grade he was speaking better English than Korean. ... His parents speak very little English ... so at times he has difficulty communicating with his parents.*
>
> *She felt that as she used English more and more she started thinking in English and her Spanish started going bad. It was hard for her because ... it was as if she didn't fit in with her own family and culture anymore.*

8.6.1.3 Cultural Conflict

Another common theme in the reflections was cultural conflict. "When children begin to discover the tremendous discrepancy between what the school proposes as accepted models of conduct and behavior ... and what they experience as life and reality at home and in their community, there cannot but be a profound inner conflict" (Ada, 1999, pp. 2–3).

Our students reflected that cultural conflict was not only caused by societal pressures toward assimilation, but also by experiences of racism and discrimination:

> *Joe is having trouble with his children questioning his authority, which creates a different kind of wedge in the family that creates tension. The children are again trying to fit in with their new culture so it's inevitable that these types of conflicts will arise within non native families.*
>
> *He felt more racism in the neighborhood he grew up in. He was and is still called a "Twinkie." He hates this racist term that his fellow Koreans call him. A Twinkie is a Korean who is yellow on the outside, but white on the inside.*

8.6.1.4 The Role of Schooling

Nieto (2003) points out that "school policies and practices—specifically, curriculum, pedagogy, tracking, testing, discipline, and hiring—can ... either promote or hinder learning among students of different backgrounds" (p. 8). As teacher educators, we need to encourage our students to question and to "confront directly the deep-seated inequalities that exist in schools" (p. 7).

The topic of schooling was present in every interview profile. As expected, the interviews reflected both negative and positive experiences with the school system. One of the prevailing themes was a sense that school had failed these individuals and their families:

> *She said that because of this accent, her son was put into special education until sixth grade.*
>
> *Her teachers were very nice to her but instead of helping her learn the language they would tell her that she didn't have to do the work.*
>
> *He thinks that the education system we have is almost like putting students in a meat grinder and having them come out the same.*

Many interviewees also shared stories of particular teachers and administrators who made a significant positive impact in their lives. These stories served as sources of inspiration for our students:

> With my interview, I learned what the most important element of ESL learning to him was. It was teachers that cared. ... I could tell how grateful he was to those teachers. He never really talked about the models they used to teach, or the content he learned, instead his focus was on how much they cared about him as a person.
>
> Teachers just need to keep in mind that all students are coming into the class with many different backgrounds. ... One blanket technique for anything isn't a good idea. We need to remember that each student is an individual and needs to be treated as one.

8.6.1.5 Use of Literature to Aid Understanding

As the students analyzed their interviewees' experiences, they constantly referred to the knowledge they had gained in class to support their interpretations. In doing so, they adopted the discourse of experts who use research and theory to support their interpretations. This type of reflection is important because it can serve as a rehearsal for future conversations with colleagues and supervisors:

> Related to the article, I can see where Robert's parents were challenged participating in Robert's school because of the language barrier, the fear of being deported, working many hours, responsibility for younger children, and lack of a welcoming atmosphere at school.
>
> I now see that it was not because his parents did not care about Robert's school, the whole reason they came to America was for their children to have a better life with better schooling. There were many, very complicated reasons why they were not active in Robert's school and I think with some programs to welcome them, they would have been much more apt to participate.

8.6.2 Relating: Personal Interpretative Phase

The fact that the students connected the interview themes to the topics being explored in our class discussions and readings is not surprising. After all, this was one of the requirements of the assignment. What was surprising was the personal tone of so many of the interview reflections. As they reflected on the experiences of their interviewees, many students contrasted them to their own experiences, often trying to place themselves in their interviewees' "shoes." In many instances, they found that this examination process helped them learn things about themselves. Making a connection at the personal and emotional level can be an important facet of critical consciousness and self-transformation:

> I had such a difficult time finding someone to interview for this project. As soon as I read this assignment in the syllabus, my mind was racing, trying to think of a person to interview. Honestly, I was embarrassed. Was I so engrained into "white America?" Did I have no friends from other countries?
>
> I haven't known suffering or poverty. I am a white female, so I have never felt different or out of place. English is my first language, so I have always understood what people are

saying. I have been able to blend or stand out when I want. To be different is not something I have experienced much in my life. Meha's life is the total opposite.

8.6.3   Thinking/Reacting: Critical Analysis Phase

For some of the students, the interviews represented an opportunity to question assumptions and even to problematize certain claims made by the interviewees. Instead of taking everything they were told "at face value," several students struggled with some of the statements, and tried to examine them from alternative perspectives:

David has a problem with illegal immigrants from Mexico. He is very outraged at these people and quick to point out that he came here legally. He works for the school district (which highly values his bilingualism) and sees the Hispanic population draining away all the resources for education. Perhaps David doesn't see the irony of the situation here. He (an immigrant from Russia) argues for the teaching of English with his superiors (immigrants from Mexico) in English at an American public school.

Although Jenny and her daughter's situation turned out to be a positive experience, I am not thoroughly convinced that total [English] immersion is the best program. If Jenny had been offered a multilingual program for her daughter, she may not have felt she was being forced to leave behind her native language and culture. Jenny's daughter seemed to be doing well in the immersion program, but she is still very young. I wish I could fast forward time and find out how she does in school later. I want to know if there are any long term effects to the immersion program.

8.6.4   Doing: Creative/Social Action Phase

A few students felt compelled to consider specific actions they could take as a result of their new sense of understanding:

As a reminder of the pain my friend has gone through due to assimilation, I am going to put up a picture of him on my desk. This will be my daily reminder in my classroom to bring in and use those belief systems and values of my non-native students.

Our District is currently holding parenting classes on Friday mornings from 9:00– 11:00 a.m. at the District Office 15 miles away. I'm curious how many working families are able to drop everything and attend these meetings? ... I'll send a copy of this article to the Parent Involvement Coordinator. I really like the idea of pairing monolingual parents with bilingual families.

As we examine our students' reflections, we conclude that the interview has been a successful introductory assignment. These dialogues have clearly fostered sociocultural consciousness in many of our students, as they have helped them see macrolevel issues (e.g., racism in society, negative views of immigration, and assimilation policies such as English-only immersion programs) manifested at the micro level through the experiences of a specific person (e.g., language loss, cultural conflict, and discriminatory schooling practices such as teachers' lower expectations and placement in special education). The quotes below capture what we believe to be a growing development of critical sociocultural consciousness in our students:

This experience has taught me the importance of additive acculturation. This is "the acquisition of knowledge and skills of a new culture without rejection of the old" (García, 2002, p. 79). In the classroom, I need to help my students by giving them opportunities to share their culture with us. They need to be given an outlet to celebrate and combine their native skills with the new skills they learn in school.

You learn all these statistics and what not, you learn the strategies to help ELLs, but when you really get out there and talk to people who are living the life, you realize you really don't know anything. I guess this assignment has opened my eyes to real life. It has shown me that when I have my own classroom I'm going to need to try a lot harder to understand my students and their families. When I have my own classroom I'm going to have to work hard to make sure my students are getting the best education possible, because that is what their families want.

However, it is also important to note that most of our students stayed at the level of naming—describing the topics and relating them to class readings. Many of them also made connections with self, and only a small number ventured into the levels of thinking, reacting, and doing. This process of critical reflection is a developmental one and as mentioned earlier, the initial phases are an important foundation for the latter stages.

We realize that development of critical sociocultural consciousness will not result from one assignment, or even one class. This close examination of the interview assignment has reinforced to us the importance of providing structures and opportunities for students to engage in the critical analysis and social action phases in all our courses throughout the program. We strive for our students to acquire the tools for ongoing critical reflection so that they will continue to examine the macro- and micro-level issues that affect their practice after they leave our program and embark on their teaching careers.

8.7 Conclusions

In an effort to combat current educational practices that emphasize reductionistic views of teaching and "one size fits all" policies such as high-stakes standardized tests and measurable outcomes set within rigid time limits, this chapter has described our efforts as ESOL teacher educators to foster our students' development of critical sociocultural consciousness.

By engaging with our students in structured critical reflection and creating assignments that require them to interact with learners and parents, we hope to encourage our students to critically examine the local contexts of their learners' lives, their classrooms, and their schools, as well as make connections to theoretical perspectives and macro-level policies. Having a framework for reflection has been useful in analyzing whether we are comprehensively meeting our goal to connect the local, micro-level issues with the macro-level, societal forces.

In addition to thinking critically about our students' outcomes, a beneficial aspect of this experience has been to compare and contrast our experiences as ESOL faculty in different courses and settings. Although we consistently structure reflection and discussion for our students, we have found that it is equally important for teacher educators to find the time to collaborate and reflect together. This collective effort has helped us replenish our own self-efficacy in advocating for educational and societal equity. We hope that fellow teacher educators, as well as preservice and in-service teachers, are inspired to utilize collaboration to more effectively reflect on their individual practices.

References

Ada, A. F. (1999). Fostering the home-school connection. In J. Frederickson (Ed.), *Reclaiming our voices: Bilingual education, critical pedagogy and praxis* (pp. 5–11). Ontario, CA: California Association for Bilingual Education.

Ada, A. F., & Olave, M. P. (1986). *Creative reading methodology. Hagamos caminos.* Reading, MA: Addison-Wesley.

Apple, M. W. (2001). *Educating the "right" way.* New York: Routledge Falmer.

Arroyo, C. G. (2007). *The funding gap.* Washington, D.C.: The Education Trust. www2.edtrust. org/EdTrust/Press+Room/fundinggap07.htm. Accessed 20 April 2008.

Bartolomé, L. I., & Balderrama, M. (2001). The need for educators with political and ideological clarity: Providing our children with "the best." In M. Reyes & J. Halcón (Eds.), *The best for our children: Critical perspectives on literacy for Latino students* (pp. 48–64). New York: Teachers College Press.

Crawford, J. (2004). *Educating English language learners: Language diversity in the classroom* (5th ed.). Los Angeles, CA: Bilingual Educational Services.

Dantas-Whitney, M., & Waldschmidt, E. D. (2006). *Moving beyond technical views of teaching and towards critical cultural consciousness in bilingual/ESOL teacher education.* Paper presented at the American Educational Research Association, San Francisco, California.

Delpit, L. (1992). Acquisition of literate discourse: Bowing before the master? *Theory into Practice, 31*(4), 296–302.

Fillmore, L. W. (2000). Loss of family languages: Should educators be concerned? *Theory into Practice, 39*(4), 203–210.

García, E. (2002). *Student cultural diversity: Understanding and meeting the challenge.* Boston, MA: Houghton Mifflin.

Garcia, O., Kleifgen, J. A., & Falchi, L. (2008). From English language learners to emergent bilinguals. Equity Matters: Research Review No. 1.

Gay, G., & Kirkland, K. (2003). Developing cultural critical consciousness and self-reflection in preservice teacher education. *Theory into Practice, 42*(3), 181–187.

González, N., Moll, L. C., & Amanti, C. (2005). *Funds of knowledge: Theorizing practices in households, communities and classrooms.* Mahwah, NJ: Lawrence Erlbaum Associates.

Jones, E. B., Pang, V. O., & Rodriguez, J. L. (2001). Social studies in the elementary classroom: Culture matters. *Theory into Practice, 40*(1), 35–42.

McNeil, L. M., Coppola, E., Radigan, J., and Vasquez Heilig, J. (2008). Avoidable losses: High-stakes accountability and the dropout crisis. *Education Policy Analysis Archives, 16*(3). Available at http://epaa.asu.edu/epaa/v16n3/.

Menken, K. (2008). *English learners left behind: Standardized testing as language policy.* Clevendon, UK: Multilingual Matters.

Mize, K., & Dantas-Whitney, M. (2007). English language development in K–12 settings: Principles, cautions and effective models. *ORTESOL Journal, 25*, 17–24

Neill, M. (2005). *Assessment of ELL students under NCLB: Problems and solutions.* FairTest. http://www.fairtest.org/nattest/NCLB_assessing_bilingual_students.pdf. Accessed 22 February 2008.

Nieto, S. M. (2003). Profoundly multicultural questions. *Educational Leadership, 60*(4), 6–10.

No Child Left Behind Act of 2001. 20 U.S.C. 6301 et seq. (2002).

Okazaki, T. (2005). Critical consciousness and critical language teaching. *Second Language Studies*, *23*(2), 174–202.

Public Broadcasting Service. (2003). *The new Americans*. http://www.pbs.org/independentlens/newamericans/quiz.html. Accessed 14 September 2005.

Siegal, J. (2008). *Finding a high school for an immigrant child is tougher than you think*. Village Voice. http://www.villagevoice.com/arts/0803,siegel,78835,12.html. Accessed 1 March 2008.

Valdés, G. (1996). *Con respeto: Bridging the distances between culturally diverse families and schools*. New York: Teachers College Press.

Whipp, J. L. (2003). Scaffolding critical reflection in online discussions. *Journal of Teacher Education*, *54*(4), 321–333.

Zeichner, K. (1999). The new scholarship in teacher education. *Educational Researcher*, *28*(1), 4–15.

Zehr, M. A. (2007). Reading aid seen to lag in ELL focus. *Education Week*, *27*(1), 20–21.

Chapter 9
Standards, Critical Literature, and Portfolio Assessment: An Integrated Approach to Critical Pedagogical Development

Glenda Moss

9.1 Introduction

The establishment of the National Board for Professional Teaching Standards (NBPTS) in 1987 and the Interstate New Teachers Assessment and Support Consortium (INTASC) in 1992 called for the development of performance-based assessment and resulted in a portfolio assessment system in the Midwestern University where I prepare secondary classroom teachers. I was completing my dissertation during the time this portfolio assessment system was being designed by professors who had never used portfolio assessment in their teaching. I was hired just in time for the initial implementation with my students who, also, had no experience with portfolios unless they were majoring in music education. For many preservice teachers, a vision of standardization came to mind as they prepared to submit their portfolios for evaluation in the spring of 2001 and 2002.

One preservice teacher's perspective captures this vision:

> *Honestly, I feel as if I'm taking a standardized test. There's one way to put together your portfolio, and those that are assessing them are grading the portfolios with a number system. So, I ask myself the question, how can I get more points, currency, for my portfolio?*

Students with this vision of standardization perceived the guidelines for writing reflections and the portfolio scoring rubric as similar to standardized testing. They approached the guidelines that require a brief description of evidence, analysis of what they learned, and a reflection on how the artifact demonstrates competence on one of the INTASC standards as a formula to follow rather than an opportunity to critically think.

This standardization vision created a barrier to my preservice teachers' ability to see the opportunity to develop critical teaching competencies within the INTASC (1992) standards and the Indiana Professional Standards Board (IPFB) (2002). For many of the professors who helped score the portfolios in the early years, the standardization vision could not be separated from the NCATE requirement to produce

G. Moss
Indiana University-Purdue University Fort Wayne

S.L. Groenke and J.A. Hatch (eds.), *Critical Pedagogy and Teacher
Education in the Neoliberal Era: Small Openings*,
DOI 10.1007/978-1-4020-9588-7_9, © Springer Science+Business Media B.V. 2009

quantitative summative data for the Unit Assessment System. However, I was interested in exploring an alternative vision, bringing critical reflection and analysis to the portfolio process. That alternative vision was for portfolios to be utilized and critiqued as a space for students to engage in a critical self-reflective process by applying a critical narrative analysis (Moss, 2003) of the standards and their experiences during their program.

This chapter brings to the forefront the importance of examining the interplay between the standards, critical literature, and portfolio assessment for critical pedagogical development. I argue this integrated practice can serve as a bridge to developing a critical framework for classroom practice. In addition, this chapter presents a beginning analysis of preservice teachers' critique of the INTASC standards through a Freirean lens within portfolio assessment. It provides evidence of the initial stage of critical pedagogical thinking and educational imagination. The chapter concludes with implications and new directions for the alternative vision.

9.2   A Critical Perspective on the INTASC Standards

I am not the first teacher educator to examine the INTASC standards in an effort to promote critical pedagogy in teacher education. Bercaw and Stooksberry (2004) analyzed the relationship "between a critical pedagogy and [INTASC] teaching standards" (p. 1) and set out to show that the standards were not framed from a critical theory philosophy. They concluded that "the Core Principles can lead toward a beginning teacher implementing a critical pedagogy" but questioned "whether the expectation of a beginning teacher to implement a critical approach is realistic" (p. 6). Their analysis was not surprising to me because I heard them present in 2002 at the Annual Meeting of the American Association of Colleges for Teacher Education (AACTE), where their initial critique criticized the INTASC standards as lacking the critical framework needed for developing a critical pedagogy.

I remember Bercaw and Stooksberry's AACTE presentation resulting in a discussion among veteran teacher educators about whether it was realistic to expect preservice teachers to engage in the reading of critical texts like Freire's (1970/2000) *Pedagogy of the Oppressed* or to develop critical teaching approaches. I argued, in my naivety as a first-year teacher educator with a biased commitment to critical pedagogical development, that underestimation of preservice teachers' potential was part of the problem in education. It was the same problem I had seen over and over in the middle school where I taught in Texas. Too often, the teachers taught for remediation and basics rather than acceleration and critical thinking. The justification was that the middle school students were not ready for thinking: they needed basic skills before they could critically think. I often wondered when they would be considered ready and if it would be too late for them to become actors in the world of school and beyond. In spite of my concerns, I acted inconsistently in my new position in higher education, where I was reluctant to use critical texts because of fear that I would not be supported.

The conference setting provided me with the space to explore my commitment to translating critical pedagogy for teacher preparation. I argued with my veteran colleagues that preservice teachers could read critical texts and engage in meaningful examination of how a critical lens might inform their teaching. I remember being excited about the analysis that Bercaw and Stooksberry presented and accepted their findings as rather obvious to anyone who was bringing a critical perspective to his or her teacher preparation work. This kind of "common sense" is troubling to me now, as it appears to be an essentialist way of viewing critical theory.

I pushed forward in my efforts as a teacher educator to move portfolio assessment in the direction of critical pedagogy development (Moss, 2003, 2004, 2005). In the back of my mind was an assumption, picked up from Bercaw and Stooksberry, that the INTASC standards were problematic in that they were not based on the core value of developing critical pedagogy for equity and democracy. It was easy to use this perspective to explain the lack of a developing critical perspective among preservice teachers. I did not consider that the problem might be students' lack of exposure to critical texts.

As I reviewed my students' products and portfolio reflections in the fall of 2001 and spring of 2002, prior to introducing them to Freire's writings, there was a visible absence of critical analysis; so I made some major changes in my curriculum and instruction for the English and social studies methods classes I was teaching. With the cooperation of an African-American principal in a local school that served a population of 85% African-American students, I implemented a service-learning field experience for the English education preservice teachers. A small group of seven preservice teachers and I taught a group of students who had all failed freshman English. My next group of three preservice teachers continued the project in the spring of 2003. I saw a marked difference in the students' portfolio reflections for the preservice English teachers in the fall of 2002 and spring of 2003 as they were becoming aware of the politics of education and their own cultural biases.

For the social studies methods class, I required students to read Symcox's (2002) *Whose History? The Struggle for National Standards in American Classrooms*, which presents a critical view of the development of national social studies standards. In the fall of 2003, we expanded the critical service-learning project to include 14 preservice social studies teachers and a group of 18 preservice English teachers. Many preservice teachers became very upset. Some female preservice teachers said it was not right for me to require them to drive through sections of town that they were not allowed by their parents to drive. Some openly expressed to me that they did not want to go into a school serving minority students because they believed Black students were dangerous.

I became increasingly conscious of the role that curriculum and instruction and students' assessment of their own learning play in the capacity to develop critical pedagogy. I used intentionality in choosing readings and in designing learning activities. I was conscious that I was framing my course within critical pedagogy theory and hoped to engage students in critical self-reflection concerning issues of racism, homophobia, and social class. It was not my goal to engage students in a process of criticizing the INTASC standards. I did not view the INTASC standards as a barrier to critical pedagogy. I did not see the INTASC standards as problematic to engaging preservice teachers in reading critical texts and using those texts for critical self-reflection and to inform the ways they looked at developing curriculum and planning instruction. Part of the problem was the fact that I had not engaged them in enough critical texts to inform their perspective on teaching.

My goal was to engage students to develop a critical pedagogical lens for viewing their own social and cultural experiences, their learning-to-teach experiences, and the INTASC standards. I acted on the theory that preservice teachers could develop a critical lens, and use that lens to critique the policies and practices they encountered in schools in terms of issues of equity, racism, and gender bias that get in the way of reciprocal teaching and learning. I also believed that preservice teachers could use a critical lens to construct instruction and interact with their students, interpreting the INTASC standards through their developing critical perspectives.

Following the fall 2003 semester, the assistant vice chancellor of academic affairs in my university heard about how upset some of my students were during their field experience with students of color and offered to assist me in better preparing White preservice teachers before they went into diverse classrooms. She and an African-American instructor on my campus worked during the spring semester and summer 2004 to help me by suggesting that I show a series of race films (Adelman, 2003) and engage preservice teachers in Diversity Study Circles during my critical reading class (Moss, 2008).

I was further encouraged when our new Dean, a critical theorist, invited Henry Giroux to our campus as a guest speaker. I immediately found the courage to add Freire's *Pedagogy of the Oppressed* to my summer curriculum in Critical Reading in the Content Areas course. Students found *Pedagogy of the Oppressed* difficult to read, so I set up times outside of class to read chapters out loud with those who were interested. Usually, about five or six White students would show up to take turns reading, and we would all discuss our understandings and implications for teaching practice. We discussed ways that we have benefited from racism that we had taken for granted.

I continued to meet with my two university colleagues in preparation for implementing the race films and Diversity Study Circles in the fall of 2004. I showed parts of all three films in the series during one class period in the fall and invited the African-American instructor to facilitate a discussion. She was very confrontational with my preservice teachers, which resulted in some becoming very resistant during the Diversity Study Circles that followed the films. The Diversity Study Circles involved separating my class of 24 into three groups of eight who were joined by additional groups of eight students of color, who were recruited by the African-American instructor from her classes and those of her daughter who taught in a local community college. Each group of 16 (eight White students and eight students of color) were led in race dialogues by trained facilitators from the local United Way organization.

In the two subsequent semesters, I showed one race film per class session and asked preservice teachers to write reflections, especially examining angry, negative, or frightful feelings they had in reaction to the films. Students were then given the opportunity the next week to discuss their concerns with me as the facilitator. These conversations became critically pedagogical in nature as some of the preservice teachers and I acknowledged the ways we have acted based on biased views. Students were more open to the films and discussion because I assured them the films were not created to make them feel guilty and because I was White.

After three semesters, the African-American instructor was no longer at the university, and I did not try to continue the Diversity Study Circles on my own. Instead, I added Nieto's (1999) *The Light in Their Eyes* and an assignment for students to work in interdisciplinary teams to create interdisciplinary units of study with a goal of implementing multicultural perspectives. Outside of class time, I conducted a workshop on racism, using the three race films. Six to 12 students attend the workshop each semester. The voluntary nature of the workshop results in a greater degree of participation in critical self-analysis.

For the most recent three sections of my course, I have asked preservice teachers to use the Universal Declaration of Human Rights as a lens for examining their Indiana State Standards and developing an interdisciplinary unit of study with a human rights theme. I continue to show the race films outside of class time and invite students to participate in a multicultural education book study. Interested students choose a book that is framed by multiculturalism or critical pedagogy, read it, and present what they learned and dialogue with peers concerning the complexity of teaching for change.

Besides these learning activities, students participate in 60 hours of urban service-learning field experiences. They design and teach several lessons for students in a school where 36 different languages are spoken. Over time, I began to see a pattern of students transforming their view of the standards and of portfolio assessment. I questioned whether my students would come to the same conclusions about the INTASC standards as Bercaw and Stooksberry if given the opportunity to intentionally analyze the INTASC standards through a Freirean lens. In keeping with critical portfolio assessment practices that create space for teacher educators and preservice teachers to engage in ongoing inquiry into the policies, practices, and standards that directly affect them and become critical actors in the process, I created a new final experience for preservice teachers in my critical reading class to examine the INTASC standards through a Freirean Lens.

Because I believe that standards, critical literature, and portfolios can be integrated for developing critical pedagogy for practice, I created the final experience to give preservice teachers the opportunity to use a Freirean lens to examine the INTASC standards. I then examined their responses to determine the impact that the critical literature had on their perspectives on the INTASC standards. I believe this is important because they will find themselves working within the pressure of standardized testing in P–12 settings. If they can integrate standards, critical perspective, and reflection, they will be more likely to engage children in critical thinking and improve education in US schools.

9.3 Preservice Teachers' Critique of the INTASC Standards through a Freirean Lens

During the last class session of the summer 2006 and fall 2006, students examined the INTASC standards through a critical lens. Using *Pedagogy of the Oppressed* (1970/2000) as a framework, students wrote about what they thought Freire would say about each of the standards. They looked for elements of the standards that provided room for practicing critical pedagogy as they understood it through their reading of Freire's work. One section of students in the summer and two sections in the fall of 2006 analyzed the INTASC standards based on their reading of *Pedagogy of the Oppressed*. I did not tell my students about the work of Bercaw and Stooksberry (2004); I simply told them this was their final reflective experience in my class and what they wrote would not affect their grade. I wondered how their critique of the standards would compare to that of Bercaw and Stooksberry (2004). Their analyses supported the conclusions of Bercaw and Stooksberry (2004) that many of the INTASC standards would "resonate in some way with the tenets of critical theory based on the multiple ways one could interpret each principle" (p. 6). It would require too much space to present an analysis of all ten standards in this narrative. For this chapter, I have decided to use standard one as an example. Standard #1 focuses on "Knowledge of Subject" (see Table 9.1 below for abbreviated summary of students' thoughts on Freirean concepts as applied to some of the INTASC Standard #1 indicators).

When I examine my preservice teachers' critical self-reflections within our School of Education's portfolio assessment system, which is aligned with the INTASC standards, I see the positive role that critical readings, critical dialogue, and critically framed projects and service-learning activities have on the development of a critical pedagogical perspective for preservice teachers (Moss, 2003, 2005).

Some preservice teachers' critical assessment of the INTASC standards resulted in reflection on the inconsistency between theory and practice they had experienced in the university setting. One social studies preservice teacher viewed Standard #1 as the best example of the inconsistency between the expectations of beginning teachers and the practice of content area teacher educators. Standard #1, Knowledge of Subject, states: "The pre-service teacher understands the central concepts, tools of inquiry and structures of the discipline he or she teaches and can create learning experiences that make these aspects of subject matter meaningful for students." The standard calls for a quality teacher who can engage students in meaningful learning experiences. The preservice teacher stated:

I agree with this and if teachers can follow this standard then they will be able to produce quality educated students.

This same preservice teacher notes that the flaw with this standard resides in practice, not in the theoretical principle:

It is also my belief that this standard is flawed only by our university educational practices. In all of my content area courses at the university level I have never witnessed a professor who has taught by the philosophy of this standard. The standard method of teaching

Table 9.1 Students' reflections as applied to a Freirean analysis of INTASC Standard #1 indicators

INTASC standard #1. The preservice teacher …	Freirean concepts from *Pedagogy of the Oppressed*	Students' thoughts/reflections
Realizes that subject matter knowledge is not a fixed body of facts but is complex and ever-evolving	Thematic investigations replace "the 'banking' concept of education, in which the scope of action allowed to the students extends only as far as receiving, filing, and storing the deposits" (p. 72)	*We can no longer treat every child the same and educate them through a lecture style of the past in which the student is more or less spoken at*
Appreciates multiple perspectives	It becomes necessary, not precisely to deny [a] fact, but to "see it differently" (p. 52)	*Dialogue was one of Freire's most emphatic points because it is a great way for students to make information meaningful. In my math classes students will work in groups for the sole purpose of dialogue*
Conveys to learners how knowledge is developed from the vantage point of the knower	Liberation is a praxis: the action and reflection of men and women upon their world in order to transform it (p. 79)	*Reflection and action achieve a transformed structure. Teach for liberation*
Sees connection between discipline(s) and everyday life	Often, educators and politicians speak and are not understood because their language is not attuned to the concrete situations of the people they address	*Students may have experienced certain aspects of life, outside of the classroom, which I as a teacher will never experience*
Is committed to continuous learning and engages in professional discourse about subject matter knowledge and children's learning of the discipline	Education must begin with the solution of the teacher–student contradiction, by reconciling the poles of the contradiction so that both are simultaneously teachers *and* students (p. 72)	*Dialogue is an essential tool for people to live, and living is a process of continued learning, therefore, dialogue must be a mainstay in learning, notably, in education. In teaching math and social studies, I desire my students to experience the content not just try to absorb words*
Develops and uses curricula that encourage students to see, question, and interpret ideas from diverse perspectives	In the name of the "preservation of culture and knowledge" we have a system which achieves neither true knowledge nor true culture (p. 80)	*Problem-posing would allow students to use their different strengths.* *This is the first time I have ever been asked to critique the standards that have been created for the education department to follow. We need the tools to create learning experiences that engage all students*

[experienced in the content classes] is what Freire refers to as the banking method. The professors lecture and try and fill the empty receptacles known as students with their knowledge. Teachers have a disadvantage from this university experience with regards to how to teach their content area.

Preservice teachers find themselves having to become cultural workers (Freire, 2005), who actively participate to change the education system. In the student's words,

[W]e cannot teach how we have been taught. That would be a great disservice to our young students. We attend education classes and learn about other techniques and hopefully can make the connections on how to use these techniques with our content areas. We are supposed to break this cycle of oppression but have been oppressed ourselves throughout our own education. Our only hope is to overcome our own oppression placed on us by society and prepare our students to fight against their possible oppression.

This preservice teacher shows the influence of critical pedagogical texts (Breault, 2003) to bring about new ways of thinking about the intersubjectivity of learning and the role that teachers play in reproducing the status quo or bringing about more democratic practices.

A look at the INTASC standards through a Freirean lens following a semester of using critical readings to reflexively examine individual social and cultural experiences and biases created a kind of productive tension that mirrors the tension that critically committed teachers experience under the pressure of standardized testing and No Child Left Behind policies. Classroom teachers face the complexity of working with the wave of standardized testing that seems to hold them hostage to continuing a pattern of oppression even if their consciousness and professionalism compel them to struggle to break the same chain of oppression that Freire talks about. Preservice teachers find themselves engaged in a fight for their own pedagogical freedom as the first step toward constructing democratic classrooms. One preservice teacher described that her Freirean pedagogy would be,

creative, interest students, adjustable to all learning styles, and give students the knowledge to free their minds. Critical knowledge of a content area would mean that the teacher can transform a subject that is normally boring to students into something that they enjoy and appreciate.

The INTASC standards look different when a Freirean lens is applied. For a teacher, the knowledge of the subject extends beyond just facts about the subject itself. A critical knowledge of a subject is necessary. This knowledge extends beyond the static facts and moves into an understanding of how the subject impacts, influences, and affects other areas of life and other disciplines. For example, a social studies teacher would not only examine the facts of history but also explore social history with his/her students, walking alongside students and growing in an understanding of historical issues and their impact on society.

One preservice teacher noted that the wording of this standard might be slightly altered through Freire's lens. It might read:

The pre-service teacher understands the central concepts, tools of inquiry and structures of the disciplines he or she teaches and MUST create learning experiences that make these aspects meaningful to students AS HE/SHE JOINS THEM IN THE LEARNING PROCESS.

This preservice teacher stresses the importance of teachers and students learning together in a community rather than the teacher narrating one way of viewing to the students. The preservice teacher goes on to draw on Freire's text and explains that oppressors are thought of as dictators who dole out static facts and rules to the students or "receptacles" and prohibit their ability to question or analyze the ideas presented. Freire's visionary curriculum has students and teachers working together to create a community of analytical thinkers and transformers of their reality who challenge themselves to address pertinent problems in their world.

Another preservice teacher imagined Freire would argue that a teacher must be aware of his or her own values, beliefs, and cultural influences and how those influences affect the ways in which he or she presents subject material in the classroom. He went on to say that a Freirean teacher must also have an understanding of the influences that affect his or her students and their prior knowledge base in order to appropriately build upon this foundation for understanding the culture in which they live. He argued that Freire would add that aside from the teacher knowing his or her body of subject matter, which is not static but ever-changing, the teacher must know himself and know or find out what his students already believe. Drawing further on the INTASC standard's text and Freire's words, this preservice teacher conceptualized that, in a manner that is fair and diplomatic, the teacher needs to use different and engaging teaching strategies that suit the needs of all students, each in his or her own way.

In critiquing the INTASC standards and keeping Freire's *Pedagogy of the Oppressed* in mind, another preservice teacher perceived "*a strong basis of [Freire's] pedagogy*" embraced in the standards. The pedagogy of the oppressed is the constant struggle in education to create a culture of equality, openness as well as understanding of diversity, and the seeking of dialogue and communication between the teachers and the students. Freire's pedagogy implemented in a school would be one rich in communication, democracy, and teachers empowering their students to succeed and getting them ready for society.

Another preservice teacher noted how the INTASC standards and portfolio had sometimes seemed like a chore until she began to view them as providing an opportunity to become a reflective practitioner. After reading Freire's *Pedagogy of the Oppressed*, she saw using the portfolio to develop her teaching voice as an attempt to move away from a testing system for teacher certification and toward a democratic classroom where she was an active participant in her development. This preservice teacher wishes that she had had this view of the standards and the portfolio at the beginning of her college education. Instead of looking at them with frustration thinking that it is nonsense and busy work, she would have looked at the potential they provide. She stated:

> *Now, I can look at each INTASC standard as a means to creating a democratic classroom. I can look at my portfolio as a way to represent myself as a teacher and democratic practitioner. Both are very important in my education and give me an opportunity to provide students with an empowering education.*

This transformation in viewing both the INTASC standards and portfolio assessment is common among my preservice teachers after a semester of reading critical texts, dialoguing in a setting where their voices are respected, and participating in meaningful field experiences where they engage with students of various cultural backgrounds, skin colors, and languages. Likewise, I continue to change along with my students and make changes in my curriculum as I understand my students' needs and the needs of the local school systems.

9.4   Continuing the Work of Developing Critical Teachers

The local school districts continue to face a vast disparity between achievement scores of white, middle-class students and those of minority students, especially African-Americans. In addition to my coursework, I also acted as co-site-director of the Appleseed Writing Project, which is housed on my campus. In this role, I had the opportunity to develop a workshop, "Focus Group Study of Teaching African-American Students to Write". Twelve participants spent a Saturday examining critical texts and issues concerning how to engage African-American students in writing. An African-American middle school teacher led participants in a focused group study of where teachers must begin if they want to close the achievement gap.

At the end of the day, participants were invited to continue the focus group study by meeting once a month to read and talk about issues of teaching in multicultural environments. I led the group in a study of Murrell's (2002) *African-Centered Pedagogy*. I invited preservice teachers to participate, providing them further experiences in diversity as three of the teachers were African-Americans, and we had no African-American professors in our department. During the second year (2005/06), we read *The Light in Their Eyes* by Nieto (1999), and I began using that book in my Critical Reading class during the spring of 2006 because I knew that Sonia Nieto was going to be the keynote speaker at the Appleseed Writing Project's inaugural conference, "Building Multicultural Learning Communities: Conversations among Educators". I hoped that many of my preservice teachers would attend the conference and that it would help them to make deeper connections to their reading of the text.

Several preservice teachers did attend the conference and began to attend the book study, then focused on *The Dreamkeepers* by Ladson-Billings (1994). It was the preservice teachers attending the book study in the fall of 2006 who strongly suggested that I use *The Dreamkeepers* as a text in the Critical Reading class. They thought that specifically looking at the complexity of engaging African-American students in learning was critical. They realized that it was wrong to blame parents and children's skin color for low achievement scores; preservice teacher preparation was a critical element.

Similar to the analysis of the INTASC standards with a Freirean lens, I asked preservice teachers to examine the standards through the lens of critical race theory out of which Ladson-Billings writes. In the fall 2007 semester, in small groups of four, one section of my students used Gloria Ladson-Billings book, *The Dreamkeepers*, to critique the standards through a lens of critical race theory.

In a second section, I asked students to get in four groups and assigned each group to examine the INTASC standards through the four educational theories that are taught in the foundation's course in our department. These include essentialism, perennialism, progressivism, and social reconstructionism (critical theory). The point of the activity was for the students to see that the standards do not drive what we do as teachers. It is the lens through which we view the standards that drives what we do with learners. Ongoing analysis of preservice teachers' critical self-analysis and reflections on their learning experiences from these activities indicates a beginning understanding of critical pedagogy and the work of teaching for equity and democracy (Moss & Lee, 2008). What kind of support new teachers would find in schools continued to be a concern, but working with several principals and three superintendents gives me hope.

9.5   Lessons Learned Concerning Critical Teacher Preparation

9.5.1   Avoid an Essentialist Approach

When I accepted a position to prepare teachers, I struggled with the issue of using critical texts to influence preservice teachers to become critical pedagogues. I model democracy in learning by allowing students a variety of opportunities to explore their own thinking rather than testing them to see if they understand my way of thinking. Students test their own theories in classroom practice and in dialogue with peers and veteran teachers. I have not given any tests in my classes since teaching at the university. Students learn more about teaching from what we model than what we say. It would be antithetical to critical pedagogy to lecture and expect students to memorize and regurgitate information. I have learned to maintain high expectations through a rigorous reading schedule and requiring that students write authentic reflective-reflexive responses and participate during class dialogues. I do use grades in an essentialist way to encourage attendance and completing work on time.

9.5.2   Utilize Field Experiences in Diverse Settings

I have learned that it is vital for White preservice teachers to spend time in classrooms with students of color if they are to become conscious of their biases. Requiring field experience in a diverse school provides my students with theory and practice for critical self-reflection. It is also important that preservice teachers recognize and examine their racial biases, and being in diverse settings makes this possible.

9.5.3   Create a Safe Environment for Dialogue

Along with experiences in the field, preservice teachers need a safe environment where they can express their perspectives and explore the ways their own biases and prejudices are influencing their expectations and interactions with students from different cultural backgrounds. While the INTASC standards are not written from a critical pedagogy framework, teacher educators can provide a setting for preservice teachers to reflect on their culture and lived experience through a critical lens to determine bias in curriculum, assessment, and instructional planning. Critical texts and space to talk across differences give preservice teachers opportunities to develop voice through a critical look at their world and society. These teacher education practices can produce critical teachers who contribute to an ongoing critique of the policies and practices where they teach to ensure dialogue among all stakeholders to build a multicultural learning community that fosters and sustains equity and democracy.

9.5.4 Understand that Philosophies of Education, Not Standards, Drive Curriculum and Instruction

Standards do not really determine how we act as educators, but our theoretical perspective or philosophy of education drives what we do and how we address INTASC and other standards intended to raise the quality of education for all children. If teacher educators hope for their preservice teachers to become critical pedagogues, they must model how to take a critical approach toward teacher education, while aligning curriculum, instruction, and assessment with the standards for which they are accountable. In my case, these are the INTASC standards. I view them through a critical lens, which informs my choices of texts and instructional strategies.

9.6 Final Reflections

As I bring this chapter to a close, I am preparing for the spring 2008 semester. I have spent many hours during the summer break reflecting and revising my plans for the fall. I sent syllabi through e-mail attachment to my students earlier today, hoping a few will come to class 4 days from now intrigued by the text titles. One student stopped by last spring to get the reading list and shared with me at that time that he already owned most of Freire's books as well as over a dozen other critical texts. I find this student's vision of actively participating in the transformation of education encouraging and hopeful.

I spent the morning in a local middle school, meeting the new principal to catch him up on the 3-year partnership I have enjoyed with the school. He was excited to continue to allow preservice teachers to come into classrooms and learn from the full-time teachers and diverse study body what it means to teach. Thirty-six different languages are spoken in this school where whiteness and poverty are visible, and where teachers engage in the struggle against oppression, trying to ensure that every child has an opportunity to become an active, participatory citizen. This is a vision of critical education in an age of standardized testing. This vision brings hope.

References

Adelman, L. (Executive Producer). (2003). Race: The Power of an Illusion [motion picture]. California Newsreel. http://www.newsreel.org/nav/title.asp?tc=CN0149). Accessed 22 September 2008.

Bercaw, L. A., & Stooksberry, L. M. (2004). Teacher education, critical pedagogy, and standards: An exploration of theory and practice. *Essays in Education, 12*, 1–13. http://www.usca.edu/essays/vol122004/Bercaw.pdf. Accessed 25 September 2008.

Breault, R. A. (2003). Dewey, Freire, and a pedagogy for the oppressor. *Multicultural Education, 10*(3),2–6.

Freire, P. (1970/2000). *Pedagogy of the oppressed*. New York: Continuum.

Freire, P. (2005). *Teachers as cultural workers: Letters to those who dare teach*. Boulder, CO: Westview Press.

Indiana Professional Standards Board. (2002). *Rules 2002*. http://www.in.gov/psb/licensing/rules2002. Accessed 1 April 2003.

Interstate New Teacher Assessment and Support Consortium (1992). Model standards for beginning teacher licensing and development: A resource for state dialogue. Washington, DC: Council of Chief State School Officers.

Ladson-Billings, G. (1994). *The dreamkeepers: Successful teachers of African American children*. San Francisco, CA: Jossey-Bass.

Moss, G. (2003). Critical self-reflective narrative of portfolio assessment in teacher preparation, *Scholar-Practitioner Quarterly, 2*(1), 45–60.

Moss, G. (2004). *Portfolio assessment for critical self-reflection: Is it possible?* Paper presented at the Annual Meeting of the American Educational Research Association, San Diego, CA.

Moss, G. (2005). *Developing a critical lens among pre-service teachers while working within mandated performance-based assessment systems*. Paper presented at the Annual Meeting of the American Educational Research Association, Montreal, Canada.

Moss, G. (2008). Diversity study circles in teacher education practice: A critical experiential learning project. *Teaching and Teacher Education, 24*, 216–224.

Moss, G., & Lee, C. (2008). A critical analysis of philosophies of education and INTASC standards in teacher preparation. Paper presented at the Annual Meeting of the Midwestern Educational Association, Columbus, OH.

Murrell, P. C. Jr. (2002). *African-centered pedagogy: Developing schools of achievement for African American children*. Albany, NY: State University of New York Press.

Nieto, S. (1999). *The light in their eyes: Creating multicultural learning communities*. New York: Teachers College Press.

Symcox, L. (2002). *Whose history? The struggle for national standards in American classrooms*. New York: Teachers College Press.

Chapter 10
Leaders-Cloaked-As-Teachers: Toward Pedagogies of Liberation

Venus Evans-Winters

10.1 Introduction

In this chapter, I utilize the concept of *leaders-cloaked-as-teachers* to describe the idea that preservice teachers must undergo a transformation process before they view themselves as teachers and leaders in the classroom, school community, and larger society. I also present the term *leaders-cloaked-as-teachers* to refer to an urgent political and pedagogical endeavor to recruit and retain teachers who view themselves as change agents in the struggle for social justice, and who intentionally adopt the profession of teaching to assist in the liberation of marginalized individuals and groups in a democratic society.

I begin each semester with the premise that before future educators can appreciate and accept for themselves the transformative nature of teaching and learning, they first must understand the nature of oppression and how they too are victims of hegemony and social inequality. Throughout the chapter, writing as an African-American female scholar, I embrace a narrative voice (embedded in the tenets of Black womanism and critical race theory) to discuss the challenges and possibilities of teaching critical pedagogy frameworks to majority White, middle-class, female students.

10.2 Formal Introductions

My name is Venus Evans-Winters. You can call me Dr. Evans-Winters, Dr. Winters, Professor Evans-Winters or Professor Winters. I am old school. I believe in showing respect to those older than you in a formal setting. Anyhow, I have a Bachelors degree in Sociology, with a focus on race, class, and gender. And, I hold a Masters degree in Social Work, with a specialization in School Social Work. I am a certified School Social Worker in the State of Illinois. My PhD is in Educational Policy Studies, with an area of specialization in Sociology of Education. In other words, I am interested in how the intersections of

V. Evans-Winters
Illinois State University

S.L. Groenke and J.A. Hatch (eds.), *Critical Pedagogy and Teacher Education in the Neoliberal Era: Small Openings,*
DOI 10.1007/978-1-4020-9588-7_10, © Springer Science+Business Media B.V. 2009

race, class, gender and location influence students' schooling experience. I use sociological and ethnographic research methods to study educational problems and issues, which is why I have a joint appointment in Educational Studies and Sociology. I have been teaching for nearly ten years, and I have experience at nearly every level of education, including early childhood education, middle and high school, community college, research and liberal arts institutions.

10.3 Setting the Stage

After teaching Foundations of Education from a critical pedagogy perspective for nearly 5 years, I have learned that preservice teachers have the tendency to perceive Foundations as the "fluff" class. So-called fluff courses in university departments signify those courses where instructors and students exchange warm and fuzzy feelings about caring for others, and participate in games and class activities that serve the purpose of learning to display empathy for others. Of course, the others in most cases typically refers to individuals who are different racially, ethnically, religiously, linguistically, physically, or mentally. The overall problem with this framework and approach to *multicultural* education is that students come to believe people who look, think, worship, and live like themselves are the norm. Those who do not fit into their little box of normality are portrayed as the other – someone in need of special attention and sympathy. Within this framework, the "fluff" class is tagged as the class where preservice teachers are instructed and encouraged to tolerate those perceived to be outside of the norm, and they leave the Foundations class believing that those who are different are potentially cool and even teachable. Students begin the Foundations class believing if they embrace a mindset of inclusivity, then they will earn an easy "A" (or at least a "B," if they simply complete the assignments, without necessarily accepting difference as something worthwhile).

Another set of students begin the Foundations class with the mindset that the course content is polluted by the instructor's personal bias and political views. Because the majority of preservice teacher education majors are from middle-class backgrounds and school settings, they may not have directly felt the impact of educational inequality. Based on my experiences, many preservice teachers enter their first Foundations class believing that the act of teaching is apolitical and culturally neutral. From these students' point of view, the act of teaching is merely comprised of a set of techniques and their manifested outcomes. The outcomes are also narrowly reduced to grades and test scores. Every now and again, teaching may lead to students' interests in, or excitement for, a subject, but rarely do these students believe the act of teaching has larger social, political, or economic consequences.

Of course, the act of teaching and the process of teaching and learning do include skill, talent, and ability on the teacher's part. However, these groups of students usually have a difficult time understanding how social relations involving authority or power may ameliorate or hinder not only what is taught, but also what is learned. Upon enrolling in the Foundations class, such students are leery of any deep discussions about racism, segregation, sexism, heterosexism, funding inequity, etc., because from their perspective, the most effective teachers leave personal biases at the door. Any discussions of social justice pose a challenge, and possibly a threat for these students, because they have already made up their minds about the intended function of education and what they need to learn to become an effective teacher.

In this same vein, often the Foundations class is viewed differently from curriculum courses in teacher education. Inevitably, at the beginning of each semester in an encounter with a new group of students, I find it necessary to demonstrate my knowledge of pedagogy, classroom practices, and educational policy. Those who teach the curriculum courses are perceived as bona fide teachers or real experts by students. It has been my experience that students are able to identify with the curriculum instructors because they are former classroom teachers who remind them of their mothers, aunts, grandmothers, or mentors from high school. Many preservice teachers have family members who are teachers, and their relatives serve as their bird's eye view into the profession. Most classroom teachers have not been afforded the opportunity or time to analyze how social conditions, historical patterns, and personal biases impact the educational system and schooling process. As a result, most preservice teachers entering the class with a putative insider's view of classroom practice may not understand the significance of Educational Foundations to their own growth as a teacher.

10.4 Let the Drama Begin

On the first day of class, students discover that Foundations is interdisciplinary in scope. Foundation instructors study and critique the social world from multiple perspectives (and for a variety of reasons), and my thinking is that preservice teachers can begin to discover pedagogical approaches that move beyond shortsighted perspectives (i.e., the bird's eye view) of teaching to more dynamic and panoptical understandings of education; hence, the mention of my interdisciplinary teaching and research background in sociology, social work, education, and anthropology. Finally, I share with the preservice teachers that "it is from these experiences and disciplinary perspectives that I approach discussions of race, class, gender, sexuality, language, and ability grouping." Another message undergirding the introduction is "I am more than competent and qualified enough to teach you." While on the one hand, I am defending the efficacy of Social Foundations as a course and program of study, on the other, I am also buffering any thoughts that a Black woman does not have what it takes to teach in a higher education classroom.

At the end of the first day of class, most students usually leave the classroom feeling eager, elated, and looking forward to the next class meeting, but other students are reluctant about the objectives of the course and the possible hidden motives of Foundation instructors. Excerpts from two journal entries exemplify student reactions:

Student A: That is what Foundations of Education is about, right? About discussions of race and class, and how certain people are mistreated in society, but as teachers we have to make them feel included at school. And, the professor is Black! Maybe we'll learn how to teach poor people.

Student B: Why do we always have to talk about race? What does race have to do with education? My mom is a teacher and she treats all of her students the same. Those people are always teaching their own political agendas.

At the end of the first class meeting, I realize that my role for the next 15 weeks is to inform students of, and embody, the principles of critical pedagogy as a way of teaching and as a way of living. My thoughts at the end of the class period read:

> How do I get this new group of excited pre-service teachers to understand and embrace the complexities of race, class and gender through a critical lens, while also recognizing my own positionality in course content and discussion? Furthermore, how do I maintain their enthusiasm for the challenge of teaching in a diverse multicultural society that privileges whiteness and middle-class status in our educational institutions? I am teaching those who have benefited from the system we are forced to analyze and critique over the coming weeks. How do I give as much space to those who are resistant, alongside those who are more open-minded? In the process, how do I maintain my own sanity?

10.5 Philosophically Speaking

At the beginning of each semester, students are assigned to read Dewey's *Pedagogic Creed* (1897) and Freire's *Pedagogy of the Oppressed* (1970/2000). As a class, we decide that Dewey theorized that education should be an extension of a child's home life; thus, the school should extend the values and lessons taught in the home. Dewey also claimed that children brought their own interests and instincts into the class, and argued that teachers should begin educating from the interests and insights of the child. Believing that the school was an extension of the larger community, Dewey also suggested that one purpose of education was to prepare students to participate and become an asset to their community. Dewey believed that one vital role of education was to involve young people in a continued critique of society in order to be active in social transformation; thus, the teacher-student role was viewed as one serving a purposeful and relational function (Dewey, 1897). After engaging the foundational beliefs of Dewey, my preservice teachers presumably begin to develop an understanding of education as an institution and social process. Pedagogically, the seed is planted that the act of teaching can be connected to a larger social purpose.

Freire (2000) extends Dewey's ideas by applying them to the social conditions affecting the poor and working class, those existing at the periphery of society. Furthermore, in *Pedagogy of the Oppressed* (1970/2000), Freire discussed his observation that education has become an act of depositing, where the teacher becomes the narrator (subject), who deposits information into the objects (students). He coined the phrase "the banking concept" to describe a method of teaching, in which the teacher talks ad nauseum and students passively listen and digest the information being delivered. Freire points out that the banking method of teaching leaves little room for student (or teacher) creativity, critical thinking, or self-reflection. Freire goes on to lay out the value of a problem-posing approach to teaching, where together students and teachers are led to examine problems that human beings produce, encounter, and may potentially counteract in the social world. From this theoretical lens, teaching and learning may lead to consciousness-raising, self-awareness, social critique and action. After introducing Dewey and Freire to the class, I paint a picture of the historical backdrop in which the two theorists were writing. At this point, I focus on the social, economic, educational and cultural shifts that were taking place in Dewey's and Freire's home countries and abroad. My intent is to contextualize theory and pedagogy, showing students that teaching and learning are situated in the politics of the day.

Interestingly, it is not until after reading *Pedagogy of the Oppressed* that students begin to connect class readings and dialogue to issues of race and class. Below is a conversation that took place during one class meeting, after reading Freire:

Female student: Who is the oppressor? And, who is the oppressed? Is Freire speaking about students who don't speak English?

Male student 1: I don't know anything about the 1970s or about Brazil. What does this have to do with today?

Class: Smirks and outbursts of laughter.

Male student 2: Is this guy a communist?

Coming from a problem-posing perspective, I welcome the first two students' comments above. They are attempting to contextualize Freire's philosophy and apply it to current issues in education, even if the first male student is sarcastic in his mannerism. On the other hand, the second male attempts to turn the conversation toward something more controversial. Knowing that most Americans hold anticommunist sentiments, the maneuver served to stray from Freire's larger message about the emancipatory possibilities of education. I cringed at the student's aggressive move. He was attempting to counter discussions of racism, classism, political, and educational disenfranchisement, by killing the messenger (Williams & Evans-Winters, 2005).

I have experienced character assassination many times myself teaching Foundations over the years. Imagine a Black woman arguing that Dewey (a White man) was in support of cultural pluralism and educational equity. Some students attack my character, as opposed to critiquing contemporary issues in education. I am human. Sometimes I fight back.

Students' journal entry: She is always making everything about race.

My journal entry: It baffles me that soon-to-be teachers can't transfer information from one social and historical situation to another. I immediately saw the relevancy of Dewey and Freire to the state of urban education today. Are these the teachers we want to teach our children? Is this lack of critical thinking developmental? Maybe it's my role to improve students' critical thinking skills.

I intentionally use Dewey to set the stage for discussions of cultural diversity and pluralism. As a White male, Dewey is safe for my majority White preservice teachers. Students think: "He must be race-neutral and objective." With Dewey, students rarely tease out sentiments of racial, ethnic, and class discord at that moment in history. I make it my responsibility to lead students in making the connection – thus, putting myself on the frontline of attacks. Overall, students view Dewey as a concerned American citizen, while Freire is the culturally biased "other."

10.6   Teaching the Oppressor?

As a supporter of critical pedagogy, I do my best to model Freirian methodologies. In this vein, after breaking students into small groups, where they briefly summarize the assigned selection or answer each other's questions, I open up a larger group discussion with the following questions: "What did you find challenging about the reading?"; "What did you find interesting about the selection?"; and "What do you disagree with in the reading?". Following Dewey's creed, my intent in raising such open-ended questions is to start where the students are in their thinking. Next, I clarify or offer my own interpretations of a selection, and follow-up by asking the preservice teachers to discuss any agreements or disagreements with my perspective or each other. After this conversation, I straightforwardly proceed by articulating the relevancy of his writing to the social conditions currently impacting African-Americans, Native Americans, Latino Americans and low-income populations.

During one class discussion on Freire and Dewey, a few of the Foundation students led a heartfelt debate about the benefits of the banking system, and thought the premises of a problem-posing pedagogy sounded nice, but not necessarily the most realistic or beneficial form of teaching. The aspiring teachers argued what many educators before them have argued: children benefit from repetition and drills; some subjects, namely math and science, require memorization techniques; and, not all students (i.e., poor urban minority children) come to school ready to learn. One male student proclaimed: "Inner-city children are not taught values at home," which hinders their learning in the school environment. I have trained myself not to react to hair-raising comments that attack me and my family members, neighbors, and role models. He argued it is the teacher's job to provide these basic fundamental skills through the most basic and rudimentary forms of instruction. The student was arguing from a cultural poverty thesis, a theory that claims families living in the "inner-city" do not value education; thus, low-income children lack the pre-readiness skills and home environment that are necessary for learning.

Although only a few students argued these points in class, after reading students' reflection journals, I learned that the majority of the preservice teachers yielded to the argument that the banking system was inevitable and valuable for certain groups of students. In a journal entry, I articulated how I interpreted the class discussion:

It was frustrating to be facing potential teachers who believed it was their job to "train" and "school" others, as opposed to allowing young people to be fully thinking and capable participants in the teaching and learning process.

Preservice teachers view students' and teachers' roles as hierarchical in nature, with the (White middle-class) teacher as the container of knowledge, and that, low-income students lack the cultural and intellectual capacity to appreciate a problem-posing pedagogy. The future educators could not conceive of marginalized students possessing the abilities to intellectually and emotionally link education to liberatory purposes and to deconstruct power relationships in everyday societal practices, such as teaching.

Other students could only compare the costs and benefits of problem-posing pedagogy, as opposed to the banking concept, based on their own experiences of teaching and learning. For instance, one female student wrote: "I simply do not have the time to sit down with a six year old and explain to him why learning how to play the piano is important. I only get paid five dollars an hour." This student appears to move beyond topics of race and class; however, her comment is concerned with larger social class dynamics. On the one hand, she is speaking from the perspective of someone with class privilege, for most low-income and urban students do not have the privilege of piano lessons. On the other hand, she is bringing forth an important topic to teachers—the value of teachers' work in our society. Like this student, many preservice teachers are already concerned with what many veteran teachers worry about—time and money. A problem-posing pedagogy appears more time-consuming and less rewarding to novice teachers of the McDonald's generation (Ritzer, 2000). Problem-posing pedagogy may be intimidating to some because it is not prepackaged, quantified, scripted, and does not yield immediate gratification like the banking method of teaching.

Beyond the required creativity and time commitment involved, some preservice teachers may not see how problem-posing pedagogy might benefit them as a part of the White, educated, and suburban middle class. Metaphorically speaking, they cannot find themselves in Freire's portrayal of the oppressed. Especially when superficially reading the selection, students assume Freire is making a claim that teachers are the oppressor and poor students are the oppressed. Nearly all of my students admit in their personal reflections that they enjoyed spending time with teachers who held their attention in class through raising critical questions and challenging their taken-for-granted assumptions about social life. These were teachers with whom students formed personal relationships, teachers who piqued their long-term curiosity about a particular subject, and teachers who inspired them to consider teaching as a vocation. But more than likely, students have had more contact with banking methods than with problem-posing methods of education.

For instance, a majority of the students maintained that "banking" benefited them in their own educational development. The common attitude in our class was as follows: "The school training I received up to this point has helped me get this far in school, for I have gained admittance into a highly esteemed institution of higher education." If throughout the majority of their schooling they have been objectified (or petrified, to use Freire's word), then it would be difficult to view teaching and learning as something extending beyond a single assignment, letter grade, classroom, or a single grade level. From this shortsighted perspective, the teacher's role is to give information and the student's role is to take it.

After a day or two of discussions on the banking concept, I was ready to link problem-posing pedagogy with the transformative nature of education; however, students were at a mental roadblock. My journal entry below unmasks my personal thoughts regarding students' unrelenting support of the banking concept of education.

> *Thursday's class discussion was disappointing. No frustrating. Students seemed stuck on the "banking" system of teaching, and focused less on the transformative aspect of teaching. It was frustrating that students could not imagine teaching and learning as process or as something tied to larger social or moral causes.*

As the all-knowing professor (i.e., narrator), I could have shifted the conversation to topics I wanted or needed to address. My rationalization for not redirecting the class discussion was because I did not want to risk silencing students for the rest of the semester; or worse yet, suppressing students' true attitudes concerning who can be taught, what should be taught, and their initial impressions of the purpose of teaching and learning. On another note, I noticed during the classroom discussions on Dewey and Freire, two male students (one from a rural school background) who passionately argued on the benefits of embracing the principles of problem-posing pedagogy. Perhaps their support should not be a surprise, since recent research in psychology and education reports that male students are becoming more disenchanted in mainstream classrooms (Pollack, 1998; Dunbar, 2001; Whitmire, 2006). It is possible that preservice male teachers' experiences with marginalization and boredom in classrooms may affect their interest in pedagogies that are intellectually, emotionally, and physically stimulating.

Despite ongoing contemplation, debate, and resistance, soon enough the preservice teachers became more interested in the most important question of the day, "What is the purpose of education?" and "What has it been up to this moment in history?" Ultimately, this was the main objective of the Dewey and Freire reading assignment—to get students thinking about the purpose of education and have them articulate orally and in writing their own philosophy of education. Intrigued or not with problem-posing pedagogy, from in-class discussions, reading student journals and students' philosophy papers, I have learned that the majority of students enter Foundation class definitely viewing themselves as "knower" and containers of knowledge. The teacher's job is to *give* knowledge to students, students' job is to receive knowledge, and banking allows them to *give* in the most efficient manner. Ironically, the preservice teachers psychologically digested the practices and attitudes of bankers, and failed to embody the attitudes and practices of those invigorating educators who led them toward the profession of teaching in the first place.

In those uncomfortable classroom discussions, I am glad that I chose not to redirect students. In addition to learning what students perceived their role to be in the classroom, and the best methods of performing that role, I also learned *why* they chose to pursue teaching. Here I struggle with students' *why*:

We all have been taught that we are the most talented and smartest of the group; therefore, it must be difficult for some of the students to perceive giving up any kind of control. Maybe that's why they have chosen teaching as a profession. Most teachers we know do control students' behavior and thinking, the classroom, their schedules, the curriculum, etc. The most resistant education students to liberatory pedagogy are typically those who are the most obedient students.

They may not envision themselves as change agents or leaders. In other words, the majority of education students typically are those who have made it to college with very few problems or struggles (i.e. social, academic, or financial). Hence, it is quite expected that they may not view schooling, or society for that matter, as in need of change. For them, teaching is a job—a simple profession; teaching is not tied to a higher purpose or moral calling; the teacher is the knower and the students are the known.

After mulling over the above journal entry and students' responses to the entry (Foundation students have access to my electronic journal), I discovered a noteworthy difference between myself and the Foundation students. The primary difference between me and the typical preservice teacher I come in contact with is that I entered the field of education with the intent of advocating on behalf of the oppressed, raising the critical consciousness of the marginalized, while at the same time fighting against the subjugation of my own mind and body.

For me, the marginalized are children, women, the poor, racial and ethnic minorities, the working class, language minorities, urban families, and the differently abled. Teaching and researching from a multiple consciousness worldview (King, 1988), I wholeheartedly believe that those of us who experience schooling at the intersection of race, class, and gender oppression are the most at risk of not having access to a free and appropriate education. The purpose of education then is to expose and ultimately eradicate social inequality through the actions of the oppressed themselves and their allies in the struggle for a just society. By building meaningful relationships with students and community members, sharpening students' basic skills, and exposing students to alternative ways of experiencing the social world, teachers become allies in the struggle.

Educated in a predominately Black school community, I looked to education as a vehicle to freedom from gender, race, and class oppression. For my peers and me, education provided choices that had traditionally been reserved for men, the middle-class, and White people (e.g., better quality neighborhoods, bigger homes, and a voice in the political economy). Education was something that extended beyond grades, entrance exam scores, prestige, and status. Based on personal experiences, I emphatically recognize that education can serve as a veil to oppression or it can serve to expose oppression in people's lives.

I carry all of the above beliefs and experiences into my classroom. At this point, a fair question to ask is: Are these beliefs and previous experiences cultural baggage or cultural capital in Social Foundations of Education? In fact, others in teacher education have discussed the culturally relevant knowledge members of minority groups bring into learning spaces (see Quiocho & Rios, 2000; Sleeter, 1992; Williams & Evans-Winters, 2005). As stated by Quiocho and Rios (2000), "[e]thnic minority teachers bring socio-cultural experiences that, in the main, make them more aware of the elements of racism embedded within schooling, more willing to name them, and more willing to enact a socially just agenda for society (generally) and schooling (specifically)" (p. 487). Hence, I am not alone in my thinking and beliefs. But, what about my Foundation students' thinking and beliefs? Even more, how does their thinking about the purpose of education complicate, interfere with, or impede social transformation?

10.7   Pomp and Circumstance

The majority of Foundation students have not needed to view education as a vehicle toward liberation. Preservice teachers are typically White, female, middle-class, from suburban neighborhoods, and have a history of academic success (Gordon et al., 2000; Trent, 1990; Jorgenson, 2000). With public education in the United States becoming more racially and ethnically diverse, preservice teachers will more than likely have had different experiences from those they will find themselves teaching (Nieto, 2004). After reviewing students' journal entries and contrasting their opinions of Freire, Dewey, and the purpose of education to my views, I have come to accept that many preservice teachers view education as a rite of passage.

A rite of passage is a ceremony or series of rituals that mark a change of status upon entry into a select group or from one stage of life to another. Education for middle-class students is ritualistic in function. Schooling (the passage) carries them from childhood to adulthood (stages of life), while granting them entry into a prestigious social class (a selective group). Coupled with their racial and educational status, they can join the ranks of the power holders in society. Most of my White students assume that education guarantees social and economic mobility. Unfortunately, for most members of minority groups, education does not necessarily lead to better homes, neighborhoods, schools, or employment (Feagin, 2001; Oliver & Shapiro, 1996; Patillo-McCoy, 1999). Therefore, education does not function well as a rite of passage for ethnic minority group members. Grade promotions, test scores, grade point averages, letter grades, graduation ceremonies and diplomas are all markers of obtained and increased status for members of the middle class. It makes sense then that aspiring teachers would want to assist members of their own groups in attaining such status in the most efficient (quick and predictable) and effective (outcome oriented) way. Once again, my journal entry communicates my private thoughts.

> For the typical middle-class student, schooling is an elongated road filled with pomp and circumstance, which eventually leads to tangible and intangible rewards. The rewards become a measure of a person's self-worth and value to society. Teaching allows preservice teachers access to the other side of the game. They go from the initiate to the initiator. The purpose of education, up until this point, was to move them from childhood to adulthood, from second class citizens to first class status. But, finally they have been graduated to the status of the knower.

As the journal entry hints, I learned the hard way that my preservice teachers were materially and psychologically invested in a meritocratic, hierarchal educational system. Moreover, they are literally *schooled* to revere and sustain a system grounded in individualism, memorization and regurgitation practices, and rituals of self-praise. This has serious consequences for the oppressed and the oppressors in society. Consequently, members of the minority group are always constructed as incompetent, while those from the dominant group are forever depicted as more than competent to participate in the educational process. Accordingly, each group perpetually plays out their role. In Freire's words:

> The teacher presents himself to his students as their necessary opposite; by considering their ignorance absolute, he justifies his own existence. The students, alienated like the slave in the Hegelian dialectic, accept their ignorance as justifying the teacher's existence—but, unlike the slave, they never discover that they educate the teacher. (Freire, 2000, p. 72)

> *In the end where does the "banking" system (Freire) of teaching fit into learning? Where does education as liberation fit into all of this discussion? Do I have a classroom full of bankees, who have been socialized (read:brainwashed) into proliferating the banking system. Banking is easier, so maybe I'll just use it this semester, and they'll find out how bankrupting (pun intended) it truly is as a teaching technique.*

There is no need for teacher educators to give in to banking methods, as I sarcastically implied in my journal entry. In conjunction with their students, teacher educators should problematize an educational system that has led many, the (over)privileged and underprivileged, successful and unsuccessful students, to view schooling as purely "ceremonial" events absent of authentic and moral meaning. An essential question at this moment in history (when racial/ethnic minority students, students from low-income families, and English language learners will be the majority in public schools) is *how* do we recruit and retain educators who have the critical skills and fortitude to foster social justice? According to Darling-Hammond (2000), the next generation of teachers must be prepared to teach a diverse group of students, which requires a deep understanding of content knowledge, the ability to be flexible and creative in student assessment, and the ability to organize a productive learning process for students. Thus, another important question is how do we open the minds and hearts of preservice teachers to see that they too have been bamboozled by the banking system, tracking and hyper-testing? Embracing a critical pedagogy stance, I posed that exact question to the Foundation students:

> How have you been affected by an educational system that divides, sorts, and selects individuals, based on race, class, gender, language, and perceived intelligence? Even more, what are the latent consequences to those who have been sorted to the lower tier of society and those who have been filtered to the top of the social totem pole? How does it not prepare you to live with the other half of America? And, how has the sort and selection process not prepared many of you (future educators) to teach the majority of our nation's school children? Do you feel deceived, uninformed, and deluded? Are you satisfied with being a pawn and puppet in processes of injustice or do you want to be one who helps lead others on the path of liberation?

First of all, embedded in the set of questions is the assumption that preservice teachers also have been exploited in the teaching and learning process. Second, the questions suggest that preservice teachers are put at a disadvantage in their careers and social life because they are not prepared to interact and live side by side with half of the US population. After making these assertions and raising these crucial questions, my students begin to see themselves in processes of hegemony.

Even more, students grow less adversarial toward me and my pedagogical style, because they come to comprehend how our plights are intimately connected.

Likewise, over time I grow less resentful of their inflammatory comments. While students hold power (e.g., White privilege), I also hold power within our Foundation class, being the credentialed authority figure. My blackness, womanness, and urbanness in front of a college classroom serve as testimony to McLaren's (2003) observation of "a world rife with contradictions and asymmetries of power and privilege" (p. 69). In our classroom setting, our privilege/power is flipped on its head. Therefore, I do not see it as "me" against "them" or "them" against "me." Instead, I view it as "us" against "them." We all learn to share the burden of exposing and eradicating the status quo through our own set of privileges.

The last question in my journal entry above—"Are you satisfied with being a pawn and puppet in processes of injustice or do you want to be one who helps lead others on the path of liberation?"—serves to provoke students' thinking about who an educator is beyond the classroom. For instance, research in education shows that high-performing schools have more than one leader in the school building and community (Furman & Starratt, 2002; Larson & Murtadha, 2002). Research also shows that successful teachers of African-American and other minority students enter their roles as teachers with confidence in the abilities of all students and care about what students experience outside of the school building (Delpit, 1995; Foster, 1999; Valenzuela, 1999; Dehyle, 1995). These findings suggest that our Foundation class is moving in the right direction. Through perpetual dialogue, tension, and contradictions, my students come to view the teacher as first a leader (one who inspires others), and second a teacher (one who instructs and transfers knowledge).

As an example of promoting shared aims in teaching and learning, the student below reflects on a memorable teaching experience that presumably served the interest of the student and teacher. Her journal entry was posted on my journal page, in response to an entry I wrote earlier.

> *After stabbing myself repeatedly and bending a needle not once, but twice, I got into a rhythm and started day-dreaming. Before that I had been thinking about when my mother had tried to teach me to sew. I'm not at the point where I've forgotten that I had to learn it (as my pointer finger is really sore, I doubt it is going to let me forget anytime soon), but now I'm confident. It's when you do something by yourself, away from the teacher that the consolidation of learning takes place. It's like you have to make sure that the knowledge was in your head and not the room or the teacher. The knowledge is part of you now, and can't be taken away.*

Ironically, the above Foundations student was one of the most vociferous students in support of banking. Nevertheless, as her journal entry reveals, she learned to appreciate the ideas of Freire and Dewey, after applying the ideas to her own life experiences. In the above entry, the student was beginning to imagine a type of knowledge that becomes second nature, because it unfolds as an extension of the home, a part of a child's everyday reality, relational, comfortable, and not intimidating or forced. Certainly, at times this type of learning can be uncomfortable (i.e., a sore pointer finger). As she told me in confidence, when her mother forced sewing on her she hated it. But, when she was allowed to explore sewing at her own pace, she began to experience the short- and long-term benefits of learning beyond self-indulging rewards or accolades. For example, in my response to her journal entry, I wrote:

> *One day you may use sewing to relax, to help others, to save money, to increase spatial reasoning, build bridges with your mother and others. You will make a great leader in the classroom, school-building and community because you understand the relational aspects of teaching and learning; and, that teaching and learning is not static and has value outside of the individual and classroom context.*

10.8   Leaders-Cloaked-As-Teachers

In her 2002 University Council for Educational Administration (UCEA) presidential address, Gail Furman pointed out that current educational research is focusing on what *"leadership is for"*. In the past, researchers were concerned with defining leadership, who does leadership, and how leadership is done. More recently, scholars are beginning to focus on the purposes of leadership. New questions are concerned with: *Why* do leaders do leadership? What are the valued ends being sought? And, how can they be achieved? Furman (2003) points out the shift to what leadership is *for*, requires educational theorists to "engage in a kind of backward mapping–starting with the purposes of leadership and backward-mapping to figure out how to get there" (p. 2). More relevant to Foundations of Education and teacher education is Furman's assertion that educational theorists need to move away from simply focusing only on the leadership skills of individuals in administrative roles and begin to address leadership development in collaboration with teacher educators. The latter have an obligation to engage future educators in leadership preparation that begins with the moral implications of teaching and learning. The critical aim in teacher education is to discover what the value of leadership can be for change agents and the marginalized.

As a framework in teacher education, leaders-cloaked-as-teachers views the role of the teacher as twofold: (1) to guide preservice teachers to envision themselves as a leader, and not simply as one who uses instructional techniques; and, (2) to foster a state of mind that is conducive to student achievement, diversity, and morality. Furman (2003) declares that the practice of leadership must be grounded in an "ethic of community" in order to achieve the moral purposes of schooling. An ethic of community calls for those in the field of education to work together on important problems, communicate and engage in dialogue with one another, and share our stories with each other in the spirit of modeling and nurturing democratic community in schools. An ethic of community is the foundation and prerequisite to all leadership (Furman, 2003).

Following the lead of UCEA, the objective in my Foundations class is to facilitate self and group empowerment; thus, we all can be full participants in a democratic society. Teachers-as-leaders serve as responsible liaisons between parents, community members, and school administrators. As cultural workers, they are empathetic to the needs of both the marginalized and the power holders present in school environments. Leaders-cloaked-as-teachers simultaneously exercise privilege (now that they understand its dynamics) to dismantle the status quo and to prepare their students to do the same. Leaders-cloaked-as-teachers also perform their social role by cultivating young leaders who will become teachers, administrators, and community activists themselves one day.

In teacher preparation programs, this means that we first need to commit to social justice frameworks. It means that education departments and teacher educators must adopt frameworks that integrate knowledge of race, class, gender, and linguistic diversity, along with discussions of inequity and oppression, enslavement, resistance, and resilience. Such critical multicultural frameworks (Kincheloe & Steinberg, 1997) might be combined with leadership frameworks. Shor (1987) reminds teacher educators that the teacher education curriculum must include critical pedagogy, desocialization, and egalitarianism in the learning process of teachers. It means that teacher educators are responsible for modeling a pedagogy of liberation.

In this modeling, we must commit to building bridges across differences with our future educators, and guide them to understand and deconstruct their own subjugation process. As I demonstrated in this chapter, such modeling benefits instructors and preservice teachers. Even though I was the professor, I still needed to be empowered in taking a stance against student resistance, while also working toward cross-cultural communication. Reflection, dialogue, and inquiry across cultural groups and contexts help shape future educators' beliefs about the purpose of education. In return, the reflection on the purposes of education may shape their beliefs about what is appropriate in their professional roles as teachers (Tatto, 1998).

In conclusion, the most important objective in Foundations is to prepare future educators to become change agents in the world, in hopes of making it a place more just for all human beings. Subsequent to sharing the daily challenges I confront as a female scholar of color teaching Foundations with majority White middle-class students, a senior White male colleague made the following point:

> Until our students are not only able to critically reflect upon their own experiences, but step outside of those experiences and demand more out of life, let alone their education, their personal fears will extend into the kind of rigid and unjust categorization of otherness that reflects the conversations you write about. (I. Epstein, 2007, personal communication)

My colleague's insight suggests, as I have argued throughout, that to adequately prepare our teacher candidates to work alongside a group of students and parents who may look, speak, think, behave, imagine, and learn differently from them, those future teachers must begin with their own de-socialization process and assist us in their preparation to become leaders-cloaked-as-teachers. The most important objective is that future leaders move beyond the simple view of teaching as a set of methods toward seeing teaching as a moral obligation to promote social justice through pedagogies of liberation.

References

Darling-Hammond, L. (2000). How teacher education matters. *Journal of Teacher Education*, *51*(3), 166–173.

Dehyle, D. (1995). Navajo youth and Anglo racism: Cultural integrity and resistance. *Harvard Educational Review*, *65*(3), 403–444.

Delpit, L. (1995). *Other people's children: Cultural conflict in the classroom.* New York: The New Press.

Dewey, J. (1897). My pedagogic creed. *School Journal, 54*, 77–80.

Dunbar, C. (2001). *Alternative schooling for African American youth: Does anyone know we're here?* New York: Peter Lang.

Feagin, J. (2001). Racist America: Roots, current realities, and future reparations. New York: Routledge.

Foster, M. (1999). Race, class, and gender in education research: Surveying the political terrains. *Educational Policy, 13*(1), 77–85.

Freire, P. (1970/2000). Pedagogy of the oppressed (30th anniversary edition). New York: Continuum International.

Furman, G.C. (2003). The 2002 UCEA presidential address. *UCEA Review, 45*(1), 1–6.

Furman, G.C., & Starratt, R.J. (2002). Leadership for democratic community in schools. In J. Murphy (Ed.), *The educational leadership challenge: Redefining leadership for the 21st century* (pp. 105–133). Chicago, IL: Chicago National Society for the Study of Education.

Gordon, R., Piana, L.D., & Keleher, T. (2000). *Facing the consequences: An examination of racial discrimination in U.S. public schools.* Applied research center. http://www.arc.org/content/view/212/48/. Accessed 18 October 2008.

Jorgenson, O. (2000). The need for more ethnic teachers: Addressing the critical shortage in American public schools. *Teachers College Record.* http://www.tcrecord.org/Content. asp?ContentId=10551. Accessed 2 April 2006.

Kincheloe, J., & Steinberg, S. (1997). *Changing multiculturalism: New times, new curriculum.* Bristol, PA: Open University Press.

King, D.R. (1988). Multiple jeopardy, multiple consciousness: The context of a Black feminist ideology. *Signs: Journal of Women, Culture, and Society, 14*(1), 42–72.

Larson, C.L., & Murtadha, K. (2002), Leadership for social justice. In J. Murphy (Ed.), *The educational leadership challenge: Redefining leadership for the 21st century* (pp. 134–161). Chicago, IL: Chicago National Society for the Study of Education.

McLaren, P. (2003). Critical pedagogy: A look at the major concepts. In A. Darder, M. Baltadona, & R. Torres (Eds.), *A critical pedagogy reader* (pp. 69–96). New York: Routledge.

Nieto, S. (2004). *Affirming diversity: The sociopolitical context of multicultural education.* Boston, MA: Allyn & Bacon.

Oliver, M.L., & Shapiro, T.M. (1996). *Black wealth/White wealth: A new perspective on racial inequality.* New York: Taylor & Francis.

Patillo-McCoy, M. (1999). Black picket fences: Privilege and peril among the Black middle class. Chicago, IL: University of Chicago Press.

Pollack, W. (1998). *Real boys: Rescuing our boys from the myth of boyhood.* New York: Henry Holt.

Quiocho, A., & Rios, F. (2000). The power of their presence: Minority group teachers and schooling. *Review of Educational Research, 70*(4), 485–528.

Ritzer, G. (2000). *The McDonaldization of society.* Thousand Oaks, CA: Pine Forge Press.

Shor, I. (1987). (Ed.) *Freire for the classroom: A sourcebook for liberatory teaching.* Portsmouth, NH: Boynton/Cook.

Sleeter, C.E. (1992). Restructuring schools for multicultural education. *Journal of Teacher Education, 43*, 141–148.

Tatto, M.T. (1998). The influence of teacher education on teachers' beliefs about purposes of education, roles, and practice. *Journal of Teacher Education, 49*(1), 66–67.

Trent, W. (1990). Race and ethnicity in teacher education curriculum. *Teachers College Record*, *91*(3), 361–369.

Valenzuela, A. (1999). *Subtractive schooling: U.S. Mexican youth and the politics of caring*. Albany, NY: State University of New York Press.

Whitmire, R. (2006). Boy trouble. *New Republic*, *234*(2), 15–18.

Williams, D., & Evans-Winters, V. (2005). The burden of teaching teachers: Memoirs of race discourse in teacher education. *The Urban Review*, *37*(3), 201–219.

Chapter 11
Regulation, Resistance, and Sacred Places in Teacher Education

David A. Greenwood, Sean W. Agriss, and Darcy Miller

11.1 Introduction: A Narrative in Three Voices

The highly regulated institutional context of undergraduate teacher education is itself a powerful pedagogical force. Ubiquitous rules, routines and rituals—epitomized by a department's faculty preparing for NCATE review—create a professional environment of self-regulation in which it becomes nearly impossible to publically confront the deep assumptions underlying the teacher education bureaucracy, or to imagine and create an alternative, decolonizing vision. Naming the experience of these constraints is an act of resistance that supports continuous learning and transformation.

This chapter makes space for the voices of two instructors working from a critical perspective within a regulatory context. David is a faculty member who developed and coordinates the course, Cultural and Community Contexts of Education, which is required in the secondary teacher education program. Sean is a doctoral student who actually teaches most sections of the course, signifying the larger trend of doctoral students and other non-tenure track faculty staffing teacher education programs. In addition to the voices of program instructors, the chapter also presents the perspective from another faculty member, Darcy, who held an administrative role during the preparations for the departmental NCATE review.

By intermingling these voices, we demonstrate the many-layered ways that the "hidden curriculum" of regulation works against the broader development of critical pedagogies that might otherwise challenge a culture of compliance. Paradoxically, we also show that even within acts of self-regulation, opportunities to develop critical praxis exist. We do not seek to cast blame for the dilemmas in our program and believe that there is, in fact, no one to blame. We want only to name our experience, which includes our own complicity in what we find to be problematic. This chorus of voices from different perspectives is also itself a form of resistance and renewal. It is not unitary; it is not sure of itself; it offers no definitive conclusion. Nonetheless,

D.A. Greenwood, S.W. Agriss, and D. Miller
Washington State University

S.L. Groenke and J.A. Hatch (eds.), *Critical Pedagogy and Teacher Education in the Neoliberal Era: Small Openings*,
DOI 10.1007/978-1-4020-9588-7_11, © Springer Science+Business Media B.V. 2009

it captures the lived experience of three program faculty in ways that contribute to their own learning and to the learning of the students in their classes.

11.2   The Institutional Context

"The greater part of what my neighbors call good I believe in my soul to be bad, and if I repent of anything, it is very likely to be my good behavior" (Thoreau, 1947, p. 266).

David: In my twelve years teaching at two universities, I have often felt let down by the regulated nature of teacher education faculty meetings. I frequently dread attending these meetings, and I often leave them feeling used and powerless. Especially this past year as my department prepared--against its will--for a visit from NCATE (National Council for Accreditation of Teacher Education), the meetings became tedious and lifeless. Each would begin with a new round of handouts, pages deep and thick with tables, matrices, and rubrics, that attempted to map compliance with the mandates from the accrediting regime that the faculty had voted overwhelmingly the year before not to submit itself to. This vote, we were told, was only advisory, and it was overruled by the administration for reasons that were never fully revealed. Some faculty in administrative roles suggested that with a new university-wide leadership focused on images of excellence and efficiency, college leaders did not want to explain the loss of externally conferred status. So as faculty we went along, meeting after meeting, dutifully enacting NCATE's ritualized vision of education, aligning our teacher certification syllabi with the prescribed student outcomes *du jour*, and collecting student evidence to be put in the examination room for the examining team. It was the "bystander effect[1]" and we were sitting in our seats instead of marching in the streets.

This Monday's meeting was typical in that it was governed again by NCATE, not by what the faculty cared most about, and not by what we might have come to together through regular meetings of imagining a teacher education program that would inspire us and our students. Such visioning seldom happens except in hallways at the grassroots; it is never sustained over time with the flush resources that legitimize the monumental commitment of preparing for accreditation review. This is one of the great opportunity costs of going along with what is externally imposed: the power of this kind of governance produces many layers of self-regulation and a culture of compliance that limits space and time for imagining and creating other possibilities.

Throughout the meeting I mostly sat despondent, trying to be positive while my need to stay inspired and hopeful in the challenging work of teaching drifted somewhere out the window looking for light and air. Just as surely as I knew that the planet was warming and that the world might possibly wake up to a time of radical transformations, I knew that this meeting would get bogged down in the details of

---

[1]The "bystander effect" describes a kind of group denial: the more bystanders there are, the less likely it is that any of them will actually respond to an emergency (Latané & Darley, 1970).

documenting compliance to the old regime. I also knew that few of us, if anyone, in the room really wanted it this way, but to object would be to obstruct an inevitable process that most everyone wanted over a soon as possible. Even those in leadership positions, those who carried the burden of ensuring a "successful" review, openly critiqued the entire ordeal. What choice did they have? What choice did I have? To openly refuse to participate would strain relationships with colleagues I care about, marking me as a poor citizen and a troublemaker. So like students disengaging from school, I mostly checked out my real thoughts and feelings, went through the motions, and waited for the bell.

Halfway through the agenda a discussion item caught my attention. I found myself reviewing the latest data from the EBI,[2] a standardized survey instrument that tracks student evaluations of our teacher education program after students graduate. While our department administration occasionally uses this assessment to rally the faculty to improve our outcomes (as measured against peer institutions), I have several times suggested that we might want to reconsider using these results to improve our program until we envision for ourselves what we want our program to become. Otherwise, I've argued, we are consenting that the EBI survey accurately represents our best thinking and that it should therefore guide our instructional choices. This objection has been met with nods of affirmation; however, the survey and its influence persist because the department uses it to show NCATE that we are using student assessments to improve our program.

The issue at this Monday's meeting was that our EBI scores from students were consistently low on an item concerning "school law." The question was put to the faculty: "Where in our program is school law taught?" Several of my colleagues responded with examples. One told of teaching the origins of IDEA (Individuals with Disabilities Education Act) and current special education law; another told of analyzing *Brown v. Board of Education* and other transformative civil rights cases; and another told of reviewing the statutes and procedures on mandatory reporting of abuse and neglect. As the person in the room responsible for the majority of the "social foundations of education," I started to feel uncomfortable with the palpable implication that I ought to be covering more school law in my classes. I began to feel guilty and defensive. I started to marshal arguments in my mind for teaching school policy over school law, but in the presence of the EBI data, I felt unsure of myself. I acknowledged that while I emphasize education policy in my classes and examine the history and tensions around policies such as the No Child Left Behind Act, I don't spend much time with school law *per se*.

Usually during such exchanges part of me starts to die inside. I want to resist, stand up and make a case for social and educational challenges more important than

---

[2]For years our department administration has referred to this survey as "the EBI," without ever naming what the abbreviation actually means. While writing this chapter I discovered that EBI is the name of the corporation that profits from producing and administering the survey (Educational Benchmarking, Inc.). That our department shorthand for self assessment ("the EBI") is a for-profit survey company is a sad and telling comment on the takeover of educational thought by the assessment industry.

how to raise our EBI scores for NCATE. I wanted to ask again, "What conversations about education does the EBI *mandate*, and what conversations does it *preclude*?" But to resist on this point, to exercise my citizenship right of free speech and my scholarly responsibility of intellectual honesty, would be to channel more energy into a conversation about compliance that I might be able to help end quickly. So instead of protesting, I proposed distributing in my classes a primer on school law and name it as such as a section in the syllabus: *A Teacher's Guide to School Law* (Essex, 2006). Everyone seemed satisfied with this solution, and it left me feeling uncomfortable about what kind of educator, what kind of person I was becoming. Instead of raising hard questions about the content of our program and the sources of its vision and re-vision, I capitulated, for the sake of expedience, to a matrix of regulatory pressures.

The faculty meeting I describe here is typical of the culture of accountability to—and complicity with—the bureaucracies that surround professional education and prescribe its "best practices." Responding to the mandates of NCATE or the state or the feds is not an occasional distraction from an otherwise intellectually free environment; it is an ever-present political and pedagogical force that constitutes undue restriction on thought, feeling, and imagination. This pedagogical force shapes the terms of schooling and remains outside of most people's volition and control. In Foucauldian terms, it is a power that circulates and is enforced everywhere as people discipline themselves and each other with its directives (Foucault, 1980).

I continue to have great passion for learning and education, but the rules, practices, and routines set in motion by an ever-more bureaucratized teaching profession wear down this passion. These routines reinforce assumptions about teaching, learning, and living that work against my own vision for myself as teacher, learner, and person. I therefore view my continued commitment to teaching as a subversive activity; however, I am frequently disappointed with myself for my inability to act outside of the very constraints that I critique and reject. I am frequently aware, for example, that the decisions I make about a teacher education course—in terms of its structure and content—are severely limited by convention and what I believe will be acceptable to my colleagues as well as to state, federal, and professional authorities. I believe this self-regulation to be ubiquitous in teaching and that the possibilities for change depend on acknowledging and problematizing the situation through collective action. How, I wonder, can I deinstitutionalize myself and my relationships, and open more and more to developing with others a vision I can embrace with more integrity?

Darcy: As a faculty member serving in an administrative role during the NCATE review process, I too felt the heavy weight of accreditation. Although faculty voted against seeking national accreditation, the college went forward. (State accreditation, on the other hand is mandatory and requires the same type of data, assessment systems, and alignment with standards.) I attended many meetings on accreditation during which the committees were either directed to complete an accreditation task, or took the lead in deciding what activities and jobs must be completed for a successful review. Instead of having the luxury of examining critical and compelling issues about teacher education, we were faced with spending many program meetings talking about accreditation, which involved among other things examining various data on our students' performance. Some of these activities were found to be extremely helpful to faculty. There were many assessments that we created and analyzed that provided us with new information about our students and our program. These findings informed our program and provided impetus for change and improvement. However, that is not to say that all of the accreditation tasks and assessments were helpful or interesting. I probably dreaded most of the program meetings as much as David. In many ways the accreditation requirements put on hold my long-held curiosity, passion, and interest in teacher education. I felt some of what we had to do was downright dreary.

I have long detested regulation but I favor "productive resistance"; resistance that actually results in an outcome – a positive outcome. As a faculty member and teacher educator, I have continually railed against regulation, especially against state mandates, although the micro-management and mandates of No Child Left Behind took regulation to a new and very disturbing level. To resist regulation, I favor working at the political level, because it is the politicians who send these mandates to education. The press for educational accountability over the past 10 years illustrates the deep distrust of teacher education. The regulation of teacher education programs is a result of political ideology, anti-higher education sentiments, angry legislators, and perhaps ignorance on the part of lawmakers. I see authentic and productive resistance occurring with hard work at the political and legal levels, not in refusing to complete a task at the department level. I have committed many hours to this type of resistance during my career.

Other faculty members were frustrated about accreditation also. A colleague recounted a canoe trip as being analogous to our situation. As a member of the canoeing party, he disagreed with the others about attempting a difficult set of rapids, but was overruled. Into the water they went. He felt more and more angry that he was overruled, especially as the rapids became significantly dangerous. But if he sat there and complained as opposed to paddling, he would put them all in jeopardy. So he paddled as hard as he could and they survived. He felt our accreditation situation was similar - we were in the water and everyone had to pull together, collaborate, and get the job done. Refusing to participate could put our program at risk - which included our jobs, our students' programs, and perhaps the college at large (i.e., loss of accreditation can equal loss of programs, especially in difficult budget times). Although I didn't agree with the accreditation requirements, if I refused to help, the tasks would just fall on others' plates - other faculty members who I respect, admire, and who are dear friends. That didn't seem like resistance, but rather like "dumping."

I identify with David's sense of despair. It was difficult to facilitate program meetings when many of the topics were regulatory. I've always loved all aspects of my profession - research, teaching and service. But faced with a completely different set of responsibilities (accreditation), my enthusiasm for my work plummeted. My colleagues are critical thinkers, creative, interesting, and hard working. To make them sit through meetings focused on regulatory issues was just as difficult for me, as it was for them.

Sean: I also feel the looming emotional drain when it is time for faculty meetings where I know regulatory issues will be the focus. On more than one occasion David and I have commiserated about the impending meetings. I am all too familiar with the process--it seems as though the accreditation cloud is following me. Prior to my return to graduate school, I was a faculty member at a tribal college engrossed in accreditation. Our meetings, like now, were constantly hijacked with expectations and guidelines in the form of charts and rubrics that were sanitized and stale, bereft of any real meaning to the faculty and students. "We're a fine arts college," we argued. "We don't want to fit into your charts and rubrics." But much like our current situation, accreditation was imposed as a necessity. I admit that now, after my third year of filling in the boxes and shuffling paperwork into the appropriate folder, cabinet, and closet, I am sufficiently jaded. This is not to say that I think accreditation can't be valuable; it can be useful when the accrediting agency shares a similar vision of education. But what is the purpose when the visions aren't aligned? It seems that dissenting voices are tuned out for the sake of the intangible thumbs up from agencies that are blindly accepted as higher powers.

As David has written, we hadn't yet received our thumbs up on the issue of "school law." Because of the faculty discussion regarding the exclusion of "school law" in our program, it is now my responsibility to make sure this item is checked off of the accreditation list. Although I initially found it difficult to find a place to crowbar this in among texts I deem more valuable, it provided the opportunity for me to see my students employ the critical skills gained in their reading of authors like Freire, McLaren, and Kozol. Students, without my prompting but empowered with a new critical framework, immediately focus on sections such as "Unwed Pregnant Teachers" and the discussion of courts considering "the community standards and the degree to which the teacher's conduct violates the ethics of the community and renders the teacher unsuitable to teach." Students point to the "Corporal Punishment" section of the text that reports the staggering 342,038 students who were hit in public schools in the 1999-2000 school year. Students question the "Family and Medical Leave Act" and ask what exactly qualifies as a family, and who isn't included (Essex, 2006).

This leads me to believe that when students are encouraged to think outside of the checklist mentality, they become interested in exploring themselves as future teachers, examining the climate of the profession they are about to enter, and asking important questions about how they fit into this system. But the current atmosphere in which we work is pushing these questions to the margins in favor of creating certified teacher clones instead of strong individuals who can have exponential influence in our classrooms.

Acknowledging the current atmosphere of institutional control, I try to recognize it when it appears and determine where I am able to resist. Passive acceptance that takes the form of instructors "going along" or "checking out" in faculty meetings, and teaching assistants implementing courses aligned with checklists, silently validates a paradigm of teacher education that needs reform. When we don't challenge the structure in place, we permit the influence to persist and expand—we are disengaged in our meetings, our students are disengaged in our classrooms, their students become disengaged in their future classrooms; professors implement what is deemed appropriate by governing agencies, teaching assistants teach courses designed by supervisors, and our future teachers become satisfied with stale prepackaged curriculum. We can't expect our students to generate the resistance; this is a job for those at higher levels of teacher education programs.

Darcy: In my administrative role, I meet regularly with teacher education student representatives. One of the complaints I've heard frequently from students is that they know nothing about educational law. So, like so many of the issues that came up around accreditation, the school law issue was more complex than merely checking off a box or interpreting EBI scores. Many of the students I met with wanted more information about No Child Left Behind, about unions, and about their legal responsibilities not because they wanted to go along with the system, but because they wanted to disrupt the status quo. One student wanted to know how he was supposed to critique the laws, if he didn't have any knowledge of the laws. After hearing similar complaints over a two year period, I told the chair of the department that I couldn't ethically meet with the students and hear the same requests, unless we began to address the issues in the program meetings. As a teacher educator, I agreed with the students - they have the right to know about the laws and policies governing their future profession. I also felt that if we want students to think critically about education, they need knowledge in order to critique. What happened in Sean's class is precisely what we would want to happen. As a result of reading Friere, McLaren, and Kozol, and then examining educational laws, students were able to ask critical questions, challenge the existing system, and begin to form independent opinions. Students in Sean's class were developing knowledge that would enable them to go beyond blind compliance, to problematizing educational structures, procedures, and requirements.

11.3 Accountability and Authenticity in Teacher Education

"The certification of teachers now constitutes an undue restriction on the right to free speech" (Illich, 1978, p. 85).

David: Many progressive and critical educators believe that education makes no sense outside of a deep examination of the social and cultural contexts in which education takes place. This idea is basic to progressive education in the tradition of Dewey, and in the more radical tradition of Freire and many other critical educators. Most courses in the social foundations of education examine relationships between practices and social and historical contexts. However, examining social and political context as a foundation for program implementation is an intellectual challenge that is utterly foreign to the bureaucracies that govern most teacher education programs. These bureaucracies are founded on sets of assumptions about schools that get reinforced and internalized as programs seek to maintain legitimacy and status in the academic marketplace.

A brief list of common assumptions about schooling might include: school purposes that are geared for uncritical participation in the growth economy; school structures that are isolated from communities and that cut learning up into small chunks of time; standards-based and teacher-centered pedagogies that frustrate the process of inquiry; and curricular fragmentation that works against holistic experience or systems thinking. Looming over all these common structures is the highly problematic assumption that school success or student achievement should be measured by test scores.

In recent years, the No Child Left Behind Act has intensified the work of educational bureaucracies, keeping them focused more than ever on compliance. This focus means that there is little room for asking questions about current practices and the relationship between these practices and the fast changing cultural and ecological contexts of local and global systems. But the problem is deeper than the lack of vision. The problem is that the discourses and practices that surround schooling function to maintain a vision that is too often uncritically embraced. In fact, schooling *is* currently tightly tied to the cultural critique and vision of the accountability movement.

Since the early 1980s and the publication of *A Nation at Risk*, trends toward standards, testing, and accountability have been linked to the perceived need to keep pace with other nations in a global economic competition. More recently, the discourse of standards, accountability, and excellence has been linked to efforts to close the historic achievement gaps between different racial, cultural, and economic groups. Thus, NCLB is invoked both as policy aimed at ending inequality of educational (and thus economic) opportunity and at strengthening the economic advantage of the entire nation. When the narratives of economic opportunity, global competition, and equity and social justice are conflated in one slick phrase—"no child left behind"—the policy environment and practices behind the rhetoric become increasingly difficult to challenge.

Intellectually, my position is that the discourse, practice, policy, and structure around teacher education programs constitute the most powerful pedagogy for new teachers. This hidden curriculum, I believe, shapes teachers' thoughts, actions, and possibilities more than the explicit or formal content of any course, perhaps even more than all of their courses combined. What can be done to problematize and interrupt this pedagogy through coursework, mine or my colleagues', is at best marginal. Our courses, with their necessary reliance on graded credits, semester hours, and state certification requirements, manifest structures that reinforce many elements of the conventional program. Furthermore, these courses are *compulsory* and are not exempt from other contradictions that I believe work against student learning. Still, many of my colleagues and I see our courses as places of resistance to a program founded on political regulation. As an instructor in the course Cultural and Community Contexts of Education, I ask students to critique and envision the profession they are about to enter. Since they have been well schooled by the profession, this is often uncomfortable, but I have learned over the years that when exposed to intellectual traditions such as critical pedagogy and place-based education, students can develop sophisticated analyses of schooling that include a vision of themselves as change agents and intellectuals in particular community contexts.

Sean: It is difficult to teach critical pedagogy within a system that, in practice, doesn't value critical pedagogy. In my teaching and in life, I have found that I am at my best when I am my full self. It is common for me to explain to students my own progression as an educator. I tell how my first few years of teaching felt more like a theater job than anything I would consider real. In the classroom I acted the acceptable role of "teacher" and only upon leaving school could I be a whole person again. My reviews were excellent and it felt dirty. I knew there was real work to do, but this work required an honesty that wasn't on any checklist or rubric. I tell this story because it establishes the necessity of honesty and openness with students, which allows classrooms to become fertile places for thought and discussion. A repercussion of practicing this honesty is that when my students, with their new critical lenses, reflect on the context of their own learning and ask specific questions like 'why' and 'for whom,' I feel obligated to explore with them the context in which we are discussing critical pedagogy.

Students in my classes are learning to ask the questions that aren't often asked. They're acquiring the skills to pay attention to aspects of their education that previously went unacknowledged. Inevitably, they consider that I am a teaching assistant who is instructing their class because it provides me a tuition waiver so I can do my PhD work. I feel some shame around this issue. I want to be fully committed to these students, but there are days when I could be better prepared, could give more extensive feedback, and could be less distracted with the demands of my own studies. It's also important to note that my situation is much better than many of my colleagues. We are all asked to step in and teach courses which we didn't design, but I'm matched with David who shares a similar philosophy of education. I'm teaching the same course for two years, and it is a course that both influences and is influenced by my own studies. Many other teaching assistants are teaching courses outside of their areas of interest, teaching different courses every semester, and sometimes teaching more than one prep each semester. Students observe this tension and experience it—they are on the receiving end of a system that values research above teaching and survives financially by using graduate students as a large portion of their labor force. What are students missing by having instructors whose energy and attention is pulled in so many directions? This is a question that students, in an open, honest, and critical classroom environment, will rightfully ask. Students are then confronted with the tensions in reading and discussing critical pedagogy as they earn their certifications from an institution where, for the most part, critical pedagogy is not a priority.

As a student in the Cultural Studies and Social Thought in Education PhD program, I see and experience the tension in studying critical social theory while simultaneously teaching in the current regulatory culture of education. It is apparent to me that the education system in this country, at all levels, needs dramatic reform, but without my tuition waiver, which requires me, in some ways, to participate in the herding of teacher education students through the various checkpoints on their way to certification, I would be unable to do the work I think is necessary to help assist in the reformation of schooling. This is difficult for me to reconcile. I want my own studies to be influencing my teaching, but I am expected to fulfill my role as a teaching assistant. The constant focus on accreditation requirements makes it difficult to conduct my class in a way I feel is appropriate. Being paired with David has made this easier, as he is one faculty member who will make the arguments I would be making if my situation didn't seem precarious, but there are times when I feel like I fall back into my first year teaching self, "acting" and conforming to a system I don't agree with pedagogically. It feels dishonest, but the regulatory culture in which we function leaves me no option but to, at times, quietly set aside my concerns and simply do what I'm told. If a large portion of the instructors in teacher education are in similar ethical dilemmas, it is important to ask what the effect is for the students in these teacher education programs.

David: Sean identifies a huge barrier to both resistance and transformation within teacher education: most classes are actually taught by temporary faculty with little status and less pay. In the last seven years, I have worked with seven different teaching assistants, which is a misnomer because they act as full instructors in the courses they teach. What this means for me is that I need to design a syllabus for someone else to teach from "successfully." The issues here are too many to unpack sufficiently. For my part, designing a syllabus for someone else creates a much different product than designing one for myself. It is a process that works against my own values in teaching, but that aligns well with department realities.

In what follows, Sean and I briefly describe key experiences that make up the content of the course that we teach. I should note that on various versions of course syllabi, I have had to comply with requests to align course objectives with the state professional education standards for teachers. This is not a difficult exercise, but the act of alignment to these mandates reinforces the idea that the mandates give the course its legitimacy (see Gruenewald, 2004). A critical pedagogy questions the legitimacy of the mandates, and searches for a higher ground of authority than the rules of the day.

Sean and I want to make it clear that our focus on our course in the remainder of this chapter does not mean that other instructors and courses in our program are uncritical of the culture of compliance that we have described above. Rather, the point is that the regulatory environment frequently limits program-wide planning among diverse instructors to conversations about program compliance.

Darcy: Most of the faculty members feel the same frustrations, constraints, and pressures experienced by Sean and David. Many faculty in our department teach their courses using a critical pedagogy lens and challenge their students to problematize the system. I agree that there is a culture of compliance in K-12 schools, as well as teacher education programs. I also agree that a deep examination of the social and political context of education should be a required focus of all teacher education programs. David and Sean's vision and perspective on their course provide an excellent example of how to address these challenging issues. Our future teachers need to take with them into the schools a critical and questioning stance - for that is the only way they can actualize their teaching to transgress.

11.4 Major Components of Cultural and Community Contexts of Education

11.4.1 Introduction to Critical Pedagogy and Place-Based Education

David: The theoretical foundation of our course rests on the convergence of critical pedagogy and place-based education, and students begin with Paulo Freire's (2000) *Pedagogy of the Oppressed.* Especially for secondary students who strongly identify with their content area specialties (i.e., English, history, biology, math, etc.), this is their first introduction to the idea that education is itself an intellectual and political arena worthy of serious study. Critical pedagogy problematizes what it means to be a teacher and a learner and blurs these roles so that beginning teachers can begin to see themselves as intellectuals and change agents in the wider culture. Introducing the critical tradition—and critiquing it—enables students to build analyses of the field of education and the business of schooling based not just on their own experience but on the social and historical record.

Sean: Many students initially find Freire difficult; most have never encountered texts of this sophistication (important to note considering this is a 400-level course and these students are usually one year away from completing coursework). Somewhere in the process of synthesizing their own educational experiences and Freire's treatment of teachers and learners, students relish the opportunity to consider themselves and the work they do as important aspects of social change. Additionally, students are able to begin seeing how and where their own instructors, including myself, fit into this model.

David: If critical pedagogy provides the foundation for the analysis of schooling, place-based education, and its convergence with a critical stance toward schooling, provides the vision (Gruenewald, 2003a, 2003b). As I often tell my students, too many educators at all levels (including myself) are long on critique and short on vision. I challenge them to develop a vision of teaching that is responsive to local and global contexts in this historical moment: a time of peak oil, global climate change, widespread social and ecological degradation, and a renaissance of grassroots movements everywhere responding to the ethical lapses of governmental and private sectors (Hawken, 2007). Place-based education is education that is responsive to particular places and the people who live there. Students begin by considering the many ways that community contexts can inform both the purpose and practice of education. We read a variety of case studies of teachers developing critical, place-based education in order to engage learners in real work that impacts their communities. Our students begin imagining how they can connect their teaching to place and to larger movements for social and ecological wellbeing (Gruenewald and Smith, 2008).

Sean: As students read case studies that examine place-based education across a wide variety of content areas, they begin to envision how to use this knowledge to transform their own philosophies of education and the communities where they reside. This takes many forms. The large university where we work is in a rural community, and this dynamic creates a very transient population where most students leave during school breaks and don't stick around after graduation. Because of this, we are forced to think about the idea of community in a variety of incarnations. Some students consider their families as their community, some the town to which they will return, some the larger regions where they travel. However students view community, they are able to think about how they can individually become change agents intimately connected to these places.

11.4.1.1 Sacred Cartography

David: In order to meet students where they are and to ground them in their own lived experience of place, one of their first assignments is to create a map of their own sacred place. Experience, especially experience that is deeply meaningful, often has a strong geographical dimension. Our memories are filled with recollections of specific places that have helped shape who we are. Our "home communities" are filled with sacred (or profane) places that make them distinctive, interesting, and sometimes horrifying and distasteful. Students create their maps out of any medium they choose and also write a narrative, in any form, that helps communicate for others the experience of the map. Each map is then digitized and assembled in a class "slide show" which is narrated by each student as his or her slide is viewed. This assignment helps build community while emphasizing the importance of place to cultural experience. It allows us to go deeper into some of the theoretical territory of critical, place-based education from the perspective of intimate experience.

   Sean: There is a need to share with others the places that helped to form us into the people we now are. One semester, without the prompting of this assignment and before we even began to delve into the concept of place, students began sharing intimate stories about meaningful places. Sharing their experiences of influential places became a visceral experience for many of them. A student wept as she told stories of childhood friends and their adventures in a wooded area near her home. Another student showed pictures and recounted a trip overseas that drastically changed his world vision. Creating space in the classroom for strong relationships to form around the idea of place facilitates camaraderie among students that I haven't witnessed in other contexts.

11.4.1.2 HB 1495 and Native American Place

David: In 2005, our state's governor signed HB 1495--"Tribal History-Common School" legislation that encourages school districts to develop relationships with the nearest federally recognized Native American tribe. The purpose of the legislation was to create culturally appropriate Native American curricula for all students, and for Native students to see themselves appropriately represented. This legislation was fortuitous for me because I want students to remember that every place in our state and country was once, and still is, Native American homeland. Through case study, we examine the history of the bill's passage and the slow progress of implementation. Students in the class then research the Native history their own homeland, or of the place they imagine themselves teaching in the near future. This research extends the idea of sacred places outward from individual experience of intimate places to a community's experience of larger eco-regions and associated lifeways. During this time, students are also introduced to the concept of education for sustainability and to contemporary conflicts between Native American rights and White society.

Sean: It is incredible for me to see how blatantly disconnected students are from the Native communities that surround them. I may be especially sensitive to this considering my tribal college experience where I had close connections with some of the local Native cultures, but many of my students have never taken note of Native American homeland. In one specific instance, a student made outright racist remarks about Native culture without any shame or inkling that there may be a problem with her comments. Other students in the room addressed her viewpoint with tact, validating that we had created a space where free expression in all forms was welcome, while decisively rejecting the racism of her words. This event serves as evidence that there is a pressing need to reconnect to what came before us, as well as to establish safe places where these issues are able to be discussed.

11.4.1.3 Media Analysis

David: Because I am interested in students developing their own analyses of education and schooling, from the first day of class I ask that they begin clipping newspaper stories, at least one each week. By mid-semester, each student has collected about 10 articles. Students then form groups of three or four and begin an analysis of 30-50 articles about schooling—a big chunk of data. Instead of asking students to write a typical research paper, I ask them sort through the data and identify emergent themes. Students then create a poster that illustrates a critique of education by connecting their thematic analysis to course themes, such as culture, place, critical pedagogy, place-based education, sustainability, and the history of policy initiatives such as NCLB. These posters are presented to the class as significant texts that contribute to teachers' understanding of their profession and its social context.

Sean: The focus of many of these projects is how education and schooling are portrayed in the media. Many students note the intense fixation on high-stakes testing and the accountability movement. The media analyses often prompt questions about why teachers have become convenient scapegoats for our nation's social ills, leading to conversations about A Nation at Risk and subsequent legislation. Considering the media portrayal of their chosen profession allows students to examine the climate of schooling which they are entering. It is important for beginning teachers to be able to figure out how to place themselves in the context of their profession.

11.4.1.4   Cultural Arts Presentation

David: When I first read *Savage Inequalities*, I remember being struck by Jonathon Kozol's (1991) report that wherever he went in struggling neighborhoods and schools, he would ask people what they thought was beautiful (one boy responded, "A baby fox"). In my class we examine the absence of attention in schooling to what Howard Gardner (1999) called the pillars of the disciplined mind: truth, goodness, and beauty. In our case, we also create space—five minutes at the start of each class period—for each student to give a brief presentation based in the aesthetic arts. The criteria for this assignment are that the student is truly moved by the work of art and that he or she reflect and comment on the work in a larger cultural context. Five minutes with the arts is an inspiring reminder of the opportunities in teaching to implement transgressive pedagogies even in small spaces. This pedagogical structure also serves to invite students to share their own creative art or passion through voice, instrumentals, visual arts, and dance. It has become one of my favorite ways of creating a structure that helps students bring parts of themselves to class that might otherwise never show up.

Sean: The arts have served as a major point of connectivity for students. It is amazing to watch students take risks by, for example, singing, playing instruments, reading poetry, and sharing artwork. Five minutes with the arts at the beginning of class establishes a particular tone that assists in the rest of the work we do in the course. It has become an essential part of what students value about the class and links students in shared appreciation for something outside of their everyday encounters with program bureaucracy.

11.4.1.5   Culture and Community Immersion Project

David: When I first began teaching critical, place-based education to undergraduates, I would complain about their lack of opportunity to experience it firsthand. Because of the logistics of teaching in a small college town in which the few available schools are already overwhelmed by university placements, students simply do not have ready access to schools while they are in my class. However, I now view this lack of access to schools as a benefit that helps me emphasize all of the other places where learning can happen in a community.

Students choose among an ever-evolving set of project ideas that challenge them to go deep, experiencing and reflecting upon the relationship between education, culture, and community. Each option requires a significant time investment, including a minimum of 12 hours community contact and a self-directed process of reflection, inquiry, action, and representation of the learning. Recent options include: 1) "Sacred place immersion"—students develop an intimate relationship with a local place and its pedagogical power throughout the semester, 2) "Oral history of learning"—students develop a "folknography" of learning with community members that focuses on cultural context, 3) "Content in the community"—students create a project that looks at the many ways of connecting the classroom to the community in content area teaching, 4) "Civic engagement"—students choose a service learning field placement through the university's Center for Civic Engagement, 5) "Investigating a local cultural or ecological issue"—students develop an issue-based inquiry project through field investigation and research, 6) "Learn a new skill"—students set out to learn a skill in a face-to-face, community-based relationship (preferably without spending money).

Sean: The Culture and Community Immersion activity is completely student driven. The project becomes valuable because students involve themselves in areas of their own interest. Some students, because the majority of their schooling has not been self-directed and has not been connected to community life, have difficulty choosing a project. Freeing students to design their own projects of inquiry and action can be uncomfortable, but by allowing students to invest themselves in what is meaningful to them, the potential for significant work is increased. At the end of the semester students share their community investments with colleagues. Students are consistently impressed with the volume and variety of work accomplished during the semester. Many projects are continued after the completion of the course and semester, and the lines separating teacher/learner, schooling/education, and work-life/home-life are blurred.

11.5   Conclusion

Although we and this course function under the regulatory umbrella, we still feel like we're doing valuable work that challenges the status quo. An invaluable aspect of the course is the coexistence of inquiry and action. Students, guided by course content and their own particular interests, begin bridging communities and schools that normally function in isolation. In an effort to create a space where students are able to explore educational conditions different from the onslaught of regulatory practices, we are attempting to deregulate this one course piece by piece. For example, in previous semesters, students have done some self-evaluation and some self-grading. We will propose officially changing this course from a "graded" to a "non-graded" or "pass/fail" course. Because we are not optimistic that this plan will be supported any time soon, we plan on continuing to interrupt grading practices as well as others that reinforce the paradigm of teacher-controlled classrooms.

Questioning the legitimacy of grades is no minor lesson. Grades and other common credentials represent the heart of what students take for granted about schooling, and it is precisely what students take for granted that we seek to interrupt and open to question. In order to transgress within or transform the current culture of schooling, future teachers need to learn about pedagogies that differ from what they have come to know as the norm. This does not mean only learning new methods that purport to be "best practices"; it also means learning to problematize the very idea of a best practice and the kinds of assumptions at work underneath everyday school lingo such as "closing the achievement gap" and "leaving no child behind." Beyond problematizing assumptions, students also need to articulate a vision for education that meets the needs of learners and the communities in which they live.

Learning about and planning for critical, place-based education provides our students with a conceptual framework that is responsive to the tensions between the needs of communities and the conventional discourses of schooling.

As we have experienced it, the regulatory power of teacher education has created a culture of compliance that severely constrains the possibilities for educators to envision, create, and enact an education that truly inspires them. Much of what we do together is governed by bureaucracy, not our best thinking. So much of our energy is wasted in compliance that we rarely get around to seriously exploring what we want our students to explore: the social, cultural, and ecological contexts of schooling, and the links between these contexts and an ethical vision for education. What kind of education do we need now? How do we maintain both our ethical and our institutional legitimacy?

The bureaucracy that governs schooling is difficult to resist because it is so pervasive, because it is always growing, and because those of us who work within institutions are often complicit in enacting the very structures and practices that work against our own hopes and vision. These are serious problems. Naming them is the first step toward developing a transgressive pedagogy. For us, the next step is to create communities of resistance within the institution, supportive spaces where colleagues can reflect on the challenges of this work and create pedagogical responses that reflect deep critique and impassioned vision. Working together to create and recreate a required course has given us, and hopefully our students, such a space.

References

Essex, N. (2006). *A teacher's pocket guide to school law*. New York: Pearson.

Foucault, M. (1980). *Power/knowledge: Selected interviews and other writings, 1972–1977*. New York: Pantheon Books.

Freire, P. (1970/2000). *Pedagogy of the oppressed*. New York: Continuum.

Gardner, H. (1999). *The disciplined mind: What all students should know*. New York: Simon & Schuster.

Gruenewald, D. (2003a). The best of both worlds: A critical pedagogy of place. *Educational Researcher, 32*(4), 3–12.

Gruenewald, D. (2003b). Foundations of place: A multidisciplinary framework for place-conscious education. *American Educational Research Journal, 40*(3), 619–654.

Gruenewald, D. (2004). A Foucauldian analysis of environmental education: Toward the socio-ecological challenge of the Earth Charter. *Curriculum Inquiry, 34*(1), 63–99.

Gruenewald, D., & Smith, G. (Eds.). (2007). *Place-based education in the global age: Local diiversity*. Mahwah, NJ: Lawrence Erlbaum.

Hawken, P. (2007). *Blessed unrest: How the largest movement in the world came into being, and why no one saw it coming*. New York: Penguin.

Illich, I. (1978). *Toward a history of needs*. New York: Pantheon.

Kozol, J. (1991). *Savage inequalities: Children in America's schools*. New York: Crown Publishing.

Latané, B., & Darley, J. M. (1970) *The unresponsive bystander: Why doesn't he help?* Englewood Cliffs, NJ: Prentice Hall

Thoreau, H. D. (1947). Walden. In C. Bode (Ed.), *The portable Thoreau*. New York: Penguin.

Chapter 12
Small Openings in Cyberspace: Preparing Preservice Teachers to Facilitate Critical Race Talk

Susan L. Groenke and Joellen Maples

12.1 Introduction

Since 2005, we have implemented the Web Pen Pals project, a university–middle school partnership pairing preservice English teachers with local middle school students in secure, online chat rooms to discuss young adult literature. The project is housed in the young adult literature course Susan teaches every spring semester at the University of Tennessee. While the course is mandatory for the English teachers enrolled in the postbaccalaureate secondary English licensure program that Susan coordinates, elementary teachers and teachers seeking middle grades licensure in language arts (grades 4–6) also take the course.

Six times during the spring semester, middle school students travel to a computer lab during their regularly scheduled reading class time. At the same time, the preservice teachers meet in a computer lab on the university campus or use personal computers at home. Once all participants have logged onto the project Web site (www.webpenpals.org)[1] discussion begins about a young adult novel both the college-level and middle school students are reading.

The Web Pen Pals project has three main objectives: 1) to provide an opportunity for preservice teachers to expand their understandings about the role of talk in learning; 2) to provide an opportunity for preservice teachers to consider using chat technology as a classroom discussion tool, and 3) to provide a safe space where preservice teachers can practice taking a critical stance toward

S.L. Groenke
University of Tennessee

J. Maples
St. John Fisher College

---

[1] This site was made possible through the support of National Science Foundation grant REC 0106552 and the Teacher Bridge project directed by Dan Dunlap in the Center for Human-Computer Interaction at Virginia Tech.

S.L. Groenke and J.A. Hatch (eds.), *Critical Pedagogy and Teacher Education in the Neoliberal Era: Small Openings*,
DOI 10.1007/978-1-4020-9588-7_12, © Springer Science+Business Media B.V. 2009

literature in online discussions with adolescents. We address the first two objectives in other work (see Groenke 2007; Groenke, Maples, & Dunlap, 2005; Groenke & Paulus, 2007); for the purposes of this chapter, we address the third objective in more detail here.

12.2   A Safe Space to Be Critical

The provision of a safe space for beginning English teachers to practice taking on a critical stance toward reading instruction becomes especially important in the current educational climate that constrains teachers' instructional choices and practices. Skrla (2001) describes this climate as a "worldwide, postmodern shift toward discourses, models, technologies, and manifestations of accountability" (p. 15). The No Child Left Behind Act (NCLB), signed into law by President Bush in 2001, is a manifestation of this movement, and has been criticized by literacy scholars and teachers for its legislated mandate of a narrow, singular definition of reading instruction that positions students as passive readers, and teachers as passive translators of "teacher proof" test-prep curriculum guides (Altwerger et al. 2001).

When the preservice English teachers take the young adult literature course, they have not yet begun their fieldwork in classrooms. As their field placement coordinator—in a state where scripted reading programs are mandated, and teachers lose jobs when students' test scores are low—Susan knows few opportunities exist for beginning English teachers to see others model a critical stance toward literature instruction—a stance that highlights diversity and difference, calls attention to the nature and role of literacy in our society, and focuses on building students' awareness of how systems of meaning and power affect people and the lives they lead (Harste et al., 2000).

If we want beginning teachers to feel confident in adopting critical teaching methods, we must provide them opportunities to see what critical literacy can look like in classrooms (Lewison et al., 2002). Altwerger et al. (2004) suggest teacher educators create "safe spaces" for beginning teachers to see alternatives and "participate in critical reflection and intellectual engagement" (p. 128). These "safe spaces" can act like the "small openings" Scott (1987) describes—openings, in our case, for resistance to NCLB's version of reading instruction. We feel like the Web Pen Pals project is one such safe "small opening," where beginning teachers can see and practice reading instruction that is responsive to difference and diversity, and respects adolescents as critical thinkers and readers.

In what follows, we describe what we do in the young adult literature course to prepare beginning teachers to talk critically with adolescents about literature; share several excerpts from a synchronous chat between a preservice teacher and her Web Pen Pals about the book *Monster*; and end with insights we have gained from the research we have conducted on the project over the past 3 years.

12.3   Young Adult Literature Course Context

In the young adult literature course, we begin our introduction to critical literacy by explaining that teaching is not an apolitical, neutral activity. As Kincheloe (2008) explains, "every form of educational practice [is a] politically contested space" (p. 2). Reading instruction is such a space, where teachers' (and more recently textbook publishers' profit-motivated) understandings of, and beliefs about, textual knowledge and meaning-making shape the choices and uses of texts in classrooms. To help make this point in class, we draw from Serafini's (2003) article on reading ideologies to compare and contrast a modernist-influenced NCLB ideology and a critical literacy stance toward reading instruction.

12.3.1   Reading Instruction NCLB-Style

Underlying NCLB's emphasis on "scientifically based" reading programs is a modernist ideology toward reading instruction. Serafini (2003) explains that a modernist perspective of reading instruction assumes a unique, single meaning resides solely in the text (which the teacher knows and the reader must "find"). This perspective positions reading comprehension and interpretation as a cognitive, skills-based process and students as passive responders, rather than active co-constructors of meaning. If students can master the cognitive skills necessary to comprehend the text, they will be successful readers.

In support of this modernist position on reading instruction, the now infamous National Reading Panel's Reading First program[2] encouraged teachers to ask fact-based comprehension questions at the end of reading selections. Specifically, teachers were encouraged to "ask questions of the why, what, how, when, or where variety" so that readers will "process the text more actively" (National Reading Panel Report, 2000, p. 40). The report rationalized that "readers are not likely to question themselves ... [or] use questions spontaneously to make inferences" (p. 87).

12.3.2   A Critical Alternative to NCLB Reading Instruction

In contrast, critical literacy theorists (e.g., Comber & Simpson, 2001) believe reading processes are not neutral. As Soter (1999) explains, "readers ... bring individual values, attitudes, and histories to their reading, but they do so framed by the cultures

---

[2] In 2006, the Reading First program was the subject of a congressional investigation into whether top advisers improperly benefited from contracts for textbooks and testing materials they designed, and whether the advisers kept some textbook publishers from qualifying for funding. In 2007, Congress—citing mismanagement concerns—cut Reading First's funding substantially. A 2008 impact study found that students in schools using Reading First scored no better on comprehension tests than their peers who attended schools that did not receive program money (see Toppo, 2008).

they are part of" (p. 87). Likewise, texts "are not simply 'delivery systems' of 'facts': They are at once the results of political, economic, and cultural activities, battles, and compromises" (Apple, 1993, p. 195). Taking a critical stance toward literature, active readers adopt a questioning stance that interrogates the choices authors make in the creation of texts, and challenges authors' positionings of characters and story lines, and readers themselves.

12.3.3 Critical Questions

Teachers can help students develop a questioning stance toward literature by posing their own critical questions in discussions of texts—questions which differ from the fact-based comprehension questions the National Reading Panel encourages. While we believe any text can be questioned from a critical stance, some texts lend themselves to this process better than others. We believe young adult literature may help teachers raise questions that help students "notice ... 'systems of domination' and 'systems of privilege','' and can "encourage readers to care" (Edelsky, 1999, p. 12). Rogers (2002) suggests teachers use texts with "built-in critiques" of oppressive social structures and institutions (p. 786) to raise critical consciousness.

One young adult novel that we believe offers such a "built-in critique" is Myers' (2001) novel, *Monster*. In *Monster*, the 16-year-old main character, Steve Harmon—who happens to be a film student at a prestigious high school—is accused of serving as a lookout for a robbery of a Harlem drugstore. The owner was shot and killed, and now Steve is in prison awaiting trial for murder. While awaiting trial, Steve struggles to prove to himself that he is not the "monster" the prosecutor, the jury, and society believes him to be.

To help the beginning teachers in the young adult literature course understand what critical questions as applied to *Monster* might look like, we introduce Lewison et al.'s (2002) "Four Dimensions of Critical Literacy" in the young adult literature class (see Table 12.1).

The "Four Dimensions" represent a synthesis of critical literacy definitions as they have appeared in the literature over the last 30 years. The dimensional perspective emphasizes critical literacy as a developmental process, moving from the first dimension's focus on problematizing the "everyday" to taking action for social justice in the fourth, and last, dimension. The process is also recursive: Lewison et al. (2002) explain the last dimension—taking action—is "*the* goal of critical literacy," but it cannot be attained without "expanded understandings and perspectives gained from the other three dimensions" (p. 384, italics in original).

Also, because many of the thematic considerations in *Monster* revolve around Steve's identity as a young Black male, and because we believe beginning teachers need strategies that help them bring race into classroom conversations, we introduce several key aspects of critical race theory (Ladson-Billings & Tate, 2006) as they relate to the four dimensions of critical literacy: (1) race is a discursive practice that constructs social relationships and personal identity; (2) racial identities are not stable or unchanging; (3) race continues to be a significant factor in determining

Table 12.1 Four dimensions of critical literacy. Adapted from Lewison et al., (2002)

Dimension	Characteristics
1. Disrupting the commonplace	• Problematizing all subjects of study (including adolescence, learning), and understanding existing knowledge as a historical product • Interrogating texts: "How is this text trying to position me?" • Including popular culture and media as a regular part of the curriculum Studying language to analyze how it shapes identity, constructs cultural discourses, and supports or disrupts the status quo
2. Interrogating multiple viewpoints	• Reflecting on multiple and contradictory perspectives • Asking: "Whose voices are heard and whose are missing?" • Paying attention to and seeking out the voices of those who have been silenced or marginalized. Making difference visible
3. Focusing on sociopolitical issues	• Going beyond the personal and attempting to understand the sociopolitical systems to which we belong • Challenging unquestioned legitimacy of unequal power relationships • Redefining literacy as a form of cultural citizenship and politics that increases opportunities for subordinate groups to participate in society and as an ongoing act of consciousness and resistance
4. Taking action and promoting social justice	• Engaging in praxis—reflection and action upon the world in order to transform it • Using language to exercise power to enhance everyday life and to question practices of privilege and injustices • Analyzing how language is used to maintain domination, how nondominant groups can gain access to dominant forms of language and culture, how diverse forms of language can be used as cultural resources, and how social action can change existing discourses

inequity in the United States; (4) racism is not a series of isolated acts, but is endemic in American life; and (5) marginalized persons must have opportunities to "voice" and "name" their own realities.

In what follows we map critical race theory onto the four dimensions of critical literacy framework as we present it in the young adult literature class.

12.3.3.1 Disrupting the Commonplace in *Monster*

Lewison et al. (2002) suggest that the first dimension of critical literacy involves seeing the "everyday" through "new lenses" and "problematizing common knowledge" (p. 383). One of the "everyday" subjects we tried to problematize in our class reading of *Monster* is the "common knowledge" non-neutral readers bring to the reading task itself—what values, assumptions, and cultural knowledge we rely on to make meaning with and from texts.

The central narrative question driving *Monster* is whether Steve is guilty or innocent. Deciding if Steve is guilty or innocent, however, requires dealing with strong prejudicial stereotypes that might affect jurors—and readers. Steve's lawyer tells him that "half of [the] jurors … believed you were guilty the moment they laid eyes on you. You're young, you're Black, and you're on trial. What else do they need to know?" (Myers, 2001, pp. 78–79). To trouble our own "common knowledge" we bring to reading *Monster*, we consider such questions in class as: Do we as readers— positioned as Steve's jury—"read" Steve the same way his jurors might? Do we prejudge Steve—assume he is a violent criminal—because he is Black? If so, what is at work in society and our own cultural frames to make us form such a prejudgment? Reading and discussing *Monster* require readers to consciously struggle with their own socially constructed and culturally framed assumptions and beliefs about persons of color, and ultimately, consider how race influences our "readings" of people.

Another aspect of the first critical literacy dimension is an emphasis on how language shapes identity and constructs cultural discourses. Language certainly shapes Steve's identity in *Monster*: the prosecuting attorney calls Steve and others "monsters" who are "willing to steal and to kill, people who disregard the rights of others" (p. 21). This haunts Steve throughout the novel: is he the monster people believe him to be? Steve writes in his journal, "I want to look like a good person. I want to feel like I'm a good person because I believe I am" (p. 62). But his lawyer reminds him, "the jury [doesn't] see a difference between [you] and all the bad guys taking the stand" (p. 116).

In *Monster*, Steve, a young Black male who is a successful high school student, cannot ignore the hardened criminals like Bobo and other men who live in his Harlem neighborhood and populate the juvenile detention center where Steve awaits trial. Does a life of crime seem attractive or unavoidable to Steve? Does he feel he has something to prove to Bobo and others in his neighborhood? Who *is* Steve, and what makes an identity as a violent criminal an (attractive) option for him? How has the media helped to create and/or appropriate the image of Black male = violent criminal (Quinn, 2000), and how does this affect how Steve is viewed by society? A larger question becomes: is racial identity a personal decision, or a social label, or both? (Rex, 2006).

Finally, in this first dimension—and in conjunction with the other aspects we have already described—Lewison et al. (2002) suggest incorporating popular culture and media in classroom curriculum to disrupt what can come to appear as "common" cultural discourses and beliefs. We want to encourage the beginning teachers in the young adult literature course to consider identity as comprised of multiple subject positions, including those influenced by one's gender (Gee, 1996). Thus, we watch the abridged, made-for-high-school version of the video *Tough Guise* (Jhally, 1999) in class—a video that examines the social construction of masculine identities in contemporary US pop culture, and makes the argument that increasing violence in American society is connected to an "ongoing crisis in masculinity." The "tough guise" is defined as a hypermasculinity that links the credibility of males to displays and postures of toughness, physical strength, and the threat or use of violence (Earp & Katz 1999).

We layer our viewing of *Tough Guise* with discussion about Steve's journal entries where he admits to wanting to be tough like King, Osvaldo, and Bobo (Myers, 2001, pp. 96, 130). We discuss the flashback scenes in the novel where Osvaldo, a gang member, chides Steve for going to a "faggot school downtown" (p. 80), and challenges/polices Steve when he says: "You ain't got the heart to be nothing but a lame" (p. 82). When King wants to know if Steve will participate in the convenience store robbery, he asks Steve: "You got the heart?" (p. 150).

We discuss in class how the "heart" King and Osvaldo refer to may be the "tough guise" described in the video, a performance that will prove Steve is a "real man" in the eyes of more hardened criminals because Steve is willing to break the law. But we do not stop there: we consider the question, where does the idea that a "real" Black man is a (violent) criminal come from?

One answer may be provided in the video, as it pays attention to how media representations of men of color (e.g., news accounts, roles in film, music videos, sports) have disproportionately shown Black men to be aggressive and violent. Other questions we consider are: What effect might these portrayals have on the gender identity formation of boys and men of color? How do these portrayals influence the way the White majority sees men of color? In what cases, or environments, do you feel a "hypermasculine" pose—one based on control, power, and the threat of violence—might be necessary? Are there such situations?

We also consider reasons why Steve and other Black men might take on the "tough guise," because—as Steve thinks at one point in the novel—violence is "normal" (Myers, 2001, p. 144), and/or "all you have going for you is the little surface stuff, how people look at you and what they say. And if that's all you have, then you have to protect that" (pp. 154–155). This last quotation, especially, has led to discussions about the need to add one more layer to the consideration of identity processes: the subject position of social class.

12.3.3.2 Interrogating Multiple Viewpoints in *Monster*

The second dimension's focus on the consideration of multiple and contradictory perspectives in texts can work in conjunction with the first dimension's attempt to disrupt common, everyday perceptions. Through the multi-genre format of *Monster*, Steve provides readers multiple and contradictory perspectives of himself and thus the "truth": in his journal entries, Steve tells us he is "surprised" to be in jail (p. 2) and says he will write a movie of his experience in jail—"not his life"—that will be "the incredible story of how one guy's life was turned around by a few events" (pp. 8–9). In his film, Steve depicts himself as a successful student at a prestigious high school in New York, and as a loving son and older brother. Yet, in other journal entries, Steve shows his fear, and questions his own innocence. He wonders if he has fooled himself and writes: "We lie to ourselves [in prison]. Maybe we are here because we lie to ourselves" (p. 203).

Thus, the reader gets different, contradictory versions of, and perspectives on, Steve in *Monster*, and this lends itself to discussion about the decisions Steve-as-author makes about how to portray himself and the other characters in his story, and how his authorial choices affect our impressions of him, other characters, and the situation. As example, Steve's lawyer tells him that it is her job to make Steve look "human" in the eyes of the jury and his job to help her do so (p. 16), and to "put some distance between yourself and whatever being a tough guy represents" (p. 216).

To look "human," to put some distance in his jurors' (and readers') minds between himself and other self-described criminals like Bobo and King, Steve juxtaposes depictions of himself as a successful film student and loving brother against descriptions of King as "the Thug" and Bobo as "the Rat" (p. 10). In the courtroom scenes, Steve describes himself as dressed in a suit and tie, but King is "sloppy-looking," and Bobo is a "big man, heavy, and ugly. His hair is uncombed, and his orange prison jumpsuit is wrinkled" (p. 172).

In addition, Steve depicts flashback scenes where he is harassed by Osvaldo and challenged by King to show some "heart." Thus, as an author in control of how we read his film script, Steve makes choices about presenting other characters so he looks more favorable. Texts, then, are constructions that position people in certain ways, and as Apple (1993) reminds us, are "results of political, economic, and cultural activities, battles, and compromises" (p. 195). Steve is certainly in a battle for his life, as he must persuade biased jurors (and readers) that Black does not equal guilty.

Another aspect of this second dimension begs the question: What if Steve had been White? Would he have to struggle to look "human" in front of the jury? And, at one point, Steve's mother wonders if she should have contacted a Black lawyer for Steve. Steve responds: "It [isn't] a matter of race" (Myers, 2001, p. 146). Why does Steve say this? Does race have anything to do with the crime that was committed? How do jurors—and readers—perceive Steve? Do readers agree? These questions lead us into the third dimension.

12.3.3.3 Focusing on Sociopolitical Issues in *Monster*

Lewison et al. (2002) explain that the third dimension of critical literacy requires readers to go beyond the personal to the sociopolitical, and interrogate how language is tied to power relationships in society that privilege some and marginalize others. Specifically, our focus for this dimension is on how language—through media representations of Black men as hypermasculine and violent—contributes to the over representation of Black males in juvenile criminal justice systems in the United States.

At one point in *Monster*, Steve explains most of the voices he hears in the detention center are "clearly Black or Hispanic" (Myers, 2001, p. 7) and he says: "[B]eing in here with these guys makes it hard to think about yourself as being different. We look about the same, and even though I'm younger than they are, it's hard not to notice that we are all pretty young" (p. 62).

In class, we also discuss statistics from an online report entitled *Juvenile Justice, Juvenile Crime* (2001) that states: (1) the proportion of Blacks under the supervision of the juvenile criminal justice systems is more than double their proportion in the general population; (2) Black offenders are referred to juvenile courts and receive institutional placement at higher rates than White offenders who commit the same severe crimes; (3) Black juvenile offenders are referred to adult courts at higher rates than White juveniles; (4) officers and judges attribute causes of crimes committed by Black juvenile offenders to *negative attitudinal traits and personality defects*, whereas causes of crimes by White juvenile offenders are attributed to *external environmental factors* (e.g., family dysfunction, drug abuse, negative peer influence); and (5) these differences in attribution contribute significantly to differential assessments of the risk of reoffending and to sentence recommendations (pp. 228–260).

We pose the question: Why might some believe African-Americans are by nature, or biology—as number 4 above suggests—inherently violent or predisposed toward crime? If we refuse to believe this, what else can help explain the statistics?

In conjunction with this last question, we also read other research literature that suggests community-level factors such as rates of joblessness, poverty, low mobility, isolation/segregation, and housing density are related to incidents of juvenile crime and violence. Sampson (1987) explains there is no other racial or ethnic group in the United States of comparable size whose members are nearly as likely to grow up in neighborhoods of concentrated urban poverty as are Blacks. Yet why do police officers and judges fail to attribute crime committed by Black juveniles to community-level factors?

The regulation of poor Blacks to urban areas, and the deliberate impoverishment of urban areas populated by poor Blacks—and thus the lives of the urban youth who live there—is not a "natural" occurrence, then, but one that can be tied to racist economic decisions made by those who hold legal and political power. But to detract from such conscious decisions, media conglomerates bombard us with images of Black males as hypermasculine, thus encouraging us to blame Black persons themselves for violent crime ("that's just how they are")—and to assume they are criminals because most (publicized) crime occurs in their neighborhoods. Some researchers say the distribution of poor Whites in rural areas and small towns may shield them from some forms of crime detection and social control found in large cities (Sampson, 1987). Television shows like *Cops* and constant media attention on Black criminality (e.g., O.J. Simpson trial, Mike Tyson and Kobe Bryant rape cases) reinforce and glamorize negative images of Black males (Reed, 2008). It is a vicious cycle, mediated by media's language of text and image. No wonder Steve has an identity crisis.

12.3.3.4 Taking Action and Promoting Social Justice

The fourth and final dimension in the critical literacy framework is that of taking action and promoting social justice. One aspect of this dimension emphasizes gaining access to dominant forms of language and culture, and using language to exercise power to enhance everyday life and to question practices of privilege and injustices. This dimension affords an appreciation of Steve as author, as one who "talks back" to the dominant discourses circulating about him (e.g., "he's Black, he must be guilty") and constructs his own narrative through a dominant form of language and culture—film.

Steve's self-construction is important to critical race theorists who believe "stories provide members of outgroups a vehicle for psychic self-preservation" (Delgado, 1989, p. 2073). Delgado explains: "One factor contributing to the demoralization of marginalized groups is self-condemnation" (p. 2073). Crenshaw (1988) explains that members of minority groups internalize the stereotypic images that certain elements of society have constructed around minorities. We see this in *Monster* as Steve struggles with being prejudged by jurors—and readers—because he is Black; he is not given the benefit of "innocent until proven guilty." At one point in the novel, Steve contemplates suicide: "I can understand why they take your shoelaces and belt from you when you're in jail" (Myers, 2001, pp. 203–204).

But ultimately, Steve decides to write about his experience. He says: "I think to get used to this I will have to give up what I think is real and take up something else. ... Maybe I could make my own movie. ... The film will be the story of my life. No, not my life, but of this experience" (pp. 4–5).

In the young adult literature course, we talk about how writing one's own story and "talking back" to dominant discourses can be a form of taking action. We talk about prominent Black film-makers like John Singleton and Spike Lee, who attempt to provide "counter-narratives" to dominant discourses through their own award-winning films. We talk about alternatives to the current US justice system, such as restorative justice programs that emphasize rehabilitation. We also talk about the kinds of place-based economic decisions (e.g., zoning laws, tax decisions, funding equity for schools, development versus neighborhood sustainability) we must advocate for if all persons are to live in safe, enriching communities.

Finally, we talk about how discussing these kinds of issues with adolescents is its own form of taking action and promoting social justice, especially in a schooling context that prefers to remain "color-blind" or "race-neutral." As Ladson-Billings and Tate (2006) suggest, teachers working for social justice make conscious decisions to problematize race in their classrooms.

12.4 What We Have Learned from Our Research on the Web Pen Pals Project

As described above, the preservice teachers in the young adult literature course get some practice talking about *Monster* through a critical lens before heading into cyberspace to talk about the book with their middle school pals. But knowing the kinds of questions to ask does not guarantee that preservice English teachers will take the opportunity to engage in critical talk with their pals.

The Web Pen Pals project provides an opportunity for beginning English teachers to practice asking questions that promote critical understandings of literature. Thus, our research on the project over the last 3 years has focused on the kinds of questions and discourse moves beginning teachers use in their conversations with adolescents in the online chats when they are encouraged to talk about literature from a critical stance (Groenke, 2008; Groenke & Maples, 2008; Maples, 2008).

What we have found—despite the National Reading Panel's belief that "readers are not likely to use questions spontaneously to make inferences" (p. 87)—is that it is often the adolescents who ask critical questions, and that teachers' follow-up comments can work to sustain the critical topics raised by students or shut them down. As the following excerpt shows, (see Fig. 12.1) it is an adolescent—Kendra—who raises the topic of race in discussion about *Monster*, while preservice teacher Amanda's follow-up questions and comments sustain and extend the topic (all names are pseudonyms:

Line #	Speaker	Turn
101	Kendra	Do you think the color of Steve has anything to do with it ?
102	Dave	Not at all
103	Sarah	I do
105	Amanda	Everyone please explain why they think what they think about the color question
106	Amanda	I think it does have something to do with things
107	Kendra	If he was White would he have a different outcome?
108	Amanda	I think his color plays a part
111	Dave	All because someone is Black does not make them any different than me or any other person in the world!
118	Amanda	We read an article that said Whites were arrested just as much, and more sometimes than Black
119	Amanda	But Blacks are more likely to be convicted and have a harsher punishment. Why do you think that is?
123	Kendra	From movies we have a certain outlook
124	Dave	People do not stop to realize things about them
127	Sarah	I think it is because they have a bad reputation
131	Sarah	Its like they were talking about [a local high school]. It has a bad reputation even though the school is not bad. I think the Black people have a bad reputation but some of them are not bad

Fig. 12.1 Excerpt 1 from chat 1

That Amanda connects one of the readings we discussed in class to the ongoing conversation about whether or not Steve's race will impact the outcome of the trial (lines 118, 119) confirms for us that the work we do in the young adult literature course is necessary and important, especially in terms of helping teachers scaffold discussion. Simpson (1996) explains critical discussions of literature often result from students' own questions and curiosities rather than from teachers' questions, and thus critical talk may depend on a collaborative exchange in which the teacher's role is to *scaffold* student talk, "making connections between our experience, the experience of others, and social structures" (Shannon, 2002, p. 422).

Having the background information we discussed in the young adult literature course may have helped Amanda make a connection that extended the topic of race relations beyond the confines of the book and individual beliefs (e.g., Dave's belief that race does not or should not matter) to larger systemic racist processes effecting the outcome of Steve's trial.

We have also found, however, that beginning teachers seem to hold beliefs, goals, and expectations for discussion (e.g., antidemocratic goals of social control) that can work against collaboration and the goals of critical literacy. One preservice teacher who has participated in our research believed there was "a time and place" for certain student-initiated topics (usually at the end of discussion about topics she initiated). Another preservice teacher believed she should be the "expert" in the discussion, and did not like it when her pals posed sophisticated text-based questions to each other.

Based on our interpretations and analysis of Amanda's post-project interviews, it seems that Amanda believed she had to cover a certain number of predetermined topics in discussion and keep the discussion moving at a quick pace. Amanda explained in an interview that she remembered her own high school English teachers leading discussions in a similar way—"keeping us on topic ... and not going on forever about one thing" (Interview transcript, December 8, 2005). As the excerpt in Fig 12.2 shows, these beliefs might have led Amanda to interrupt potential critical talk with questions that posed new, unrelated topics.

Line #	Speaker	Turn
132	Dave	Blacks are more of my friends than most White people
133	Amanda	Awesome Dave that means you are more open-minded than some other people
135	Amanda	We need guys like you in the world to help stop the craziness
142	Kendra	People are afraid of things they cannot explain or understand
144	Amanda	Great job Kendra
155	Sarah	People judge people by what color they are; even if they do not try to they still do it
156	Sarah	Its hard not to
157	Amanda	And that is why we need to recognize this and effect the world what do you think?
158	Kendra	People go by what statistics say
160	Amanda	Can you explain to me why you chose the line from the book you did?

Fig. 12.2 Excerpt 2 from chat 1

In this excerpt, in the midst of potentially rich conversation, Amanda posed a question which initiated a new and unrelated topic: "Can you explain to me why you chose the lines from the book you did?" (line 160), referring to a previous conversation where Amanda had asked her pals to share lines they felt important to the text. Thus, Amanda missed an opportunity to develop and sustain critical talk about race and race relations with her adolescent pals.

As Lewison et al. (2002) suggest, opportunities for development of critical understandings are crucial if students are to consider ways to take action and work for social justice in their own lives. Understanding why these opportunities are missed, then, is necessary if we are to help beginning teachers facilitate critical development with their students. In what follows, we consider several possible explanations for these missed opportunities, and their implications for our future teaching.

First, Amanda and other project participants may be using their own former high school English teachers' discussion practices as models for their behavior in the chat rooms. McCann et al. (2006) explain that one of the most influential resources that prospective English teachers have for learning how to facilitate discussion is "the years of watching their own English teachers trying to lead discussions" (p. 2). Smagorinsky and Whiting (1995) suggest novice teachers will revert to images of themselves as students as guides for their own behaviors in the classroom.

Thus, one of the things we will need to do in the young adult literature course is provide opportunities for beginning teachers to consider and voice their expectations for teachers and students in discussion, and to consider how their beliefs are formed. In addition, if the process of becoming critical involves "becoming conscious of one's experience as historically constructed within specific power relations" (Anderson & Irvine, 1993, p. 82), we must consider how teachers come to be positioned as disciplinary (and disciplined) bodies in schools, expected to maintain order and control (Foucault, 1979).

Scripted reading programs and Initiate-Response-Evaluate (IRE) models of discussion help teachers maintain control, but at the price of student silence and disengagement. In the young adult literature course, we can talk with the preservice teachers about how traditional, teacher-controlled discourse may (or may not) be challenged in virtual environments and why challenges might be desired. We can then ask the preservice teachers to pay attention to times during the chats when they feel their beliefs being challenged and/or confirmed, and how they act on these feelings. Ultimately, as teacher educators, we need to encourage preservice teachers to trouble existing cultural knowledge about teachers' roles in discussion (Manke, 1997), and to request, listen to, and validate their students' contributions to discussion, understanding that students are capable of critical talk when talk is a collaborative process.

In addition, we understand, as McLaughlin and DeVoogd (2004) remind us, that teachers cannot just "become critical," that it is a "process that involves learning, understanding, and changing over time" (p. 55). We understand that the preservice teachers who come to our young adult literature course may not be familiar with a critical stance toward reading instruction, and we realize that even with practice at critical talk in the young adult literature course, the preservice teachers may not thoroughly understand critical literacy, may not be comfortable with such a stance, or may resist the stance in the chats.

We also understand that—as other researchers have suggested (cf. Greene & Abt-Perkins, 2003; LeCompte & McCray, 2002; Chapter 6, Flynn et al., this volume)—it is often difficult for White preservice teachers to talk about, or much less, facilitate discussion with adolescents about race. In her journal, Amanda wrote that she "stopped the talk [about racism] because she noticed one of her pals was "quieter." She furthered, "I am still unsure where the boundaries are," and explained that she felt her web pals might be "offended or hurt by our talk." Thus, we realize we may need to slow down the process of "becoming critical" in our young adult literature course, attending more patiently and collaboratively to beginning teachers' beliefs about race and racism, and their feelings about discussing such topics with adolescents before heading into cyberspace.

We do struggle as teacher educators and researchers with the feeling that we impose a critical literacy stance, rather than allow it to "generate" (Freire, 2000/1970) from the beginning teachers' own intellectual curiosities, questions, and dilemmas, or the adolescents' questions that often emerge in the chats without teacher prompting. We are continually looking for ways to balance our desire to provide alternatives to NCLB reading instruction with our respect for students' individual readiness and varying levels of commitment to social change.

Finally, it is important for us to remember that not all of our students are "tech savvy"(Kajder, 2003). We are guilty of assuming that our beginning teachers would have access to computers at home and be comfortable in virtual learning spaces. But several of the teachers involved in the Web Pen Pals project did not have access at home, and thus had less experience than others—including their adolescent pals—with chat technologies. Several preservice teachers struggled to keep up with the rapidly paced chats. Thus, we realize we need to be more conscious of technology access as an equity issue, and more cognizant of, and reflexive about, the ways we position our students, both as potential critical educators and as technology users. Ultimately, we need to keep in mind that "safe spaces" may not always feel "safe" to all students.

12.5 Conclusion

Altwerger et al. (2004) use the metaphor of a "collision" to describe the tensions literacy teacher educators experience when their desire to maintain critical, intellectual spaces in their classrooms meets the current NCLB classroom realities beginning teachers are certain to face (p. 121). A "collision" can be defined as a violent crash—as something that causes harm to some or all involved. We like to think of "collision" as a physicist might, as a "meeting of bodies in which each exerts a force upon the other, causing the exchange of energy or momentum" (Dictionary.com, 2008).

NCLB certainly exerts its force upon teacher educators and beginning teachers, with its legislated definition of reading process and instruction, but literacy teacher educators can create dissonance—can "exert force"—by providing beginning teachers with alternatives to NCLB's circumscribed notion of reading instruction.

In our young adult literature course, we strive to create a "safe space," a "small opening" where beginning teachers can see and practice an alternative kind of reading instruction that respects students as active, capable readers, and teachers as intellectuals. Ultimately, we envision our beginning teachers as professionals who go into their classrooms well aware of the curricular expectations they will face, but also aware that NCLB's definition of reading instruction is not the *sole* definition. Critical literacy offers an alternative for teachers who understand that beliefs about who our students are, and what they can become must also shape decisions about reading instruction.

References

Altwerger, B., Arya, P., Jin, L., Jordan, N.L., Laster, B., Martens, P., et al. (2004). When research and mandates collide: The challenges and dilemmas of teacher education in the era of NCLB. *English Education, 36*(2), 119–133.

Anderson, G.L., & Irvine, P. (1993). Informing critical literacy with ethnography. In C. Lankshear & P.L. McLaren (Eds.), *Critical literacy: Politics, praxis, and the postmodern* (pp. 81–104). Albany, New York: SUNY.

Apple, M.W. (1993). Between moral regulation and democracy: The cultural contradictions of the text. In C. Lankshear & P.L. McLaren (Eds.), *Critical literacy: Politics, praxis, and the postmodern* (pp. 193–216). Albany, New York: SUNY.

Collision (n.d.). Retrieved September 8, 2008, from Dictionary.com.

Comber, B., & Simpson, A. (2001). *Negotiating critical literacies in classrooms*. Mahwah, NJ: Lawrence Erlbaum.

Crenshaw, K.W. (1988) Race reform, retrenchment: Transformation and legitimation in anti-discrimination law. *Harvard Law Review,* 101, 1331–1387.

Delgado, R. (1989). Storytelling for oppositionists and others: A plea for narrative. *Michigan Law Review, 87,* 2411–2441.

Earp, J., & Katz, J. (1999). *Tough guise: Violence, media and the crisis in masculinity*. Media Education Foundation. http://www.mediaed.org/videos/MediaGenderAndDiversity/ToughGuise/studyguide/ToughGuise.pdf. Accessed 15 September 2008.

Edelsky, C. (1999). *Making justice our project: Teachers working toward critical whole language practice*. Urbana, IL: NCTE.

Foucault, M. (1979). *Discipline and punish: The birth of the prison*. New York: Vintage.

Freire, P. (2001/1970). *Pedagogy of the oppressed*. New York: Continuum.

Gee, J. (1996). *Social linguistics and literacies: Ideology in discourses*. London: Taylor & Francis.

Greene, S., & Abt-Perkins, D. (2003). Introduction: How can literacy research contribute to racial understanding? In Greene, S. & Abt-Perkins (Eds.), *Making race visible: Literacy research for cultural understanding* (pp. 1–31). New York: Teachers College Press.

Groenke, S.L. (2007). Collaborative dialogue in synchronous CMC? A look at one beginning English teacher's discourse strategies. *Journal of Computing in Teacher Education, 24*(2), 53–59.

Groenke, S.L. (2008). Missed opportunities in cyberspace: Preparing pre-service teachers to facilitate critical book discussions through computer-mediated communication. *Journal of Adolescent and Adult Literacy, 52*(3), 224–233.

Groenke, S.L., & Maples, J. (2008). Critical literacy in cyberspace? A case study analysis of one pre-service teacher's attempts at critical talk about *Monster* in online chats with adolescents. *The ALAN Review, 36*(1), 6–14.

Groenke, S.L., & Paulus, T. (2007–2008). The role of teacher questioning in promoting dialogic literary inquiry in computer-mediated communication. *Journal of Research on Technology in Education, 40*, 141–164.

Groenke, S.L., Maples, J., & Dunlap, D. (2005). Understanding and unlocking the potential of virtual talk in cyberspace. *English Leadership Quarterly, 28*(2), 3–9.

Harste, J. C., Breau, A., Leland, C., Lewison, M., Ociepka, A., & Vasquez, V. (2000). Supporting critical conversations. In K.M. Pierce (Ed.), *Adventuring with books* (pp. 506–554). Urbana, IL: National Council of Teachers of English.

Jhally, S. (Director/Producer) (1999). *Tough guise: Violence, media and the crisis in masculinity.* [DVD]. Northampton, MA: Media Education Foundation.

Juvenile justice, juvenile crime. (2001). Commission on Behavioral and Social Sciences and Education (2001). http://www.nap.edu/openbook.php?record_id=9747&page=228. Accessed 8 September 2008.

Kajder, S. (2003). *The tech-savvy English classroom.* Portland, ME: Stenhouse.

Kincheloe, J. (2008). *Critical pedagogy primer* (2nd ed.). New York: Peter Lang.

Ladson-Billings, G., & Tate, W.F. (2006). Toward a critical race theory of education. In Dixson, A.D., & Rousseau, C.K. (Eds.), *Critical race theory in education: All God's children got a song* (pp. 11–30). New York: Routledge.

LeCompte, K. and McCray, A. (2002). Complex conversations with teacher candidates: Perspectives of whiteness and culturally responsive teaching. *Curriculum and Teaching Dialogue, 4*(1), 25–35.

Lewison, M., Seely Flint, A., & Van Sluys, K. (2002). Taking on critical literacy: The journey of newcomers and novices. *Language Arts, 79*(5), 382–392.

Manke, M.P. (1997). *Classroom power relations: Understanding student-teacher interaction.* New York: Lawrence Erlbaum.

Maples, J. (2008). *Investigating critical talk between pre-service English teachers and middle school students in online literature discussions.* Unpublished doctoral dissertation, University of Tennessee, Knoxville, TN.

McCann, T.M., Johannessen, L.R., Kahn, E., & Flanagan, J.M. (2006). *Talking in class: Using discussion to enhance teaching and learning.* Urbana, IL: NCTE.

McLaughlin, M., & DeVoogd, G. (2004). Critical literacy as comprehension: Expanding reader response. *Journal of Adolescent and Adult Literacy, 48*(1), 52–62.

Myers, W.D. (2001). *Monster.* New York: Amistad.

National Reading Panel Report. (2000, April). Report of the National Reading Panel: Teaching Children to Read. Washington, DC: National Institute of Child Health and Human Development, National Institutes of Health, U.S. Department of Health and Human Services. www.nichd.nih.gov/publications/nrppubskey.cfm. Accessed 3 August 2007.

Quinn, E. (2000). "Who's the Mack?": The performativity and politics of the pimp figure in gangsta rap. *Journal of American Studies, 34*(1), 115–136.

Reed, I. (2008). *Mixing it up: Taking on the media bullies and other reflections.* New York: De Capo Press.

Rex, L. (2006). Acting "cool" and "appropriate": Toward a framework for considering literacy classroom interactions when race is a factor. *Journal of Literacy Research, 38*(3), 275–325.

Rogers, R. (2002). "That's what you're here for, you're suppose to tell us": Teaching and learning critical literacy. *Journal of Adolescent and Adult Literacy, 45*(8), 772–787.

Sampson, R.J. (1987). Urban black violence: The effect of male joblessness and family disruption. *American Journal of Sociology 93*(2), 348–382.

Scott, J. (1987). Weapons of the weak: *Everyday forms of peasant resistance.* New Haven, CT: Yale University Press.

Serafini, F. (2003). Informing our practice: Modernist, transactional, and critical perspectives on children's literature and reading instruction. Reading Online. http://www.readingonline.org/articles/art_index.asp?HREF=serafini/index.html. Accessed 20 October 2007.

Shannon, P. (2002). Critical literacy in everyday life. *Language Arts, 79*(5), 415–424.

Simpson, A. (1996). Critical questions: Whose questions? *The Reading Teacher, 50*(2), 118–127.

Skrla, L. (2001). Accountability, equity, and complexity. *Educational Researcher, 30* (4), 15–21.

Smagorinsky, P., & Whiting, M.E. (1995). *How English teachers get taught: Methods of teaching the methods class*. Urbana, IL:NCTE.

Soter, A. (1999) *Young adult literature and the new literary theories: Developing critical readers in middle school*. New York: Teachers College Press.

Toppo, G. (2008, May 5). Study: Bush's Reading First program ineffective. USA Today. http://www.usatoday.com/news/education/2008-05-01-reading-first_N.htm. Accessed 6 August 2008.

Chapter 13
Teaching for Democracy and Social Justice in Rural Settings: Challenges and Pedagogical Opportunities

Lydiah Nganga and John Kambutu

13.1 Introduction

The College of Education at the University of Wyoming has a unique mission that focuses on preparing "competent and democratic professionals." As faculty in the college, we are committed to advancing this mission by teaching our preservice teachers principles of democracy and social justice. In addition to teaching our students about the process of socialization (Harro, 2000), we explore the meaning of knowledge, that is, how and why knowledge is constructed. Knowledge is not neutral. Rather, it is a constructed instrument of "domestication," utilized effectively by the dominant culture to preserve its power and privilege. Freire (1997, p. 44) argued that such an education "in the service of domination cannot cause critical and dialectical thinking; rather it stimulates naïve thinking about the world." To teach for democracy and social justice, which we contend is a form of critical pedagogy, educators must utilize a pedagogy that seeks critical understandings of reality.

Critical pedagogy is based on educational theories and practices that help learners to achieve critical consciousness around democracy and social justice. In a critical pedagogy, the focus is rarely on instructional approaches and content (Freire, 1997), but on why, how, and what reality is constructed, legitimized, and celebrated by the dominant culture (McLaren, 1998). A critical pedagogy requires a different kind of thinking and teaching. Indeed, critical pedagogy does not depend on teaching in its usual form (Freire, 1997). It must contend with many complexities, such as classroom cultures, curricular structures, professional and community ideologies, and assumptions imbedded in historical contexts (Steinberg & Kincheloe, 1998).

Teaching for democracy and social justice in rural United States of America has its own unique problems. For example, due to isolation from metropolises with diverse racial and ethnic groups, many rural communities are intolerant toward democracy and social justice work. The conservative values and a strong belief in meritocracy (bootstrap phenomenon) that are common in many rural settings in the

L. Nganga and J. Kambutu
University of Wyoming/Casper Center

S.L. Groenke and J.A. Hatch (eds.), *Critical Pedagogy and Teacher Education in the Neoliberal Era: Small Openings*,
DOI 10.1007/978-1-4020-9588-7_13, © Springer Science+Business Media B.V. 2009

United States are reasons for stiff resistance to diversity and equity efforts. Notwithstanding the challenges involved, however, educators are required ethically to implement critical pedagogy because public schools are still charged with the responsibility of preparing productive and civic-minded citizens (Dewey, 1916.) In this chapter, we discuss the challenges and opportunities we have experienced while teaching for democracy and social justice in a teacher education program in rural United States.

13.2   Democracy and Social Justice Curricula

People are not born with the knowledge, skills, and dispositions necessary for full participation in a democratic society. Rather, attributes such as fairness, kindness, justice, and equity are acquired (Goodlad, 1984; Goodlad et al., 2004). These attributes, also espoused in social justice work, are the foundation of a social democracy (Goodlad, 2004). In a social democracy, citizens are engaged fully not just in voting (political democracy), but also in the process of protecting all citizens' rights and freedoms without regard to human differences. In others words, a social democracy ensures the elimination of all unjust practices in order for all citizens to enjoy the rights and privileges such as life, liberty, and the pursuit of happiness guaranteed by the US Constitution and the Bill of Rights. Thus, human differences such as gender, sexual orientation, class, age, religion, ability/disability, ethnicity, language, and race do not interfere negatively with human interactions. In the absence of social justice, however, democracies ultimately fail (Goodland, 2004). Public education, then, has the important mandate to teach for "Publicness," that is, teaching "what it means to be a public" with a "common national and civic identity" (Goodlad et al., 2004, p. 35). Traditionally, however, public schools in the United States have failed generally to teach for publicness, opting rather to promote distinct levels of injustice against different groups (Nieto, 2000).

Schooling in the United States is generally unjust. An examination of educational policies, practices, curriculum, and instructional strategies and materials reveals definite systemic injustices (Kozol, 2005). Different levels of injustices have contributed significantly to the academic achievement gap that exists between different groups. As a result, the Federal Government passed the No Child Left Behind Act (NCLB) of 2001 to "close the achievement gap between high-and low performing children, especially the achievement gaps between minority and nonminority students, and between disadvantaged children and their more advantaged peers" (U.S. Department of Education, 2008). Without finding viable solutions to unjust educational practices, however, the NCLB Act will not close the achievement gaps in education. One problem with dire implications is that of school segregation based on race and class.

School segregation in the United States is disheartening. Due to segregation, children of color attend segregated schools with inferior facilities and inexperienced teachers (Burant et al., 2002; Orfield & Lee, 2004). As a result, minority children are being left behind. Schools have a moral responsibility to practice educational policies that support equal educational opportunities for all people (Banks, 2002). An education for democracy and social justice is an ideal place to start because it benefits everyone, not just the marginalized groups (Davidman & Davidman, 1997; Dee, 2004).

Studies have shown that many educators have biases. Common among teachers, for example, is the tendency to make "idiosyncratic judgments" on students' potential for success, especially when they come from "different cultural, linguistic, and socioeconomic backgrounds" (Obiakor, 2001, p. 20). Instead of applying idiosyncratic judgments, a social justice curriculum that is balanced and empowering to all learners is needed. In a democracy and social justice curriculum, responsive teaching, in which instructional strategies that engage students in a culturally relevant manner, are the norm (Nieto, 2000). Culture influences learning in many dramatic ways and is, therefore, critical in the planning and teaching processes (Kambutu & Thompson, 2005; Smith, 1998). Meanwhile, current demographic changes in the United States (Rios, 2007) are likely also to alter dramatically the national cultural landscape, thus generating additional impetus for a democracy and social justice education.

13.3 Teaching for Democracy and Social Justice in a Rural Teacher Education Program

Teaching for democracy and social justice in a rural teacher education program, isolated from major cities, is a daunting task. Due to isolation from major metropolises that are racially and/or ethnically diverse, most rural communities lack the impetus to advance democracy and social justice work. In rural communities, the dominant group (usually White, Anglo-Saxon, and protestant) sets the agenda for human interactions. In Wyoming, for example, social justice work is generally unappreciated; people simply believe there is no diversity in Wyoming.

To summarize, there are several challenges to enacting democracy and social justice efforts in rural settings. First, because rural communities are isolated from major cities, individuals, and communities are less conscious of social justice issues. Second, rural communities tend to be conservative, and are, therefore, likely to resist change (Atkins, 2003). Third, a prevalent strong sense of community and loyalty to religious, cultural, racial, and occupational groups tends to favor the dominant culture. Fourth, children in rural communities attend the same schools their parents and grandparents did. Thus, educators are expected to teach to established community values (Morrison, 1997). Fifth, most rural communities are generally dominated by people of European heritage. There are expectations that other cultures will simply melt or assimilate into the dominant culture (Diazi-Rico & Weed, 1995). Teaching for social justice in the face of such factors is challenging indeed.

13.4   Preservice Teachers in the Wyoming Teacher Education Program

We teach in an outreach education program that is affiliated to the University of Wyoming. The Wyoming Teacher Education Program (WTEP) has sole responsibility for preparing educators for all the public schools in the state. A predominantly monoracial rural state (88% White, non-Hispanic), Wyoming has one of the lowest percentage of ethnic minorities in the United States (Wyoming, 2007). Thus, the preservice students enrolled in WTEP have little or no exposure to issues related to cultural complexity or social justice. Upon completing college, many students are employed in rural communities across Wyoming. Our experience is that they are therefore less motivated to develop skills that promote social justice and democracy. Collins (1999) had a similar observation and added that most educators in rural schools were raised close to where they now teach. Meanwhile, although Wyoming is a generally White state, people of color are gradually migrating to different parts of the state (Liu, 2007). According to the 2006 U.S Census Bureau, for example, a third of Wyoming's population growth between 2000 and 2006 was from minority groups. As a result, most public schools in the state experienced an influx of children whose first language was other than English, thus creating an additional impetus for WTEP to prepare teachers for democracy and social justice.

As educators of color in rural settings, we face unique obstacles. The exclusive nature of rural settings is especially problematic for educators of color (Sleeter, 1992). In Wyoming, educators of color teaching for social justice are likely to contend with strong conservative cultural values (Rios, 2007). Common also are "hidden or closet" forms of social injustice, not easy to label or recognize. These covert and insidious forms of injustice are "chameleon" in nature—disguised and ever-changing, depending on situations and circumstances. A negative "undercurrent," that takes form in always being watched and insidiously judged causes us to feel powerlessness and to doubt our ability to function effectively. Nonetheless, we do not have a choice because WTEP requires our preservice students to master the outcomes relating to "issues of access to education including diversity, gender, and inclusion." The implementation of pertinent activities to accomplish these outcomes, however, is determined by individual faculty and departments. For example, in the department of Elementary and Early Childhood education, where Lydiah's course is housed, an "infusion of multicultural education" model is emphasized. But in John's department, Educational Studies, there is no formal structure to ensure consistent implementation of democracy and social justice outcomes.

Due to the inconsistent manner in which democracy and social justice outcomes were being addressed, we (Lydiah and John) decided to collaborate because our courses run in succession (i.e., students complete John's foundations course before enrolling in Lydiah's methods course). We adopted an infusion model that allowed Lydiah to build on the foundation laid during the "Teacher as Practitioner" course. In addition to establishing continuity, we wanted to collect evidence that our preservice students were mastering various democracy and social justice outcomes. Additionally, we wanted to provide multiple opportunities for our students to rethink schooling in the context of critical pedagogy, that is, education that seeks critical understandings of reality. As a result, we used instructional strategies that help our preservice teachers to question and challenge unjust practices and beliefs. We prepare students to understand the ways in which formal education is utilized to perpetuate the values and norms of the dominant culture. In other words, we implement a form of critical pedagogy that shows our students that schooling in general is not neutral. Rather, previous decisions by people operating with different values, ideologies, and cultural assumptions about their historical contexts are still influential (Steinberg & Kincheloe, 1998). Nonetheless, professional educators do possess agency and must, therefore, be prepared to challenge existing paradigms, while exploring how societal organization and dominant ideologies provide justification for oppression.

Generally, the infusion model to teaching for democracy and social justice outcomes has been a success. For example, in their end-of-semester course evaluations for faculty, students have described our courses as "challenging and causing them to think out of the box." Nonetheless, a number of students are opposed to democracy and social justice. We understand that members of the dominant culture are likely to resist any pedagogy that challenges dominant values, and we suspect that these resistant preservice students are responsible for the negative course evaluations we receive. Notwithstanding the unfavorable evaluations, our job is an intellectual enterprise that helps our students to reflect on their subjective, multiple identities within the borders of human differences, and on their roles in the schooling process. This is a challenging task for us as teachers of color in rural settings. In response, we have developed a variety of coping strategies.

13.5 Managing Instructional Challenges

To cope with the many challenges we experience as teachers of color in a rural teacher education program, we have developed unique strategies such as having a "thick skin" or making the decision not to allow unpleasant feedback from students and other stakeholders to influence negatively our work for democracy and social justice. Social justice work requires an examination of societal practices that confer power and privilege to certain dominant groups, while creating social injustice for marginalized individuals and groups. Thus, the privileged are usually opposed to social justice efforts. For example, after studying racism as a social construct that confers power and privilege based on skin color (Cameron & Wycoff, 1998), a White student defended her privilege thusly: "Blacks are taught to blame all their problems on Whites. It is time everyone gets off the race issue and sees each other as just people." Unable to accept the notion that she enjoyed privileges as a White person, whether she knew it or not, that the dominated groups lacked, she blamed the oppressed for causing their predicament. Teaching for social justice is typically challenging because it requires students to change their cultural values and assumptions (Thompson, 1995). The level of resistance that is experienced in rural communities is, however, sometimes debilitating. To cope in the past, we reverted to individualism or a teach-alone approach.

Individualism comes from the "bootstrap" phenomenon that is popular in most rural communities. Due to a strong belief in meritocracy (Gollnick & Chinn, 2006), success in rural communities is viewed frequently in the context of hard work, usually by individuals doing their "thing." By adopting an individualistic approach in our own teaching, we were simply conforming to the prevailing attitude that hand work will bring success (Castañeda et al., 2006). As we worked individually, however, we exercised caution so as not to aggravate the dominant community in these rural settings where, like "flies in the milk," we live and work. However, individualism was not a practical coping strategy because it added to our social and professional isolation (Quiocho & Rios, 2000). Instead of individualism, teamwork and institutional support is what we needed (Nieto, 2000). As a result, we developed inclusive interdisciplinary collaborative teaching, moving from individual to collective teaching with notable success. We consider this approach to teaching a form of critical pedagogy.

13.6 Inclusive Interdisciplinary Collaboration

We use an interdisciplinary approach to teach for democracy and social justice. As noted earlier, the Teacher as Practitioner and the Humanities methods courses have a social justice strand. Notwithstanding the program's goals, preservice students were generally resistant to social justice curriculum as is evident in the following excerpt from a student in the Humanities methods course:

> I really do not know why we were learning stuff about diversity. Wyoming does not have diversity. The instructor was biased. We are forced to read an article on White teachers and racism and the professor seems to agree with it. This was a total waste of my time and I feel we should have learned other more important information, not about racism and diversity.

To minimize students' resistance, we considered various pedagogies that could increase learning. Derman-Sparks and the A.B.C. Task Force (1998) recommended instructional strategies that support active activism. To be active activists, however, students must be involved fully in their own learning (Wenger, 1998); and students are more likely to be actively involved in a student-centered learning environment (Arends, 2007). As a result, we developed inclusive interdisciplinary collaborative teaching, a form of critical pedagogy consisting of the following components: (a) student inclusion, (b) faculty cooperation within and across academic disciplines, and (c) collaboration between faculty and students.

13.6.1 Student Inclusion

We believed that students should be involved in making curricular decisions in the classroom. Students learn more if they have ownership in the learning process (Glickman, 1993). When students are empowered to take charge of their education, meaningful learning occurs. Taking charge of learning motivates students to develop a community of practice that gives them a sense of knowledge ownership (Wenger, 1998). Students are more likely to take charge in a student-centered rather than a teacher-centered learning environment. There are many student-centered strategies such as experiential and/or cooperative learning (Johnson & Johnson, 2006), problem-based learning (Gordon et al., 2001), discovery learning (Wilson, 2002; Strike, 1975), and discussions (Angelis, 2003) that help learners to personalize and make meaning of the knowledge gained (Dewey, 1938).

After several discussions, we realized that the preservice teachers in Lydiah's methods course had difficulty transferring democracy and social justice understandings they learned in John's foundations course. In our effort to improve transfer, we identified common readings with social justice themes. We also used research projects, videos, and reflective writing. We shared two videos to help explore the meaning of a social justice curriculum that is anti-biased: *Starting Small: Teaching Children Tolerance* (1997) and *Prejudice: Answering Children's Questions* (1994). The books we selected for common reading had an implicit social justice theme. These were *Holler If You Hear Me* by Gregory Michie (1999) and *Anti-bias Curriculum: Tools for Empowering Young Children* by Derman-Sparks and the A.B.C. Task Force (1998). We also used selected readings from *Teaching for Diversity and Social Justice* (Adams et al., 1997).

From our experiences, students are likely to resist when faculty identify or label issues. We, therefore, allow the students to select topics of interest for common readings, conduct research, and present findings to peers. Inquiry projects are intended to give students the opportunity to study further a social justice issue of their choosing. In addition to following conventional research methodologies such as framing study questions, reviewing available literature, and collecting and analyzing data, students personalize the knowledge gained by showing the ways in which the new knowledge would help them become better educators and citizens. Students study different topics, but the influence that gender, economic class, poverty, culture, race, ethnicity, ability/disability, assessment, special education, parental involvement, and learning resources have on learning is popular. Equally studied are issues around quality learning and culturally proficient teaching, differentiated instruction, antibias curriculum, extracurricular activities, multiage classrooms, holiday celebrations, and the No Child Left Behind Act.

We have found that learners are less resistant when they sense ownership, that is, a feeling that they, not faculty, had actually identified the issues. The readings students select are usually easy-to-read books (e.g., *Holler If You Hear Me* by Gregory Michie (1999) about teaching and teacher experiences. As students read, they identify in writing the qualities of good teaching exhibited by different educators. There are no right or wrong responses; but we are keen at recognizing students' responses with a social justice theme. During class discussions, we are careful to clarify misconceptions of issues. Again, from our experience, students are likely to resent teacher-centered lectures that elucidate the injustices committed by the group they belong to. Rather, a caring, non-blaming, and nonthreatening learning environment is desired. In all, in an inclusive student-centered instructional approach such as the one we have established, learners' interests are respected and they are given responsibility for directing their own learning.

13.6.2 Interdisciplinary Faculty Collaboration

Faculty collaboration within a program and across academic disciplines is beneficial. Collaboration transforms learning into a "communal human effort and creative imagination that is directed at many different objectives" (Bess, 2000, p. xiii). In other words, faculty collaboration is likely to cause the development of a community of learners that increases intellectual exchange across disciplines (Frost & Jean, 2003). Interdisciplinary collaboration is rooted in the premise that knowledge does not fit into neatly packed, mutually exclusive subjects (Palmer, 1983). Rather, when there is collaboration between two or more subjects and/or disciplines, significant learning occurs. Interdisciplinary collaboration, however, is rare in institutions of higher learning because it takes effort and hard work (Gardner & Southerland, 1997). Instead, many educators prefer to teach alone, rarely speaking to teachers within their home departments and/or programs (Boyer, 1990). Faculty collaboration is desirable, but there are challenges as well.

Successful faculty collaboration requires commitment. In the absence of the following levels of commitment, for example, collaboration will certainly fail: (a) curiosity, (b) passion, (c) time, and (d) respect (Gardner & Southerland, 1997). Lack of adequate time was a challenge for us, yet there was need for us to meet as often as necessary to measure progress, which for us meant weekly. Another issue that almost derailed our collaboration was the concept of academic freedom. Faculties in higher education resent practices that infringe on their freedom to utilize content and teaching strategies consistent with their areas of expertise. We were, therefore, very mindful of these academic "territories." Thus, we reminded ourselves of our rights and resolved to withdraw freely from collaborative activities at any time we felt our academic freedoms were in jeopardy. We have found that faculty collaboration has multiple benefits. For example, the professional support system that emerged, an essential tool in challenging resistance to social justice work, was an impetus for continued collaboration in our teacher education program.

At the end of each semester, students complete an end-of-semester written course evaluation. These evaluations have considerable weight during faculty tenure and promotion decisions. Teaching for social justice, however, is likely to engender resentment in some students, hence the likelihood for faculty to receive negative course evaluations. The following is an example of a negative evaluation that John received from his course:

> On a number of occasions we spent up to two hours off subject. I feel this off- task time was a waste of my time and it short-changed the content that needed to be discussed. Those off-task discussions on topics such as racism and multicultural issues may be valuable, but are not part of the course content. We were a captive audience.

Lydiah received similar negative course evaluations as is evident in the following excerpt:

> I felt that the materials we covered were a waste of time. It seemed like the professor most of the time was talking about slavery, modern-day slavery, and social justice and nothing else. Even though these topics are important, I felt we should have spent more time covering Wyoming history.

Through our collaboration, we have realized that negative course evaluations can be typical feedback for faculty teaching for social justice. The negative evaluations we received once our collaboration began helped us to reflect on our teaching approach. It was apparent that our approach before collaboration was not working. We wanted our students to "just get it" and move on. We wanted a "quick fix." However, through collaboration, we realized that teaching for democracy and social justice was going to be a process. We could have given up, but we did not. Instead, we opted to learn together how to teach for democracy and social justice. This is how the process of collaboration between stakeholders, a form of critical pedagogy, was conceived.

13.6.3   Collaboration with Learners

Collaboration with learners meant cooperation between students and faculty. This type of collaboration has the potential to transform teaching into a collective enterprise. In a collective enterprise, educators relinquish their traditional roles of truth-telling. Instead, they facilitate the devolvement of a learning community where learners are actively involved in their own learning. The learner is the most important element in a collaborative effort; hence the need to ensure a learner-centered environment is established. Reflecting on the value of active learning, a preservice student in John's course reported that the research project she completed was most meaningful because "I was able to study an issue that was important to me. Researching the topic I chose really helped me gain knowledge and respect for a culture that I knew very little about." Collaboration can help create ideal spaces for learning and knowledge retention. Because collaboration leads to the development of a nonthreatening learning environment, learners are able to personalize knowledge.

When learners feel emotionally safe, they are likely to develop a willingness to study issues that confer power and privilege to certain dominant groups while generating social injustices for individuals and marginalized groups. For example, a student in the Teacher as Practitioner course initially viewed education for illegal immigrants as an unnecessary burden to taxpayers. Adopting a "supremacist" form of resistance (Sandoval, 2000), the student believed strongly that education for illegal immigrants should not be funded by taxpayers. As she studied the issue, she learned about the complexities involved. Data showed that the school dropout rate for illegal immigrant children was 43% higher than that of other groups due to interruptions, limited English language proficiency, poverty, and health issues (Clare et al., 2005; Duarte & Rafanello, 2001). The new information about the status of illegal immigrants transformed the student from a resistant supremacist to an advocate for human rights, as is evident in the excerpt below:

> Generally, people have little knowledge about illegal immigrants. Illegal immigrants play an important role in our society by filling low paying, yet necessary jobs like harvesting the food we eat. Educators must be informed about the issues illegal immigrants face. I feel that there needs to be more multicultural education in our community. The most important thing for educators is to know their students regardless of where they come from. Teachers need to know their students' strengths and weakness and be informed so they can educate all students to the best of their ability.

We believe this apparent transformation is unlikely in a non-collaborative, teacher-centered learning environment where the teacher is the truth-teller. Most important is the ability of collaboration to motivate students to not only become aware of their beliefs, experiences, and biases, but to also become agents of social change, as is evident in the following student comments:

> I was scared at first to write about why Blacks are angry and Whites are frustrated, but then I said "be honest." To start to understand racism we have to first know our prejudices, work through those and decide the changes we need to make. I feel that this issue will never be resolved unless we put away all past hurts and discrimination and talk freely about why Blacks are angry and Whites are frustrated.

Collaboration is likely to increase knowledge retention and transfer. For example, after experiencing active learning in John's course, preservice students in Lydiah's methods course were prepared and willing to study sensitive topics such as democracy, globalization, justice, equality, and equity. The opportunity to personalize knowledge through written reflections and research projects helped preservice teachers to retain and transfer the knowledge and skills learned earlier. Knowledge transfer made social justice curriculum enjoyable to Lydiah's students, as is shown in the following excerpt:

> I really loved the activities in my Humanities class. I enjoyed the deep research about a country that I was interested in. Interviewing someone from another culture and learning from them was a great experience. The food gave a visual presence of the country and of course a taste of the country. The whole project including peer presentations helped me to see cultural similarities and differences between countries. My study on Egypt helped me to become aware of the richness of Egyptian cultures. This unit reduced my ignorance. I will definitely do this unit with my students.

Collaboration requires a heightened level of respect for students' prior knowledge and interests. To that end, students in John's course responded in writing to the question, "What do you already know?" about a particular issue before studying it. Later, students responded in writing to the following additional questions: (a) What did you learn? (b) What questions do you still have? (c) How has the knowledge gained helped you become a better educator and/or person? Student responses were explored in detail during class discussions, but reflective writing enabled them to personalize knowledge and to change their views as needed. For example, a strong believer in creation theory was agreeable to evolution theory after learning more about it. Although this student still believed in humans' common ancestry (i.e., from Adam and Eve), she broadened her views thusly, "We are not common, similar or the same. We are different in ways that should be acknowledged, shared experienced, and appreciated." Apparently, because of validating the students' belief in creation theory, she was willing to engage in social justice work. Meanwhile, a student in the Humanities course who believed strongly in evolution theory was willing to listen to other points of view and added:

> I feel teaching for social justice should start early. If children are aware how similar we are, and what makes us different, then they may become more accepting to people who are different from them. Children have a hard time understanding that we are very alike because when they see that someone doesn't look like them, then they automatically think they are different, and then stereotypes, racism, etc. come into play. I feel it is important to teach our children about how similar the human race really is.

Different teaching strategies are necessary in a collaborative setup. For example, the use of electronic media with a social justice agenda increased knowledge retention. After watching two videos with a social justice theme, a student in Lydiah's course was shocked to see that "[e]veryone in this world is 99% alike. I did not know that. I was very surprised that we are all that close to being alike. I think we learn racism and teachers must teach children to respect and accept differences." A critical piece of information from the watched videos was the fact that children are not necessarily taught discriminatory attitudes at home. Instead, children learn biases from the general society through lived experiences (Aboud & Doyle, 1996). The reflection below captures one student's understanding of this important concept:

> I have realized that children form biases from society (peers and media). As educators, we need to be aware of how our children are coming up with certain biases towards certain people. We also need to know that many children are not learning their biases from home, so we can't be so quick to judge their home life. We need to take a deeper look into what types of leisure activities and community attitudes may be creating their biases. Another important point to me was that children form biases from their experiences.

When there is trust, students are able to express their struggles freely. For example, preservice teachers expressed a lack of confidence in their ability to teach a social justice curriculum. Generally, students were afraid to teach because social justice is "such a difficult area." Other preservice teachers wondered how practical it was to teach for social justice and at the same time meet the requirements of the No Child Left Behind Act. These are legitimate concerns, but rather than ignoring social justice work, they should be concerned with identifying teaching strategies that help students to acquire the necessary knowledge, skills, and dispositions to be full participants in a democratic society. Inclusive interdisciplinary collaboration can be part of the solution.

13.7 The Advantages of Inclusive Interdisciplinary Collaboration

Inclusive interdisciplinary collaboration has multiple benefits. For example, although we, as faculty of color teaching for democracy and social justice in a rural teacher education program, experienced many challenges, inclusive interdisciplinary collaboration reduced students' resistance at the same time it increased learning and knowledge transfer from a foundations of education to a methods course. Successful teaching for social justices is critical especially because of the goals of schooling in the United States, the demands of the NCLB, and demographic changes in the United States. As a result, educators should utilize pedagogies that maximize learning. Because inclusive interdisciplinary collaboration focuses on changing teaching from a teacher- to student-centered enterprise, learners were actively involved in setting their educational goals. It is also important to note that in any curriculum, it is up to educators to implement critical pedagogical elements that not only support education for democracy and social justice, but also meet institutional guidelines.

We believe collaboration between faculties increased our students' transfer of social justice knowledge, skills, and dispositions. Equally helpful was our cross-discipline collaboration because it increased our knowledge repertoire. We have new insight about working collaboratively across disciplines. Although we encountered resistance to our social justice work and sometimes were demoralized by students' negative evaluations, we also experienced success after changing our teaching approaches. In teaching for democracy and social justice, we directed our own learning and that of our students on issues directly related to critical pedagogy. We continue to address issues of social justice and more so to appreciate the rights of our students as active participants of their education. We have learned to not be the sole owners of knowledge in the classroom, but to be aware consciously of the need to create ways to bring democracy and social justice into the curriculum. One of the greatest lessons for us as faculty was that teaching for social justice is best undertaken as a collaborative effort. Although it is a time-intensive process, we are confident we improved our teaching and our students' abilities to learn, retain, and transfer democracy and social justice knowledge, skills, and dispositions from their coursework to action in real classrooms in rural settings.

References

Aboud, F., & Doyle, A. B. (1996). Parental and peer influence on children's racial attitudes. *International Journal of Intercultural Relations, 20*, 371–383.

Adams, M., Bell, L. A., & Griffin, P. (1997). *Teaching for diversity and social justice*. New York, Routledge.

Angelis, J. I. (2003). Conversation with the middle school classroom: Developing reading, writing, and other language abilities. *Middle School Journal, 34*(3), 57–61.

Arends, R. I. (2007). *Learning to teach* (7th ed.). New York: McGraw-Hill.

Atkins, C. (2003, July). The influence of rural culture on post-sixteen pathways from school. *Journal for Continuing Liberal Adult Education*. http://www.cont-ed.cam.ac.uk/BOCE/AdLib24/article2.html. Accessed 17 July 2007.

Banks, J. A. (2002). *An Introduction to multicultural education* (3rd ed.) Boston, MA: Allyn & Bacon.

Bess, J. L. (2000). *Teaching alone, teaching together: Transforming the structure of team for teaching*. San Francisco, CA: Jossey-Bass.

Boyer, E. L. (1990). *Scholarship reconsidered: Priorities of the professoriate*. San Francisco, CA: Jossey-Bass.

Burant, T., Quiocho, A., & Rios, F. (2002). Changing the face of teaching: Barriers and possibilities. *Multicultural Perspectives, 4*(2), 8–14.

Cameron, S. C., & Wycoff, S. M. (1998). The destructive nature of the term race: Growing beyond a false paradigm. *Journal of Counseling and Development, 76,* 277–285.

Castañeda, R. C., Kambutu, J., & Rios, F. (2006). Speaking their truths: Teachers of color in diasporic contexts. *The Rural Educator, 27*(3), 13–23.

Clare, M., Jimenez, A., & McClendon, J. (2005). Toma el Tiempo: The wisdom of migrant families in consultation. *Journal of Educational and Psychological Consultation, 16*(1 & 2), 95–111.

Collins, T. (1999). Attracting and retaining teachers in rural areas. Eric Clearinghouse on Rural Education and Small Schools. http://www.ericdigests.org/2000-4/rural.htm. Accessed 20 October 2008.

Davidman, L., & Davidman, P. (1997). *Teaching with a multicultural perspective: A practical guide* (2nd ed.). New York: Longman.

Dee, T. (2004). Teachers, race, and student achievement in a randomized experiment. *Review of Economics and Statistics, 86*(1), 195–210.

Derman-Parks & the A.B.C. Task Force. (1998). *Anti-bias curriculum: Tools for empowering young children.* Washington, DC: National Association for the Education of Young Children.

Dewey, J. (1916). *Democracy and education.* New York: Macmillan.

Dewey, J.(1938). *Experience and education.* New York: Macmillan.

Diaz-Rico, L., & Weed, K. Z. (1995). *The cross-cultural, language, and academic development handbook.* Needham Heights, MA: Allyn & Bacon.

Duarte, G., & Rafanello, D. (2001). The migrant child: A special place in the field. *Young Children, 56*(2), 88–93.

Freire, P. (1997). *Pedagogy of the heart.* New York: Continuum.

Frost, S. H., & Jean, P. M. (2003). Bridging the disciplines: Interdisciplinary discourse and faculty scholarship. *Journal of Higher Education, 74*(2), 119–149.

Gardner, S. A., & Southerland, S. A. (1997). Interdisciplinary teaching? It only takes talent, time, and treasure. *The English Journal, 86*(7), 30–36.

Glickman, C. (1993). *Renewing America's schools.* San Francisco, CA: Jossey-Bass.

Goodlad, J. I. (1984). *A place called school: Prospects for the future.* New York: McGraw-Hill.

Goodlad, S. J. (2004). Democracy, schools, and the agenda. *Kappa Delta Pi Record, 41*(1), 17–20.

Goodlad, J. I., Mantle-Bromley, C., & Goodlad, S. (2004). *Education for everyone: Agenda for education in a democracy.* San Franci sco, CA: Jossey-Bass.

Gollnick, D. M., & Chinn, P. C. (2006) *Multicultural education in a pluralistic society.* Englewood Cliffs, NJ: Pearson Merrill Prentice Hall.

Gordon, P., Rogers, A., & Comfort, M. (2001). A taste of problem-based learning increases achievement of urban minority middle-school students. *Educational Horizons, 79*(4), 171–175.

Harro, B. (2000). The cycle of socialization. In M. Adams, J. W. Blumenfeld, R. Castañeda, W.H., Hackman, L. M. Peters, X. Zuniga (Eds.), *Readings for diversity and social justice (pp. 15–21).* New York: Routledge.

Johnson, D. W., & Johnson, F. P. (2006). *Joining together: Group theory and group skills* (9th ed.). Englewood Cliffs, NJ: Prentice-Hall.

Kambutu, J., & Thompson, S. (2005). Exploring processes that help adult learners become culturally responsive. *Journal of Adult Education, 34*(2), 6–19.

Kozol, J. (2005). *Shame of the nation: The restoration of apartheid schooling in America.* New York: Random House.

Liu, W. (2007). *The changing faces of Wyoming Population.* Cheyenne, WY: State Department of Administration.

McLaren, P. (1998). *Life in schools: An introduction to critical pedagogy in the foundations of education* (3rd ed). New York: Longman.

Michie, G. (1999). *Holler if you hear me: The education of a teacher and his students.* New York: Teachers College Press.

Morrison, G. S. (1997). *Teaching in America*. Boston, MA: Allyn & Bacon.

Nieto, S. (2000). Placing equity front and center. Some thoughts on transforming teacher education for a new century. *Journal of Teacher Education, 51,* 180–1287.

Nieto, S. (2000). *Affirming diversity: The sociopolitical context of multicultural education* (3rd ed.). New York: Longman.

Obiakor, F. E. (2001). *It even happens in "good" schools: Responding to cultural diversity in today's classrooms*. Thousand Oaks, CA: Corwin Press.

Orfield, G., & Lee, C. (2004). *Brown at 50: King's dream or Plessy's nightmare?* Cambridge, MA: The Civil Rights Project.

Palmer, J. C. (1983). Interdisciplinary studies: *An Eric review*. *Community College Review, 11,* 59–64.

Prejudice: Answering children's questions. [VHS]. United States: ABC News.

Quiocho, A., & Rios, F. (2000). The power of their presence: Minority group teachers and schooling. *Review of Educational Research, 70,* 485–528.

Rios, F. (2007). La Casa de esperanza: The house that multicultural education built. *International Journal of Multicultural Education, 9*(2), 1–15.

Smith, G. P. (1998). *Common sense about uncommon knowledge: The knowledge bases for diversity*. New York: AACTE Publications.

Sandoval, C. (2000). *Methodology of the oppressed*. Minneapolis, MN: University of Minnesota Press.

Sleeter C. (1992). Keepers of the American dream. Bristol, PA: Falmer Press.

Steinberg, S. R., & Kincheloe J. L. (Eds.) (1998). *Students as researchers: Creating classrooms that matter*. Bristol, PA: Falmer Press.

Strike, K. A. (1975). The logic of learning by discovery. *Review of Educational Research, 45,* 461–483.

Starting small: Teaching tolerance in preschool and the early grades. [VHS]. Montgomery, AL: Teaching Tolerance.

Thompson, L. (1995). Teaching about ethnic minority families using pedagogy of care. *Family Relations, 5*(44), 2, 129–135.

US Department of Education (2008). No Child Left Behind Act of 2001. (NCLB Public Law 107–110). http://www.ed.gov/nclb/landing.jhtml. Accessed 30 July 2008.

Wenger, E. (1998) Communities of Practice. Learning as a social system systems thinker. http://www.co-i-l.com/coil/knowledge-garden/cop/lss.shtml. Accessed 30 May 2007.

Wilson, H. C. (2002). Discovery education: A definition. *Horizons, 19,* 25–29.

Wyoming (2007). Just the facts. http://eadiv.state.wy.us/Wy_facts/facts07.pdf. Accessed 18 June 2008.

Chapter 14
Adjusting to Rose-Colored Glasses: Finding Creative Ways to Be Critical in Kentucky

Lane W. Clarke

14.1 Introduction

Jones (2006) describes critical literacy as "a pair of eyeglasses that allows one to see beyond the familiar and comfortable" (p. 67). It was precisely this lens that my pre-service teachers were sorely missing as they entered my literacy courses and one that I was determined to help them find through my classes. This, of course, was a tall order considering that our literacy department had just reorganized an already-packed curriculum to meet the many external local, state, and national expectations. This was also going to be harder than I thought because many of my students had never been out of the tristate in which we lived and seemed perfectly content with the familiar. Fresh out of my progressive doctoral program, I soon realized that I had on rose-colored glasses, expecting to create critical thinkers who were going to interrogate educational issues and be committed to fighting for more equitable schooling.

I now know that I was naïve in my initial expectations because it was harder than I imagined to translate my ideals into a prescriptive teaching environment. While I was looking for openings to engage my students in critical pedagogy, I realized that hairline fractures were more realistic. However, by being creative and finding these fractures, I was able to begin to encourage my students to adjust their lenses and see issues through a more critical gaze. In my exploration of critical pedagogy in my preservice teacher education classroom, I have learned a lot about myself and my students, the challenges of teaching at a comprehensive university, and the difficulties of engaging in critical pedagogy. I hope that by sharing my journey I will not only make myself a better teacher, but will also help others who also have to adjust their critical pedagogy lenses without losing focus.

L.W. Clarke
Northern Kentucky University

S.L. Groenke and J.A. Hatch (eds.), *Critical Pedagogy and Teacher Education in the Neoliberal Era: Small Openings*, DOI 10.1007/978-1-4020-9588-7_14, © Springer Science+Business Media B.V. 2009

14.2 Putting on My Rose-Colored Glasses

When I started my career, I was very similar to the typical beginning teacher. I was a young, White, middle-class female teaching in a suburban community not unlike the one in which I was raised. I had no reason to think beyond my comfort zone as I seldom encountered experiences that did not seem familiar. The idea of even considering multiple perspectives and that I might be perpetuating a White middle-class power system did not even enter my consciousness. No one had ever challenged this status quo for me, and none of my personal experiences lent themselves to a thoughtful consideration of the inherent inequities that were part of this vision of education.

This may have remained the case until everything changed when I moved from my safe suburban New York school to one in rural South Carolina. All of a sudden I was faced with an entirely different environment that forced me to start to interrogate issues of race, class, gender, and power in ways that I had never considered. I felt as if I had entered a whole new world, and I struggled to make sense of how to relate to my new surroundings. Moving from an environment that mirrored my own middle-class upbringing to a rural poor mountain community shook my understanding of the world and the purposes that I had set out for educating my students. I began to wonder why the strategies that I had used in my suburban teaching were not as effective. Why did I feel uncomfortable using the same books, the same cultural references, and the same approach with this new group of students? I was suddenly aware that something had changed, but at the time I was not sure what this was or how to confront the unsettling feeling that I was experiencing.

This feeling of discomfort only intensified when I then moved to an urban school in Ohio. Teaching in an inner-city working poor community with students whose backgrounds were definitely nothing like my own provided a whole different shock to my system. I realized I was very far from my comfort zone, and I again struggled with how to be an effective teacher to students whose experiences seemed so different from my own. Luckily during this time I entered a doctoral program and began to read critical theorists such as Freire, Macedo, McLaren, Giroux, hooks, Kincheloe, and Apple. Critical theory and pedagogy gave me a tool to make sense of these very different surroundings and to consider my positioning as a teacher—not just in relation to my students, but to schooling in general. I began to see how although public education appears to have the ultimate goal of educating all students for the greater good, this did not look the same in all schools and in practice sometimes did the reverse. The system that I thought worked well in my upper-middle-class setting actually oppressed and marginalized the students in the other communities in which I worked—not to mention did nothing to challenge these students to think beyond their hegemonic communities. In my new schools where I thought I was "empowering" students, I realized that I was actually perpetuating a structure that kept these students marginalized. I also began to realize how my own race and class background blinded me to seeing past what society deems as "normal."

With this new pair of critical "eyeglasses", I was able to interrogate not only my long-standing positions on education and entitlement, but also see how these ideologies were shaped by my privileged upbringing. Once I saw through this lens, my eyes felt opened for the first time to the myriad social forces that effect everyday encounters in my classroom and beyond. I felt that as a result of this awareness I became a better teacher for all students and a more critical and self-aware individual. I entered the world of teacher education with the desire to help my future students reach the awareness that I had gained through numerous years of wandering aimlessly. I naively thought that I could save my students years of blindly espousing hegemonic school rhetoric and reproduction before they too had their eyes opened to the discourses of power and social inequities.

The goals that I had for my students were bold. I wanted them to develop a "critical consciousness" (Kincheloe, 2008, p. 13) that would enable them to interrogate how factors such as culture, race, gender, and social class impacted how education was embodied in their classrooms. I wanted them to consider our country's goals for education and how these contrasted with enacted public policies that impacted their day-to-day teaching lives. I wanted them to speak out for the marginalized and work toward social justice. But what I failed to realize at the time was that my turn to critical pedagogy was born out of necessity and discomfort. If I had remained within the safety of my suburban New York classroom, I probably would have never have put on these critical glasses. How was I going to inspire my young preservice teachers, many of whom had never made it past their own neighborhoods, to do the same? I quickly realized that critical pedagogy had to involve a necessity to go out of your comfort zone. I could talk about this from my experience, but how could this translate into an awakening for my students? This became a challenge for me as I engaged in critical pedagogy with my students. It is one thing to put the glasses on yourself, but another to try to place them on the eyes of others.

14.3   Conflicting Discourses

It is one thing to realize that critical pedagogy had to be born out of a personal awareness; it is another thing to facilitate the type of environment that fosters this critical gaze. And it is still another thing to create this type of engaged inquiry within a highly rigid and prescribed setting such as my preservice education classroom. I realized that although my intentions were good, I had many obstacles that hindered the accomplishment of my goal. As I started to work in teacher education, I realized that incorporating critical pedagogy was going to be difficult because my university classroom was nested within many powerful contexts that converged to create multiple competing discourses. In order to situate this learning, I needed to consider the multiple influences of my university, the demands of our state, the influence of federal legislation, and the unique characteristics of my students. The way that these contexts were layered created unique challenges for me in this mission.

14.3.1   University Challenges

When I first started in my position, the department had just reorganized its under-graduate courses to block together courses that fit thematically. I was teaching the literacy block—a grouping of two courses: literacy and a practicum. The plus side was that I essentially had the same 20 students 4 mornings a week for 3 hours a day. This was a wonderful opportunity to build relationships and create the type of sup-portive environment I would need to engage in critical pedagogy with my students. On the downside, there were two other professors who also taught the courses, and we shared a common syllabus that designated books, assignments, topic order, and content. Furthermore, it was well known that all the students talked about the teach-ers and compared experiences across the three sections. This cafeteria-like gossip found its way onto course evaluations and to the department chair, and I certainly did not want to start my new career off on the wrong foot. I felt like I was back in elementary school where all the teachers had to be on the same page on the same day, and this felt stifling and antithetical to what I wanted to accomplish in the classroom. I also knew that getting the other sections on board with what I wanted to do was not going to be an easy task. I felt brave taking on this challenge with my students, but also isolated.

To make matters worse, a report by the National Council of Teacher Quality, "What education schools aren't teaching about reading and what elementary school teachers aren't learning" (Walsh et al., 2006) came out, and we were one of the schools that did not make the "grade." As a result, there had been numerous meet-ings between the dean, local superintendents, faculty members, teachers, and other stakeholders to discuss what we could do to remedy this situation. All the profes-sors in the literacy block squeezed in working lunches, power sessions, reviewed our syllabi, aligned our content with the list of the "acceptable" texts, and revised our syllabi to more closely align with these recommendations. We adopted "approved" texts that espoused scientifically valid rhetoric on the teaching of reading. We made sure that everything was aligned. In addition, our university's mission now required that a service learning component be in place for each of our classes. Now I also needed to add a class-wide service learning project to the syllabus.

14.3.2   State Challenges

In addition to university demands, my class also needed to prepare these future teachers for Kentucky's rigorous first-year internship program, align our content with Kentucky's Core Content for assessment, incorporate Kentucky's New Teacher Standards, and improve our students' Praxis test scores—all in one semester. My assignments had to reflect a teacher work sample that consisted of teaching learning contexts, specific lesson plan templates, and lengthy reflection on lessons and units. The students needed to be familiar with the state's reading and writing core content and how to effectively teach each strand in order to prepare their future students for the rigor of state testing. They needed to be able to demonstrate the New Teacher Standards and document each of these ten standards and their corresponding criteria through the creation of electronic portfolio artifacts and reflections. Furthermore, the state compared the Praxis scores of all its universities, and our college wanted to improve the score for our students—so I had to add Praxis review, Praxis test questions, and Praxis case studies to my class. All of a sudden my six-page syllabus was bursting at the seams. There were so many "required" elements that I had no idea how, in 16 weeks, I would cover all of this and also give time to start to develop my students' critical consciousness.

14.3.3 Federal Challenges

In addition to the challenges that I faced from my university and from my state, I was also constrained by the national movement of only supporting "scientific" research and the promotion of high-stakes testing. I had to now teach my students the five components of reading instruction as delineated by the National Reading Panel. I had to make sure these future teachers knew how to cover the entire curriculum in order for their students to pass the "test" so that their school would make Adequate Yearly Progress (AYP) and continue to receive federal funding. I was feeling the pressure of how to equip these teachers to navigate the paradoxes of teaching all students but not having the time to really get to know their students, understand where they are from, and how to connect the curriculum to their lives. I was realizing that there were a lot of competing discourses that were in direct contrast to the critical mission that I had originally planned for my future teachers.

14.3.4 Student Challenges

I had anticipated that I would have challenges imposed from above, but I was surprised to find that my students also presented a significant challenge. When I started teaching, I had visions of empowering young and impressionable minds. I would inspire them and create exciting learning opportunities that would provoke, excite, and stimulate these students. I would draw upon my own experiences and work with them to help them see past their immediate worlds. However, I was not anticipating the resistance that I would experience from these soon-to-be teachers. One of my miscalculations was that I thought these students would be like I was when I was in their shoes—young, middle-class, and privileged. However, unlike the small liberal arts private college that I attended, I was teaching at a public comprehensive university. Many of my students were from working-class backgrounds, were nontraditional, and many were first-generation college students. Most of them worked full-time jobs in addition to taking a full course load, and many were single mothers, or had the additional responsibility of taking care of families and loved ones. These students were hardworking and cared about their education, but they really saw their education as a means to an end—to get a job and earn a living. It was hard to get them to buy into learning for knowledge sake, and they were hesitant to go out of their comfort zones. They worked hard and wanted results and relevancy.

I had to confront the realization that my privileged background afforded me with the luxury of engaging in intellectual endeavors. I began to wonder if critical pedagogy was something that the privileged could think about because we had the economic capital to do so. Or perhaps it was the marginalized and oppressed who engaged in critical pedagogy because they had to for survival (Freire, 1970). But what about those in the middle—what would be their impetus to make these critical engagements? This is reminiscent of how Bourdieu claimed that each habitus embodies material conditions differently—especially as it relates to the possession of capital. For my students, education could be considered more of a "choice of necessity" (Bourdieu, 1991); since they hold less capital, they must confront practical needs such as making a living. I had to ask how critical engagement would fit into this "choice of necessity."

14.4   Reframing the Lens

As I considered my goals as a teacher educator, I became bewildered with how I would approach critical pedagogy in this incredibly rigid and almost hostile environment. And in all honesty, I actually shrank from this responsibility during my first year of teaching. I felt so completely overwhelmed with e-portfolios, lesson plans, standards, Praxis, service learning, practicum hours, and getting to know this new community that I did not even come close to addressing my critical goals. However, as I began to become more comfortable in my new surroundings and increasingly committed to inspiring my students to put on critical glasses, I started to find ways to embed critical pedagogy into my already-packed semester. It was important to me that critical awareness was an integral part of my class and not seen as an add-on. I knew that the students had a class called "Race, Class, and Gender in Education," but I was afraid that by isolating this type of inquiry, these new teachers would have no sense on how this awareness pervaded every part of the teaching day. I knew how important it was to show the students that all of our decisions—curricular, teaching, or interactions with children—were impacted by sociocultural factors like race, class, and gender.

Teaching is not a neutral practice, and I felt strongly that through this class they would expand their understandings. With this in mind, I created a critical issues project as one of my focal points for the semester. At the end of this first project, I reevaluated what I learned from my successes and failures. The second year I modified this project and again reevaluated it. I learned that it is not easy to engage in this type of approach in my teacher education program, and although I know that I only began to help my students see through a more critical lens, there is much room for growth. By sharing how I found small openings, I hope that others are inspired to share and continue this exploration.

14.5 Year One: Finding Small Cracks Through the Critical Issues Project

My first attempt at trying to raise my students' "critical consciousness" in my courses happened through my creation of a "Critical Issues Project." One of the goals of including this type of project was to facilitate the type of environment that would foster a critical gaze on relevant issues in education. I treated this project as I would any class assignment and on the syllabus provided the following description:

- **Critical Inquiry Project**—70 points

  There are many critical issues facing educators today that impact our teaching and how we create effective instruction and relate to our students. During this semester you will be working in groups to explore a critical issue topic as it relates specifically to literacy instruction. Each group will choose a topic, come up with a list of driving question, and work collaboratively to investigate this topic. Topics may include gender, social class, race, nonnative English speakers, diverse learners, and social relationships in the classroom. There are a number of parts to this project and some of the work will be done in the class as well as on your own time.

- **Book Resource List**—10 points

  Each group will prepare a book resource guide to distribute to the class on their topic. This guide should include book titles, authors, grade level, and possible activities for each book.

- **Writing Portfolio**—50 points

  We will be learning about each type of writing genre that is mandated by the State of Kentucky. As many of you know the culminating assessment piece for students is the creation of a writing portfolio. Each of you will also be creating a writing portfolio but the writing samples (your choice of genre) that you include should reflect the theme of your inquiry topic.

- **Service Learning Project**—10 points

  You will need to think of a way that your knowledge of this topic could benefit the larger community.

It was important to me that I embedded this assignment into the class in a seamless manner. It was not just a matter of "killing two birds with one stone"; I wanted the students to see the relevancy of these issues to the everyday world of educators. Since there was a children's literature component to this course, I had each group compile a list of literature that related to their chosen issue. Also, writing was a big focus, and I streamlined our writing portfolio requirement to incorporate this approach. Finally, I connected the service learning requirement to this assignment in hopes that students would use their learning to engage in an activist project.

On the first day of the semester, I put headings around the room identifying topics that the students could choose from to guide their inquiry projects. The students organized themselves into groups, and I gave them a children's book that related to each of the topics to get them started. I asked them to read the book and create a list of questions that could guide their inquiries. Many groups came up with relevant questions that guided their investigations throughout the semester. For example, the group that was looking at gender came up with both simple and more complex questions such as:

- *Are boys called on more than girls?*
- *How do social relationships of different sexes change with age and school setting?*
- *How can teachers encourage equal interaction and opportunities for both genders in the classroom?*
- *Are there any benefits/disadvantages of same-sex classrooms/schools?*
  The group looking at race came up with questions such as:
- *How do you deal with parents of different races?*
- *How do you keep discrimination out of the classroom?*
- *How do you discipline negative racial comments that are made in the classroom?*
- *How do you prepare a nonbiased lesson?*

Interestingly, the group that chose social class had the most difficult time, coming up with only a few questions, such as:

- *How do we know more about a family's background?*
- *How can a teacher relate to children of different social classes?*

14.6 Hairline Fractures of Success

Although this project did not go perfectly, there were some parts that I believe led to the beginnings of critical consciousness. As the students started to make their book lists, they began to notice the lack of diversity in texts they found in the classrooms where they were doing their practicum. This also helped them see how White middle-class norms were portrayed in many of the books published for children. Looking at book series like *Henry and Mudge* (Rylant, 1995) and *Magic Tree House* (Pope Osborn, 1998) increased the students' awareness of how some children's lives are marginalized by not being included in popular texts. Also, they started to become more aware of books that they could use in their classrooms to approach topics of diversity and social awareness with their students.

The biggest areas of success were found in the students' work for the writing portfolio. After making book lists, following up on their questions, making observations, and interviewing teachers, I then had the students write about their topics using any genre of their choice. Some of the students took this opportunity to critically reflect on their own upbringing as it related to their issues.

One of the most powerful pieces was a reflective letter and poem on social class by Beth.[1] In her letter she commented: "After participating in the group reflection, I realized that many teachers deny the existence of social class issues amongst their students. I have always known that social class is not just homelessness or living in the ghetto. It exists among all students who differ from each other and makes social class inequities inevitable in the classroom." Beth then followed with a personal poem about how social class became salient to her when she moved from a rural public school to a more exclusive private school. By writing this poem and reflecting on her inquiry question, she began the process of putting on the critical eyeglasses I had been encouraging. She especially related to using writing to assist her in this exploration. For example at the end of her reflective letter, she commented that this opportunity gave her "a chance to return to elementary school and relive not only my own experiences with social class but encouraged me to use my pen to speak and make my voice heard." After this semester ended, I kept up with this teacher as she continued to grow into a critical educator. She began to read more books about social class and become more active in advocating in her community for equity for all students.

Another student, Nora, was able to use this assignment not only to explore how race impacted classroom interactions, but also how it impacted her personal relationship with her African-American boyfriend (a topic that she seldom discussed). When her group interviewed educators, the students noticed that, "many of us never realized that race is still a big issue in the educational world. Just because we don't discriminate personally toward a person of color or another background; doesn't mean that it does not happen. We have learned that we need to be conscious of this in our classrooms." Personally, Nora wrote how this assignment helped her confront some of the emotions that she had experienced in her own dealings with racism as she commented, "people give him a hard time about being with me. I am often stereotyped and immediately written off by some of his friends when they meet me or find out that I am White." With these reflections she made an overt commitment to creating a nonbiased classroom in her own teaching. She used this assignment to connect her own experiences to the need to push herself and her students beyond what is comfortable and familiar.

There were also pieces of this project that were not as successful. For example, the students had a hard time translating their critical issues work into meaningful service learning experiences. Perhaps it was too soon to ask them to become advocates since they were just beginning to develop their critical understandings. Perhaps the assignment was too open-ended, which made it difficult for them to come up with a clear objective for this part of the project. Perhaps the students still did not have the necessary framework for thinking and talking about these issues. Perhaps I needed to be more explicit on what critical awareness could look like in practice. As Martino (2001) found in his study with boys and questioning stereotypes of masculinity, sometimes it is not enough to merely present the material, but it is often necessary to be explicit and overtly question students in order to expose issues that may otherwise stay under the surface.

---

[1] All names are pseudonyms.

All of these questions converged as I reflected on this first year's experience. Although there were glimmers of hope, there were also many frustrations. First, although I tried hard to make this project fit within the confines of this course, by making it an actual assignment, I found that the students and I treated it as such—another assignment to be crossed off the list. I wanted this to become a way of looking at the world—not something on the to-do list. I also felt uncomfortable with the lack of guidance that I provided in this project. I wanted this to be inquiry-based with opportunities for self-discovery, but in doing so I think I missed my opportunity to share some of my experiences and structure more powerful activities that would open their eyes to being critical about issues in education. In addition, I felt that although I did start with the students' own experiences, I still needed to do a better job of helping them "cultivate the intellect" (Kincheloe, 2008, p. 21) to become more engaged intellectually with the many sociocultural issues facing our nations' classrooms. With these reflections in mind, I altered this project a bit for the next year and tried again.

14.7   Year Two: Cracks Getting Smaller Instead of Bigger

As mentioned above, one of my biggest concerns was how this project seemed to become just another assignment, which seemed antithetical to what I was hoping to accomplish. I struggled with not relegating deep critical thinking to one project. Furthermore, I felt that I needed to provide more initial scaffolding to assist the students in their journeys toward heightened awareness. Therefore, the next year I framed this project in a different way, hoping that this would provide a more powerful way to approach critical pedagogy in the classroom. Although these were two of my goals for this second year, I also knew that due to the high-pressure nature of this course, if I did not have this on the agenda then there would be a good possibility that my students would not engage in this type of investigation. Therefore the second year's description for the critical issues project was as follows:

- **Critical Inquiry Project**—50 points

  During this semester we will be thinking critically about social issues such as politics, gender, race and social class in our classrooms. Towards the end of the semester I will ask each of you to come up with an inquiry question dealing with either one of the issues that we covered or an issue of your choosing. You will create a way to answer this question and write a short paper and share with the class your thinking on this question.

I was hoping that by embedding this inquiry into the everyday topics and issues, it would become more of a way to think about the world, versus only an assignment to be covered. I also wanted to maintain the inquiry nature of investigating these issues, as well as wanting the students to take the lead in deciding what topic that they felt passionate about (much like Beth and Nora from the previous year). I started off the year modeling what it meant to read the world through critical eyeglasses. I first engaged the students in some lessons on looking at issues through multiple perspectives. I started by reading *Voices in the Park* (Browne, 2001), which is a book that tells all sides of a simple encounter at the park but through the eyes of several different actors. We deconstructed the voices in this text, since the power and positioning of each person shifted dramatically according to influences such as gender, social class, and age. We used this multiple perspectives frame to look at issues in education, and I coupled the "acceptable texts" that we were using with other perspectives from journals like *Rethinking Schools* and editorials and articles from newspapers. The students and I investigated policies related to "No Child Left Behind" and "The National Reading Panel" and tried to interrogate these from different sides. They then looked at how these influences impacted the day-to-day enactments of their classrooms. I then paired this investigation with children's literature around topics like gender, social class, and race in the classroom. The students discussed in literature circles how these children's books connected to larger themes and issues that they were seeing in their practicum environments. I was hoping that this multiple perspective frame would help them more deeply interrogate the critical issue of their choosing. I was feeling more optimistic at how this was starting off; however, my positive feelings were quickly extinguished.

Although this semester started off much better than the previous one and I was feeling better about how I was embedding these types of interrogations and becoming more proactive in situating myself as one who can lead the class on this exploration, the semester took several unexpected turns. First, I had to cancel some classes due to an unexpected hospital stay and then a freak spring snowstorm blanketed Kentucky and shut down classes for an extended period of time. To top it off, the school district where our students were in practicum placements readjusted their calendars due to the snow and ice, which impacted my students in completing their required teaching hours. Finally, the service learning project that the students designed ended up taking much more time than I had allotted. By the time in the semester when the students should have been taking this structure and engaging in their own inquiries, I was forced instead to reevaluate this assignment. Unfortunately, the pressures of unit plans, teacher work samples, electronic portfolios, PRAXIS, service learning, and myriad other requirements resulted in this critical issues project being compromised. After such high aspirations and a strong start, I was devastated by how my high ideals fizzled and embarrassed at how I capitulated to these external forces (as I can barely force myself to admit this in print). I learned that critical pedagogy is not for the faint-hearted, and I seriously questioned if I had what it takes to actually facilitate this type of awareness in my students. With my proverbial tail between my legs, I retreated to my own reflections and vowed to examine what had gone wrong and confront those rose-colored glasses that now seemed so dramatically misplaced.

14.8   Adjusting My Rose-Colored Glasses

Experimenting with critical literacy has left me asking many questions about how such an approach could look in my undergraduate preservice teaching classroom. I learned that I needed to become stronger and more assertive in my goal to truly help others develop the ability to see beyond the comfortable and familiar, going to a place where deep learning about education can occur. This experiment has left me with many questions, but also many new directions. A few lingering questions that I have are:

- How do we assess critical consciousness? How do I know if my students have put on these glasses? How do I know if they keep them on?
- How can we include critical pedagogy in our classrooms but still maintain the current structure—or are they too much the opposite? Is this even possible to do? Are these hairline fractures good enough or do we have to radically restructure our courses?
- How do I get my colleagues to come on board and reinforce this perspective in their classrooms? Is it possible to make this approach mainstream in all of my students' preservice classrooms? Does making it mainstream negate what critical pedagogy is all about?
- How do we inspire others to want to go out of their comfort zones—especially when they are content to stay there?
- How can I get my students to create their own issues of inquiry that will propel them deeper into critical thinking about issues of education that are important to them?

Next semester I will be back at it trying things differently. I believe that what makes good teachers is the ability to reflect and continually refine their practice. Some parts of my critical issues project will change and some will stay the same. Two of ideas that I have to further grow this project are:

- I plan to do a better job at having students come up with their own critical inquiries. I want to support students as researchers and model my own investigation as I work with them. Freire talks about true critical pedagogy being generative, emerging from the students' own questions, tensions, and issues. I would like to model for my students how to come up with these inquiry questions. I hope that by engaging in my own critical inquiry, I can support the students in their investigations as I can turn an action research project into a meaningful project for us all.
- I feel strongly that critical pedagogy is born out of a necessity to go out of your comfort zone. Perhaps I can include more detailed community investigations-similar to what Lazar (2004) does with her classes in urban education, where she has her students spend more time on the context of teaching—both in traditionally diverse and non-diverse placements. Also, it is important that many of my students see their own whiteness as a space for investigation. Because whiteness is normalized in our society, many of my students have trouble seeing the many layers of diversity within their own culture (me included as a beginning teacher). By starting an investigation within their own surroundings, perhaps this will help them see through the veil of normalcy and get a richer understanding of how power and privilege impact education.

The fact that this investigation is not complete is part of what makes it critical. I hesitated to write about my failures and works-in-progress, but then realized that this is exactly what pushed me toward critical pedagogy. If I just kept on my rose-colored glasses without constantly refocusing them, then nothing has been learned. I hope that sharing stories—both the frustrations and the small cracks of success—can be generative to us all as we figure out how to work within and among a variety of settings to create teachers who are socially aware and engaged intellectual advocates for the marginalized and supporters of fair and just educational policies.

References

Bourdieu, P. (1991). *Language and symbolic power*. Cambridge, MA: Harvard University Press.
Browne, A. (2001). *Voices in the park*. New York: DK Children.
Freire, P. (1970). *Pedagogy of the oppressed*. New York: Continuum Publishing.
Jones, S. (2006). *Girls, social class and literacy: What teachers can do to make a difference*. Portsmouth, NH: Heinemann.
Kincheloe, J.L. (2008). *Critical pedagogy primer* (2nd ed.). New York: Peter Lang.
Lazar, A.M. (2004). *Learning to be literacy teachers in urban schools: Stories of growth and change*. Newark, DE: International Reading Association.
Martino, W. (2001). "Dickheads, wusses, and faggots": Addressing issues of masculinity and homophobia in the critical literacy classroom. In B. Comber & A. Simpson (Eds.), *Negotiating critical literacies in classrooms*. Mahwah, NJ: Erlbaum.
Pope Osborn, M. (1998). *Magic tree house: Day of the dragon king*. New York: Random House.
Rylant, C. (1995). *Henry and Mudge and the best day of all*. New York: Aladdin.
Walsh, K., Glaser, D., & Wilcox, D.D. (2006). What education schools aren't teaching about reading—and what elementary teachers aren't learning. Washington, DC: National Council of Teacher Quality.

Chapter 15
Becoming Critical in an Urban Elementary Teacher Education Program

J. Amos Hatch and Wendy B. Meller*

15.1 Introduction

The authors share the experience of introducing critical pedagogical approaches in a teacher education program for students preparing to work in urban elementary schools. This chapter is an account of parts of that experience and our reflections about what it is like to become more critical in our work with pre-service teachers. As a professor and an advanced graduate student, we are strongly committed to infusing the instructional experiences we provide with opportunities for our students to learn to "critically read"(Quintero & Rummel, 2003, p. 12) the complex social, economic, and political processes that impact urban schooling. As we have worked toward this aim with others in our urban multicultural teacher education program, we have learned a great deal about ourselves. Because we work very closely with small groups of students over an extended period of time, we also have learned something about how future teachers respond to our efforts to raise their consciousness about social issues and lay the foundations for applying critical pedagogies in their own urban elementary teaching. In addition, each of us has conducted independent qualitative research projects related to the development of critical perspectives in our urban multicultural teacher education students.

This chapter recounts the transformative journeys we have taken in our efforts to prepare elementary teachers to work in urban settings. Our journeys are marked by highs and lows along the path to adopting critical perspectives, applying critical pedagogies, and encouraging the development of critical consciousness

J.A. Hatch
University of Tennessee

W.B. Meller
Rowan University

---

*This chapter was completed while Wendy was a doctoral candidate at the University of Tennessee. She is now an Assistant Professor at Rowan University.

S.L. Groenke and J.A. Hatch (eds.), *Critical Pedagogy and Teacher Education in the Neoliberal Era: Small Openings*, DOI 10.1007/978-1-4020-9588-7_15, © Springer Science + Business Media B.V. 2009

in future urban teachers. We use data from our research projects to bring to life
the difficulties, paradoxes, and rewards associated with becoming critical in university, school, political, and social contexts that are dominated by powerful
conservative forces. Examples of activities that we have used with preservice
elementary teachers are presented, and lessons learned along the pathway to
adopting critical pedagogical approaches in an urban teacher education program
are detailed.

15.2   Contexts

Knowing something about the contexts in which we work is important to understanding
our experience of introducing critical pedagogy to preservice urban teachers.
We work in one of several K–8 licensure programs at the University of Tennessee
in Knoxville. The expressed purpose of the urban, multicultural program is to
prepare teachers who will be effective in urban settings, and who will stay in those
settings as their careers unfold. As required by all the teacher education programs
at the University of Tennessee, urban multicultural students earn their licenses upon
completion of a 5-year program that includes a full year's internship in local
schools. Students enter the professional studies portion of their preservice programs
with bachelor's degrees (with arts and sciences majors) and do at least one semester
of pre-internship coursework as part of an undergraduate minor in education.
Students apply for admission into the urban multicultural program, participate in an
interview process, and compete for slots. Accepted students go through their urban
teacher preparation as a cohort group, working with the same team of faculty
throughout their pre-internship and internship.

The urban multicultural teacher education program has a history of being
grounded in a strong orientation toward preparing individuals to teach in a
complex, multicultural society. The theoretical foundations of the program have
expanded over the years to include elements related to multicultural education,
culturally responsive teaching, urban education, and (most recently) critical
pedagogy. Our attraction to critical perspectives on preparing urban teachers
has increased over the past 2 or 3 years, as has our willingness to be more open
(with ourselves, our students, and our colleagues in other programs) about our
motives and methods. A core group of three professors (Gina Barclay-
McLaughlin, Susan Benner, and Amos Hatch) along with graduate teaching
assistants and clinical instructors (most recently, Wendy Meller and Susan
Newsom) spend lots of time planning the content and delivery of the urban
multicultural program. Infusing critical pedagogical approaches into our students' experiences has been an important focus of late. The authors of this
chapter, Amos and Wendy, have had direct experience implementing critical
pedagogical approaches with the most recent urban multicultural cohorts. Our
reflections on that experience follow next.

15.2.1 Amos's Story

I am a White male who grew up in poor, mostly homogeneous, White communities in Utah. I have been working in teacher education for almost 25 years, the last 20 at the University of Tennessee. My own teacher preparation and my 14 years of urban elementary and early childhood teaching did not include much critical pedagogy. In my doctoral program at the University of Florida, I encountered and admired the work of important critical theorists, but I didn't count myself as a critical educator. Over my years in higher education, my interest and admiration for critical approaches to understanding the world and doing research about it grew. I learned a great deal about alternative perspectives from colleagues around the world, especially those involved in the Reconceptualizing Early Childhood Education group that has been active since the early 1990s.

During most of my tenure as a professor, I have taught and written about critical perspectives as a kind of intellectual outsider, valuing the ideas and contributions of critical approaches, but naming myself as more of a liberal than a critical theorist. Over the past 5 or 6 years, I have returned to my roots in urban education and found opportunities to work with graduate students and other scholars who have challenged me to reexamine my philosophical, political, and pedagogical assumptions. I have begun to internalize and enact my intellectualized understandings of critical thought, and my writing and teaching have changed as a result. My approach to bringing about change has always been to work from inside organizations and institutions, rather than to stand on the fringes and throw rocks at the middle. I continue to write for mainstream audiences, but my message and its tone are changing. I continue to teach in ways intended to move pre- and in-service teachers and graduate students toward richer understandings of themselves and their profession; but I am much more interested in engaging them in consciousness-raising and transformative action than in the past. I am lucky to have found colleagues who share my commitments to social justice and critical pedagogical approaches and who are willing to explore possibilities for transforming what we do in our university teaching.

My goals for the instructional experiences I share with preservice teachers include helping them see that (a) the deck is stacked against many of the children and families with whom they will be working in urban schools; (b) structural constraints, not personal problems, are the source of most of the barriers that limit the life chances of poor, urban students and their communities; (c) teachers and schools are often complicit in maintaining an inherently unfair socioeconomic system; and (d) we as educators have opportunities to challenge the status quo and empower others as we work for social change. The urban multicultural teacher education program is fortunate in that we get to select from among students who apply to our program. Some come to us with deeply held commitments to social justice, and a few have been involved in social action in various arenas. For most of our teacher education students, however, accomplishing these goals is a long stretch. The usual case is that the values of their families, their home communities, and the schools our students attended run counter to those at the core of the goals listed. My approach is not to blame them for viewing oppression and inequality differently from the way I do, but to help them explore other ways of thinking about how the world is ordered and their place in it. Some of the activities I have tried are described next.

I have tried a variety of ways to utilize popular culture as an avenue for helping preservice teachers explore urban schooling and its place in perpetuating the diminished life chances of poor children in our society. With one cohort, I joined a small group of students in presenting a seminar that included showing and analyzing examples of television shows, movies, and pop music that portrayed urban schools. For my part, I passed out the words to the Pink Floyd song "Another Brick in the Wall Part II," played the song, told a story of my own urban teaching, explained how the song and story have influenced my own thinking about myself as an educator, repeated the playing of the song, and led a discussion of their reactions to the song and my story. The song contains the haunting refrain, "We don't need no education, we don't need no thought control." The story recounts my confrontation with someone who argued that, as a new White teacher in an all-Black urban school, I was being duped by the system, that schools were set up to ensure that children like the ones I was teaching would never succeed; and that the more teachers are committed to helping children improve their chances for success, the better those teachers are at appearing to offer oppressed people the chance to succeed when none exists. I told how the "Brick in the Wall" song always reminded me of that conversation and the doubt it planted in my mind about the real value of the education I was trying so hard to provide. Following the seminar, two sets of reflective e-mail exchanges took place between me and the students. I responded to each student in writing, reacting to what he or she had written. An analysis of those interchanges is reported in an upcoming article (Hatch, in press), and excerpts from student reactions are presented later in this chapter.

Another set of strategies I use involves assigning readings that address critical issues in urban schooling to small groups of students, then making them responsible for using the readings to plan instructional activities for their preservice peers. I try to select articles and book chapters that stretch students' thinking without overwhelming or intimidating them. I have used some of my own articles, including one on the necessity of making learning a subversive activity in contemporary schooling (Hatch, 2007). Another piece that has worked is Kivel's (2004) chapter on "The Ruling Class and the Buffer Zone," which locates teachers in the space between those in power and those who would almost certainly rebel without the mollifying effects of a number of workers who unwittingly provide a buffer. And I have assigned chapters from *Literacy with an Attitude* (Finn, 1999) and *What Keeps Teachers Going* (Nieto, 2003), texts that challenge conventional understandings of teacher roles in urban schools. I distribute a reading to a designated group, give students a chance to process it and think about ways to engage their peers in understanding the ideas in the reading, then I meet with them to help shape the instructional experiences they will be responsible for conducting. All students in the larger cohort read the assigned article or chapter in preparation for participating in the activity.

Another example of a critical pedagogical strategy I have used is setting up role-playing activities in which students are assigned positions on controversial issues that they have to defend in a confrontational situation. The contexts for role-playing have been settings like school board meetings, meetings with parents, and cocktail parties. I try to set up situations that are real enough so that students can feel themselves defending tough positions in places in which actual conflicts arise. I assign them to a position, give them time to prepare their case and anticipate the case they expect their opponents to bring, and insist that they stay in role throughout the role-playing activity. I frequently use point–counterpoint readings to help them prepare, and I always give them a chance to debrief about their real positions and how they felt about the interchange.

I have mixed feelings about the effects of my own and our team's efforts to become more critical. Because we work so closely with them, we have a pretty good idea of how our students are receiving the experiences we provide, and because we stay with them over the course of a full year's internship, we get to see what they use and don't use during what is essentially their first year as urban teachers. In addition, I have implemented a longitudinal qualitative study of one of our recent cohorts, tracking them from their pre-internship, through their internship year, and now into their first year as fully employed teachers. Not all of the data for that study are directly tied to critical pedagogy, but I do have some data-based outcomes that tell me something about the effects of our attempts to integrate critical pedagogy into our teaching. Both my impressions and research-based conclusions are mixed in terms of gauging the impact of our work.

Most of our preservice teachers struggle to understand and apply critical pedagogy. Most seem to get that resources in our society are unevenly and unfairly distributed across socioeconomic and cultural lines. As a group, they feel deep compassion for the children they plan to teach. They select urban teaching because they are committed to making a difference in the lives of children they see as underserved and disadvantaged by society. Many feel as if they are called to this work and are acting out a kind of moral imperative. We see this kind of commitment when we interview students who want to join our program, and it is clear in the first round of data collection in my longitudinal research. As one student explained in an open-ended interview conducted soon after entering the program:

> I decided that I could not stand back and watch these children turn into statistics. I see the tears of these children I work with and their outbursts of anger, and it would be wrong to turn my back and look the other way.

As a faculty, we share many of these same feelings, and we want to nurture and support our students' caring and commitment. We worry though about some of the assumptions many of our students seem to be making about the issues that urban students, families, and communities face. Many of our students come to us with a deficit model for understanding phenomena such as poverty, racism, immigration, and school failure. This is understandable, given the powerful influence of the society at large and their families and communities in particular on explaining away social issues by blaming the victims of systemic oppression. Our students' comments during class discussions, in their written reflections, and in one-on-one conversations reveal the difficulties they have moving their explanations for the difficulties they see their students experiencing from personal problems to social issues. We see breakthroughs and epiphanies among our students, but because changing this perspective is one of the goals of my critical teaching, I am especially sensitive to the frequency with which students revert to long-held assumptions about what it means to be an urban student, parent, or teacher. For example, when one preservice teacher in my study reflected on the meanings of the "Brick in the Wall" activity described above, she essentially denied any possibility that schools might be abetting the maintenance of the socioeconomic status quo, writing:

> The idea that urban schools serve as a sorting mechanism is something I had never even considered. If it were true, then everything that I hope to accomplish as an educator would be undermined. My goal as an urban educator is to enable children to lift themselves out of poverty and ignorance. If there was a covert force working against those ideas, then my efforts would be in vain, and my profession a sham. I would be devastated if I knew that my life's efforts contributed to any child's failures, or misled them with false hope.

Yes, we are working to challenge the thinking that many of our students bring to their understandings of schooling and social justice, but it is often difficult, sometimes frustrating, and occasionally disheartening.

A related tension that we experience is some of our students' concern that they are being placed in a position that often contradicts the values of their parents, their religion, and their culture. We encourage and support open dialogue about the sensitive issues we raise, and we are clear that we are trying to open up alternative ways of understanding rather than requiring them to adopt our perspectives. We are careful to cultivate a climate in which everyone's point of view is valued, and our best discussions happen when students process disagreements among themselves. Still, some students feel genuine anxiety when confronted with ways of thinking that blur the Black-and-White world they are used to seeing. One of our recent pre-interns cried to one of the faculty that her parents were worried that her professors were "radical Democrats trying to poison her mind."

The most recent data from the longitudinal study mentioned above indicate mixed outcomes as the cohort in the study is finishing its first year of teaching. When asked if and how they had applied critical approaches or actively sought social change in their professional work so far, responses were uneven. Most of these new teachers seemed to be committed to critical approaches and social change, but they offered a variety of reasons for why they had done little or nothing by way of utilizing the critical pedagogical approaches they had been exposed to in their teacher preparation. Explanations for not doing more included statements such as:

> The expectations for teachers are very high. The support is not as high. We are expected to make so many different ends meet.

> As far as seeking social change, I am far from it because there are so many politics. I am under the _____ system, so they have their own way of enforcing social change. We teach them that they can graduate on time and how to effectively communicate with others, but they are doomed to a system that they are co-dependent upon.

A few of the teachers in the study are comfortable including critical approaches, especially critical literacy strategies, in their teaching. Most, like those above, are making a slow start for understandable reasons associated with the insecurities of starting a teaching career, incredible pressures on teachers, and constraints tied to implementing the canned programs that dominate urban schooling. These issues are real, and part of Wendy's story below includes a description of what happens when university personnel work to support a new teacher as she implements critical literacy activities in an urban first-grade classroom.

Like the new teachers in my study, I have mixed feelings about the efficacy of my critical pedagogical efforts. I am committed to our team's efforts to move future urban elementary educators toward a more critical approach in their teaching. I enjoy the challenges and learn from my students and colleagues everyday. I worry that I may be "just another brick in the wall," but I plan to keep trying to facilitate experiences and elicit insights that improve the possibilities for creating a just and equitable society.

15.2.2   Wendy's Story

Growing up in Philadelphia, many of my schoolmates were from diverse backgrounds, even though I lived in a primarily White, middle-class neighborhood. My first teaching position was at a charter school in Philadelphia. I taught kindergarten, and the only White student in the school was a little girl in my class. At the time, Jessica was living in a shelter with her mom, who was escaping an abusive relationship. Kaya, another little girl, lived with her dad and never saw her mother who was addicted to crack when Kaya was born. Daniel was raised by both his grandparents and never saw his mother either. Their stories were like those of many others I would teach over the years in Philadelphia and New York City.

My teacher preparation program did not emphasize a multicultural or critical perspective. It was not until I was in my own classroom and faced with students of different backgrounds than my own that I begin to look at who I was and how and where I might fit in. When my first kindergarten students began to question whether or not Jessica was White or Black, I knew I was entering unchartered waters. When I learned that a student had a parent in jail or when another was living in a shelter, I did not know what would be appropriate for discussion with them, especially because they were young.

While working on my Ph.D. in Literacy Education at the University of Tennessee, I found a missing element in my own education: developing a critical perspective. I discovered critical literacy and came to realize that this pedagogical approach could support preservice teachers as they confronted the same issues I faced as a new teacher. I was fortunate to work within the urban multicultural teacher education program with colleagues who supported critical pedagogy. They allowed me to go through my own self-discovery as we worked together to support future urban teachers.

Discovering the children's book *Visiting Day* (Woodson, 2002) launched the beginning of how I came to introduce preservice teachers to critical literacy and have critical conversations with them. Woodson's story is of a young African-American girl, living with her grandmother. Together they board a bus in their community to visit the girl's father in jail. The story captures the love and bond between the daughter and her father and the sadness that comes with their separation. Engaging the preservice teachers in questions about what was missing, or how power was distributed among the characters made this conversation "critical." To me that story was a mirror image of many of my students' lives. In discovering this book and this genre of text, I felt that I found something to connect children's lives, literacy, and the world.

My goals for the instructional experiences I share with preservice teachers have developed based on my own experience as an urban elementary school teacher and a teacher educator who prepares teachers for urban contexts. I want to help preservice teachers understand that

(a) Developing a critical perspective is a process, one that does not happen in a day, a week, a month, or a semester. It continues to evolve as they become teachers.
(b) There is never one right answer or a single solution to critical situations. The more opportunities students have to share in dialogue, the more they learn, and the more they will be able to find their own comfort zone.
(c) Their experience and background are the foundation for their own knowing. Their understandings may differ from their peers, yet hearing others' stories and histories can change their perspective.
(d) Engaging students in critical conversations should include more than just cultural/racial insiders. If we hope to change the world, we need to include individuals from all groups in confronting the effects of social injustice.

Developing a critical perspective is a process that starts with, and builds on, students' background knowledge and supports them in making connections with the world. As they introduce critical literacy, I believe teachers should start with discussions around texts that highlight diversity and difference. These texts can be used in place of basal and/or leveled readers or in conjunction with them, depending on the school literacy program and how the teacher chooses to incorporate the texts. Multicultural literature allows students to make personal connections, learn new perspectives, and question the content. Cai (2008) believes that analyzing multicultural texts serves as a starting point in developing a critical perspective.

Cai (2008) argues that rather than being distinct from transactional theories of reading (Rosenblatt, 1978, 1995), critical literacy builds on them. I agree with Cai's view that text criticism is anchored in what Rosenblatt called the reader's aesthetic response, which serves as the primary step in literary transaction. Cai believes the reader's aesthetic response is a necessary first step toward critical literacy because of the personal and political nature of critical understandings of literacy. Based on Rosenblatt's (1995) theory, once a reader scrutinizes her response to text, she can have a better understanding of her personal attitudes. This provides for richer responses to text, allowing her to move forward with this process. Teachers particularly need to examine their own aesthetic response in order to support student transactions. If we bypass this crucial first step, we "run the risk of imposing a certain critical point of view on the reader, without the reader understanding and accepting it" (Cai, 2008, p. 218). Once a reader has established an understanding of her aesthetic response to text, she is able to take on a more critical perspective. I will now share some examples of how I start the process of engaging preservice teachers in critical conversations through the use of children's literature.

As I attempt to implement critical literacy with preservice teachers, my hope is that I am modeling practices that will be transferred into their own instructional approaches. I initially immerse preservice teachers in children's critical literacy literature. I start the process by reading aloud a children's book. Most recently, I have been reading *A Shelter in Our Car* (Gunning, 2004), which is about a little girl from Jamaica now living in a car in the United States with her mother. There are issues such as death, immigration, bullying, and poverty throughout the story; yet, the overarching theme is the bond of love between this mother and daughter. This story raises many points for discussion, and students later reflect in their journals about that story and their personal connections to it. Throughout the reading of the story, I pose critical questions such as "Whose voice is missing?" "What is the teacher's role?" "Should this family stay together?" Engaging the group in considering these kinds of questions provides them an opportunity to go deeper into the text than just asking who, what, why, when, and how.

Similar to Amos, I also use role-play as an instructional approach. However, I have preservice teachers confront critical issues based on a text. For example, I have used the same book, *A Shelter in Our Car* (Gunning, 2004), and chosen five participants to be part of a talk show. I take them into the hall and have them decide which role they would like to play: Zettie (the little girl), Zettie's mom, the police officer, the teacher, and the talk-show host. The host is to engage the audience in critical questions posed to the guests. This activity elicits rich questions from the group, for example:

Teacher: Why did you not step in and offer support? Did you know they were homeless?
Mom: How did you stay so strong and resilient?
Zettie: How did it feel being homeless?
Mom: Where are you today?
Policeman: Would you have treated Zettie different if you knew her situation?

This story and particularly this activity have brought out different view points about how this child should be raised. Recently, I read it to a group that included one preservice teacher who experienced homelessness as a child and another who was a foster mom. They had very different opinions about what should happen to Zettie based on her living situation. I have preservice teachers reflect in writing about this experience in order for them to explore their own history and connections to the story. Each time the group reflects in their journals, I respond back, encouraging them to think carefully about having these kinds of conversations with children.

Another activity I engage my preservice teachers in is called carousel reading and reflection (Sluys et al., 2005). The idea is to have the students see multiple texts in a small amount of time as they develop an understanding of the characteristics of critical literacy texts. I bring various children's books to class, spread them around the room, and put a sheet of paper by each text. I pose some questions on the papers, such as Whose voice is missing? Who has the power? Is this a "happily ever after" ending? Who benefits? The group then moves around the room, spending a few minutes with each book. This provides them with enough time to see what critical literacy texts look like. It also allows them to see their peers' reactions to the texts, helping them gain insight into other readers' responses. After the group has a chance to look through and comment on the books, I have someone read the reactions aloud as we discuss a few of these stories as part of a dialogic process.

As Amos stated above, we are lucky to work closely with a small cohort of preservice teachers throughout their teacher education program. Working with our students from start to finish has enabled me to see some patterns in their reaction to critical literacy. I also designed a pilot study to explore how preservice teachers confront issues of diversity through children's critical literacy literature. The study examined preservice teachers' reactions to a two-phase instructional approach. I first read aloud children's critical literacy literature to the group and engaged them in discussion. Later in the year, the preservice teachers took on a leadership role in small groups by selecting and reading a book aloud. Some of their reactions to this process are expressed in the following statements:

> I don't know the situations of all my students. Eventually I will feel comfortable to read a non-traditional book to my students.

> When we have these discussions on race, I feel a little uneasy because I have seen and experienced racism firsthand.

> It was not until I shared the book with my group, that I gained a new perspective. Mark, being of another race and gender, received the book much more negatively than I had. I had not thought of the full-time fathers.

My data show that our preservice teachers initially were unsure about their ability to engage students in critical conversation through texts focusing on critical issues. It was important for them to know their students and feel comfortable in the school setting before having this kind of dialogue with children. However, as they were immersed in critical literacy through read alouds, reading professional literature, discussion, and reflection, the cohort of students began to move away from rejecting this approach to looking forward to sharing stories of how they were incorporating critical literacy literature in their own classrooms. I found that being exposed to critical literacy over a year was an effective way to support preservice teachers in gaining comfort in talking about critical issues. The next step in this process would be to extend the discussions to include the role of language, literacy, and power. I will now share additional reactions to critical literacy instruction from my dissertation study (Meller, 2008), which grew out of the pilot project.

Our field continually expresses concern that we rarely follow preservice teachers from theory to practice. My pilot study left me wondering what would happen to these preservice teachers once they were in their own classrooms. Would they engage children in critical conversations? If so, how would they do so, what would it look like, and how would that influence their beliefs and understandings about critical literacy? Amos and I both were fortunate to be able to follow the same cohort of students as they went into the classroom as first-year teachers. I decided to venture on a journey with one of the teachers (Jennifer) from the pilot study. Together, this first-year teacher and I co-constructed our knowledge of critical literacy as I sought to raise her consciousness of this process. During the study, as

Jennifer engaged her students in critical literacy read alouds, I helped her construct her lesson plans. In the data, she expressed the following thoughts:

> I try and go around what I know my kids have going on.

> I use critical literacy because I don't know what to say in a lot of those situations.

> It makes my stomach irritated to even think about having to talk about that stuff without having something to go to.

> Most of my critical literacy books are books that I call the "untouchables" because it's stuff that I wouldn't feel comfortable with.

The study revealed that early on Jennifer chose books aligned with her students' situations rather than her specific desire to raise their consciousness about social issues. She felt that she could have critical conversations only if there were books that could help her breach the subject. Toward the end of the study, a shift occurred in her thoughts about this process. The following are examples of the change in her thinking about critical literacy.

> Now it's awesome because not only does it help the students, but it helps me.

> It's so funny because now that I've done critical literacy, there's so much better reading out there; you just have to find it.

> I'm kind of learning through my children and I'm learning myself through the critical literacy and responding with the kids when they're getting into it.

My own understanding of critical literacy developed over time, progressing from making text connections and exploring my aesthetic response to critically examining and questioning text. I am therefore very mindful of that developmental progression as I work with preservice and in-service teachers. Having the opportunity to be a part of Jennifer's critical development enriched my understanding of this process. I found that she needed to reflect on her own background and beliefs; learn about her students' backgrounds; explore her understanding of, and comfort with, multicultural literature; and develop an identity within the existing school culture. I believe she needed to examine these aspects with herself first, before having deeper discussions with her students. Although there was apprehension and occasional reticence, she never shied away from having critical literature book talks with them. Once she moved past this exploratory period, Jennifer had a better understanding of a reader's response to literature, enabling her and her students to become more critical.

This ongoing process is how teachers come to find their "voice" in critical conversations with others. Once I discovered critical literacy, I wanted to know what it would be like for someone like me (White, middle-class, and female) to engage children in conversations around these texts. What I did not know was that there was so much more to be uncovered when pursuing these conversations. As I became immersed in professional literature about critical literacy and pursued conversations with like-minded educators, I came to find that becoming critical is a never-ending journey. There are moments when you think you have "defined" critical literacy only to discover there is more to be uncovered.

Am I more comfortable in having critical conversations with others about issues of difference? Yes, but that does not mean that I am totally at ease. I experience moments of anxiety even today as I present critical literacy workshops to groups of teachers. I am always presented with "what if" questions. I know I don't have many definitive answers, but what I can offer is that there is a personal level of comfort we all have to find in ourselves before engaging our students. That is why we work so hard to develop critical understandings with our preservice teachers before they are out on their own and confronted with these difficult issues.

15.3   Lessons Learned: Becoming Critical in an Urban Elementary Teacher Education Program

Based on an extensive review of research on preparing urban teachers, Hollins and Guzman (2005) concluded that "unless prospective teachers have opportunities to rethink and change their attitudes and beliefs, the students who are in the greatest academic need may also be the ones least likely to have access to rich learning opportunities" (p. 482). We concur, and conclude by offering the following "lessons" we have learned in our efforts to get urban preservice teachers to think reflexively about their own attitudes and beliefs, and to move toward a more critical perspective on schooling, society, and social change. We hope these lessons and the experiences described in the chapter will help teacher educators who seek to be more critical in their pedagogical approaches to better understand where their students are coming from, and what needs to happen to move them forward. Lessons are divided between (a) generalizations that characterize preservice teachers' development of critical pedagogy and critical literacy perspectives, and (b) implications for facilitating the development of those perspectives.

15.3.1   Generalizations

- Many preservice teachers are deeply committed to teaching in urban settings, but some bring a deficit approach to understanding issues in urban families, schools, and communities.
- They feel uneasy about confronting issues of diversity.
- It is difficult for them to see beyond personal/psychological effects (as opposed to social/structural influences) as they consider explanations for urban issues.
- They find it hard to critically reflect on their own behaviors and attitudes in relation to urban teaching.
- It is difficult for them to recognize and deal with the paradoxes associated with adopting a critical perspective in urban public school settings.
- New urban teachers' chances of being successful at initiating critical pedagogical approaches are improved with support from teacher educators.

15.3.2 Implications

- Urban teacher educators should use tools like the data collection strategies of the studies in this chapter to gauge preservice teachers' development of critical knowledge, skills, and dispositions.
- They should accept preservice teachers where they are and move them forward in their development as critical educators, building on their students' commitment to urban teaching and their desire to make a difference.
- They should apply the principles of critical pedagogy to the instructional experiences provided in their teacher education programs (i.e., walk the talk).
- They should integrate critical approaches throughout program experiences, providing a wide variety of instructional opportunities (on campus and in schools and communities) for developing critical pedagogical perspectives.
- They should explore ways to continue to support critical pedagogical development once preservice teachers find jobs in urban schools.

References

Cai, M. (2008). Transactional theory and the study of multicultural literature. *Language Arts, 85*(3), 212–220.

Finn, P. J. (1999). *Literacy with an attitude: Educating working-class children in their own self-interest.* Albany, NY: State University of New York Press.

Gunning, M. (2004). A shelter in our car. San Francisco, CA: Children's Book Press.

Hatch, J. A. (2007). Learning as a subversive activity. *Phi Delta Kappan, 89,* 310–311.

Hatch, J. A. (in press). Pre-service teachers' perspectives on critical pedagogy for urban teaching: Yet another brick in the wall? *Teacher Education and Practice.*

Hollins, E., & Guzman, M. T. (2005). Research on preparing teachers for diverse populations. In M. Cochran-Smith & K. M. Zeichner (Eds.), *Studying teacher education: The report of the AERA Panel on Research and Teacher Education* (pp. 477–548). Mahwah, NJ: Erlbaum.

Kivel, P. (2004). *You call this a democracy? Who benefits, who pays and who really decides.* New York: Apex.

Meller, W. B. (2008). *A Critical literacy case study: The journey from pre-service exploration to in-service implementation.* Unpublished doctoral dissertation, University of Tennessee, Knoxville.

Nieto, S. (2003). *What keeps teachers going?*. New York: Teachers College Press.

Quintero, E. P., & Rummel, M. K. (2003). *Becoming a teacher in the new society: Bringing communities and classrooms together.* New York: Peter Lang.

Rosenblatt, L. M. (1978). *The reader the text the poem.* Carbondale, IL: Southern Illinois University Press.

Rosenblatt, L. M. (1995). *Literature as exploration* (5th ed.). New York: The Modern Language Association.

Sluys, K. V., Legan, N., Laman, T. T., & Lewison, M. (2005). Critical literacy and preservice teachers: Changing definitions of what it might mean to read. *Journal of Reading Education, 31*(1), 13–22.

Woodson, J. (2002). Visiting day. New York: Scholastic Press.

Afterword

Susan L. Groenke and J. Amos Hatch

> *Persons of all ages are rejecting mere acquiescence to tradition;*
> *they are struggling to name the relations of power, to open*
> *spaces where they can be free.*

(Maxine Greene, 1993)

Reflection on Themes in the Book

Christine Sleeter (2008), writing about the neoliberal assault on teacher education, has said that teacher educators are often unaware of what neoliberalism is and how it is impacting a range of social institutions. The chapters in this book reflect that many teacher educators are aware of what neoliberalism is and how it is impacting public schools and university-based teacher preparation programs. The chapters in Part I explain various facets of the neoliberal assault on public and higher education. Chapters 1, 2, and 4 describe the loss of public services, including public schools, as a goal of neoliberalism; the havoc NCLB has wreaked, especially on historically under-served and impoverished school communities; and the pressures university-based teacher preparation programs feel to align themselves with neoliberal agendas.

Chapter 3 critiques the discourses of professionalism, rationality, and egalitari-anism espoused in national teacher preparation standards for their "political sym-bolism," rather than their attempts to enact real equity-minded educational reform. Chapter 5 describes the limits to doing critical pedagogy that teacher educators feel in the neoliberal era, including frustration that critical work is not valued, sup-ported, or understood, and consequent fears of not being promoted/tenured.

Sleeter (2008) also says teacher educators must "become more aware of linkages between macro-level shifts in power and local realities, to engage in the long-term work of pushing back [neoliberal forces] collectively" (p. 1955). The stories of practice included in Part II of the book show that teacher educators are aware of the

S.L. Groenke and J.A. Hatch
University of Tennessee

effects of macro-level, neoliberal forces on the local and particular teaching contexts where they are trying to do critical work. Chapters in Part II describe education students questioning the necessity and practicality of social foundations courses, and the legitimacy of minority, non-White professors; NCATE's domination at teacher education department meetings, and ensuing low faculty morale; and the removal of critically oriented courses from teacher preparation curriculum.

However, all of the authors in this section *persist*, finding or creating the "small openings" in their contexts that foster critical reflection, intellectual engagement, and examination of alternative paradigms that help beginning teachers pursue deeper understandings about schooling in a democratic society. Whether these small openings are dialogic classroom spaces (see Chapters 6, 7, and 14); the contact zones afforded by interview assignments, focus study groups, and role-playing activities (see Chapters 8, 9, and 15); sacred, indigenous, and rural places (see Chapters 11 and 14); or cyberspace (see Chapter 12), they represent teacher educators' efforts to not only bear witness to the deleterious effects of neoliberalism in teacher education, but also to resist—to push back—those forces. Indeed, as the epigraph that opens this writing claims, persons of all ages—in many places—are struggling to open spaces where they can be free.

Thus, this book serves as a collective act of resistance to the forces currently limiting critical teacher education efforts. And collective acts are necessary, if the histories of grassroots movements in the United States (e.g., the Women's Rights and Civil Rights movements) are any indication. But we could be doing more collectively than writing about what we do in scholarly journals and books, like this one. In what follows, we consider some gaps and omissions in the critical pedagogy work in teacher education represented in this book, and in so doing, outline future considerations for more effective, locally collaborative forms of collective resistance to the neoliberal forces threatening public schools, university-based teacher education programs, and indeed notions of the "public good" altogether (Weiner, 2007).

These considerations envision college-level collaborations; local school and community collaborations; and finally, collaborative relationships with our students that do not blame them for their historical and sociopolitical innocence, but require a shared responsibility to know the histories of oppression and resistance that mark our country's narratives. Carlson (2008) suggests this responsibility, for teacher educators, must include moving "beyond assigned texts and course syllabi, to [engaging] young people in the politics of everyday life and [connecting] the inside and the outside of the university" (p. 105). The idea of connecting the "inside and outside of the university" marks all of the considerations we describe below.

Gaps, Omissions, and Future Considerations

One of the first things that strikes us as we read the chapters in Part II as a whole is the lack of any concerted *programmatic* efforts to do critical pedagogy in teacher education. Most of the authors work within their own individual courses to find the "small openings" they describe. Granted, teacher educators are constrained by shrinking university budgets, resources, and time (that is why the openings are small), but where are the program-wide approaches to developing future critical teachers?

As many chapters in both parts of this book make clear, becoming critical is a process that involves beginning teachers (1) recognizing the political complications of schooling, (2) understanding the origins of deficitism, (3) becoming aware of cultural investments in whiteness, (4) participating in desocialization processes, and (5) critiquing their own life stories. These processes require time and recursivity, or opportunities to struggle through resistance, revisit contradictory ideas, and reflect on one's own and others' personal narratives, through multiple and diverse interactions.

Neither time nor recursivity is possible in one single equity-oriented or critically oriented course, and as researchers suggest, single courses have little impact on beginning teachers' beliefs and attitudes. Brown's (2004) research on beginning teachers' cultural diversity awareness development in one multicultural course found that students needed at least eight class meetings just to reduce resistance to course material. Mueller and O'Connor (2007) suggested that because "issues of multiculturalism and diversity were not emphasized programmatically" and because "for many students, this was the first (and the last) time … they would struggle with these issues," the (predominantly White, upper-middle-class, female) students' meritocratic beliefs about why they succeeded in school remained unchanged (p. 852).

Thus, rather than succumb to pressures to align (read: narrow) teacher preparation programs with neoliberal reform agendas, teacher educators must also look for and create "small openings" in which to engage colleagues (including those in other programs and departments), department heads, and college deans, as well as state educational policy officials in efforts to reenvision and articulate a programmatic commitment that takes critical pedagogy in teacher education more seriously.

As part of this reenvisioning process at the University of Tennessee, the faculty in the College of Education, Health, and Human Sciences have begun a discussion group on "Neoliberalism in Education." Meeting several times over the course of a semester, various discussion group members suggest readings and videos (e.g., Davies & Bansel, 2007; Friedberg, 2005; Piazza, 2007; Leistyna, 2007; Weiner, 2007), and facilitate discussion about them. Action goals of the group include monitoring local and federal school policy, getting involved in local and federal educational policy decisions, sharing ideas/strategies for interrupting and "talking back" to neoliberal discourses in our own classrooms, and collaborating with school leaders and teachers to initiate communitywide forums on neoliberalism and public schooling. The discussion group has helped faculty meet other colleagues from different departments within the college who struggle with similar issues, and has helped faculty members know they are not alone in their efforts, but instead have allies who can support them.

In addition, the Department of Theory and Practice at the University of Tennessee will soon begin a series of workshops for all secondary education students on public school issues unique to East Tennessee. For example, one workshop called "Crossing Borders in Our Classrooms" will address the neoliberal forces at work behind the movement of Mexican immigrants and Burundian refugees to East Tennessee, share strategies for debunking myths about immigrants to the United States, and provide resources for beginning teachers to make their classrooms and school communities welcome and equitable places for these students and their families.

Part of this reenvisioning collaborative process at the university level must also include stronger partnerships between teacher educators and local schools. Surprisingly few of the chapters in this book describe university–school partnerships, or "small openings" occurring outside of academe, between teacher educators, classroom teachers, and/or community centers. This is problematic for several reasons. First, as described in Chapter 1, early social reconstructionists believed teachers and students had to be taught to care about building a good society, that it wouldn't happen naturally. They believed that implementing "practice schools" in university-based teacher education programs, where beginning teachers were expected to be in "contact" with diverse people in diverse situations, would help make teachers care about defeating capitalism and turning schools into something other than worker factories. Rodgers (2006) and other educational historians attest to the significant impact such "practice" programs had on developing critically oriented and equity-oriented teachers.

However, "practice" in the majority of today's teacher preparation programs often consists of one (increasingly shortened) field experience, usually in schools satisfied with maintaining the status quo (and not jeopardizing test scores), and rarely in low-income and/or cultural or language minority schools, or other community sites. Sleeter (2008) suggests "multiple … field experiences in historically-underserved areas, in both classrooms and communities, with guided inquiry, has a reasonable track record for disrupting stereotypes, helping teacher candidates learn about students' cultural backgrounds, and helping them learn to connect student behavior and learning with what teachers do" (p. 1949). The kinds of "practice" experiences Sleeter suggests—especially those in nonschool, community settings—are crucial if beginning teachers are to gain insight, especially, into the economic realities of today's public school students and their families, and engage in dialogue about students' experiences and perspectives defined by social class. As Lipsitz (1997) explains, "out-of-school experiences often offer rich storehouses of evidence, insight, and eloquent expression about social class" (p. 11). No stories of practice included in this book draw attention to social class as it intersects other subject positions (e.g., race, gender), and inhabits the classroom—a place where "labor is socialized, where people learn the requisite values, attitudes, and behaviors needed to make them docile, compliant, and productive workers and citizens," and "upward mobility" is promised (Lipsitz, 1997, p. 10)

The omission of social class in teacher education has been noted before: Linda Brodkey (1989) speculated in the late 1980s that classroom practices and pedagogies tend to support middle-class norms and ideologies that suppress class tensions and work to erase class differences. Middle-class ideologies of upward mobility affirm competition, individual ambition, and the pursuit of personal material gain as the central purposes of schooling.

Once again, the social reconstructionists understood that a "new social order" required teachers and teacher educators to take responsibility for disrupting these kinds of ideologies and the forces of capitalism at work in our classrooms and communities. Today—with an economy in recession, stagnated or lost wages for all but the very rich, and neoliberal capitalism working to dismantle social welfare programs that benefit the working class—teacher educators must collaborate with schools and communities, especially with those schools and communities that need our resources most, if we are to begin to imagine education as creating social possibilities rather than curtailing them.

Ultimately, the social reconstructionists envisioned public schools as "neighborhood [centers] to which [adults] may come for recreation, companionship, and for constant help in the solution of their community problems" (Brameld, 1947, p. 139). The reconstructionists believed if teachers and teacher educators took part in community affairs and allied with other progressive forces they could build a collective resistance against outside pressures (Bowers, 1969). But the social reconstructionists failed to garner the support of classroom teachers and community members, so their ideas remained just that—ideas.

Contemporary educational researchers (see Achinstein & Ogawa, 2006; Auerbach, 2001; Hursh, 2005; Thompson, 2003) describe teachers' frustrations with "teacher-proof" curriculums, parents' anger at the "deskilling" and lack of critical thinking they see occurring as a result of an overemphasis on standardized testing, and working-class community members' frustrations over job losses and home foreclosures. These teachers, parents, and community members need and want allies; working side by side with them, teacher educators can begin to help craft a counter-discourse to NCLB's deficit-oriented notions of student achievement and teacher quality—a discourse supported by policymakers' calls for educational and economic productivity in an increasingly globalized neoliberal economy (Hursh, 2005). Just as importantly, teacher educators, parents, and classroom teachers can ask local government officials and educational policymakers to engage in dialogue with them about the purposes of public schooling in a democratic, civil society.

Finally, as the findings of our survey study in Chapter 5 warrant, and the authors of Chapter 6 suggest, teacher educators must consider working more collaboratively with beginning teachers to better understand their resistance to alternative paradigms that challenge their worldviews and understandings about difference, and the roles of schooling in creating, mediating, and resisting difference. We can't keep blaming our students for "not getting it," for not having the right "background knowledge or cultural experiences" to appreciate and consider critical paradigms, and for being reluctant to talk about sensitive issues like racism and social class. Our privileged, college-level students—like us—are victims of the same socialization processes that make it difficult to argue with the seemingly commonsense, moral logic that rationalizes privilege for some to the detriment of others (Mueller & O'Connor, 2007).

But that does not mean we have to let them (or ourselves) off the hook. Instead, we can admit to our own innocences (if not ignorances), take responsibility for what we do not know, and begin the hard work of learning (and unlearning) together. Perhaps if our students begin to see us as allies rather than strangers, as collaborators in the attempt to understand what makes it hard to *be* critical and *do* critical work— *and it is hard*—then some of the resistance that characterizes so much of the critical pedagogy work in teacher education will begin to soften. Then we can get on with the work of stemming the neoliberal bankruptcy of public schools and university-based teacher education programs, and perhaps our small openings might become, as Maxine Greene says, "doorways, through which we can move in a new-found solidarity in search of a somewhat better world" (1993, p. xi).

References

Achinstein, B., & Ogawa, R. T. (2006). (In)fidelity: What the resistance of new teachers reveals about professional principles and prescriptive educational policies. *Harvard Educational Review*, *67*(1), 30–63.

Auerbach, S. (2001). From moral supporters to struggling advocates. *Urban Education*, *42*(3), 250–283.

Brameld, T. (1947). Workers' education in America. *Educational Administration and Supervision*, *33*, 129–140.

Bowers, C.A. (1969). The progressive educator and the depression: The radical years. New York: Random House.

Brodkey, L. (1989). On the subjects of class and gender in *The Literacy Letters*. *College English*, *51*, 125–141.

Brown, E. L. (2004). What precipitates change in cultural diverse awareness during a multicultural course? *Journal of Teacher Education*, *55*(4), 325–340.

Carlson, D. (2008). 2007 AESA Presidential Address. Conflict of the faculties: Democratic progressivism in the age of "No Child Left Behind." *Educational Studies*, *43*, 94–113.

Davies, B., & Bansel, P. (2007). Neoliberalism and education. *International Journal of Qualitative Studies in Education*, *20*(3), 247–259.

Friedberg, J. (Producer/Director). (2005). Granito de Arena (Grain of Sand). [DVD]. Seattle, WA: Corrugated Films.

Greene, M. (1993). Foreword. In C. Lankshear & P.L. McLaren (Eds.), *Critical literacy: Politics, praxis, and the postmodern*. Albany, NY: SUNY Press.

Hursh, D. (2005). The growth of high-stakes testing in the USA: Accountability, markets and the decline in educational equality. *British Educational Research Journal*, *31*(5), 605–622.

Leistyna, P. (2007). Neoliberal nonsense. In P. McLaren & J. Kincheloe (Eds.), Critical pedagogy: Where are we now? New York: Peter Lang.

Lipsitz, G. (1997). Class and consciousness: Teaching about social class. In A. Kumar (Ed.), *Class issues: Pedagogy, cultural studies, and the public sphere*. (pp. 9–21). New York: New York University Press.

Mueller, J., & O'Connor, C. (2007). Telling and retelling about self and "others": How preservice teachers (re)interpret privilege and disadvantage in one college classroom. *Teaching and Teacher Education*, *23*, 840–856.

Piazza, C. (2007). If you think language is neutral, think again! *English Leadership Quarterly*, *30*(2), 12–16.

Rodgers, C.R. (2006). "The turning of one's soul"—Learning to teach for social justice: The Putney Graduate School of Teacher Education. *Teachers College Record*, *108*(7), 1266–1295.

Sleeter, C. (2008). Equity, democracy, and neoliberal assaults on teacher education. *Teaching and Teacher Education*, *24*, 1947–1957.

Thompson, G. L. (2003). *What African American parents want educators to know*. Westport, CT: Praeger.

Weiner, L. (2007). A lethal threat to US teacher education. *Journal of Teacher Education*, *58*(4), 274–286.

Author Bios

Sean Agriss (sagriss@wsu.edu) is a doctoral student in Cultural Studies and Social Thought in Education at Washington State University. He teaches an upper level undergraduate course titled "Cultural and Community Contexts of Education," which draws from the fields of educational foundations and cultural studies to examine schooling, teaching, and education in the context of place. His research interests include social justice issues in higher education, specifically focusing on discriminatory policy affecting faculty outside of institutionally established and accepted norms.

Cristian R. Aquino-Sterling (cristian.aquino@asu.edu) earned a BA in Western Philosophy from Fordham University and an MA in Latin American and Spanish Literatures from Columbia University. He is currently a Ph.D. Candidate in the Mary Lou Fulton College of Education at Arizona State University (ASU) and was a recipient of ASU's Graduate College Dissertation Fellowship Award (2006-2007). His academic and research interests pertain to discourse and ideology in scholarly critiques of NCLB and the practice of schooling/education in culturally and linguistically diverse contexts.

Maggie Bartlett (mabartle@asu.edu) is a doctoral candidate in Educational Leadership & Policy Studies, concentrating on international and comparative education, at Arizona State University. Her research interests include policies and education for children with disabilities in sub-Saharan Africa. She situates her work within critical and emancipatory frameworks while investigating the cultural complexities and intersection of disabilities, education, policy, practice, and society. Based on her experiences as a Peace Corps volunteer, her current fieldwork is situated in rural Namibia, Africa.

Lane W. Clarke (clarkel1@nku.edu) is an Assistant Professor of Literacy at Northern Kentucky University. She also has been a classroom teacher and reading specialist in New York, South Carolina, and Ohio. She has had articles published in journals such as *Language Arts, English Journal, Journal of Literacy Research, The Reading Teacher* and *The Journal of Adolescent and Adult Literacy*. Her interests include reading comprehension, literature circles, struggling readers, critical literacy, and instructional technology.

Maria Dantas-Whitney (dantasm@wou.edu) is Associate Professor of ESOL/bilingual education at Western Oregon University in the United States. Her professional interests include language teacher education, critical reflective practice, and classroom-based research. She is co-editor for TESOL's *Classroom Practice Series*, and is currently a Fulbright scholar at the Universidad Autónoma Benito Juárez de Oaxaca, in Mexico.

Venus Evans-Winters (vwinters@iwu.edu) is an Assistant Professor at Illinois State University in the Department of Educational Administration & Foundations. Her areas of research interest are urban education, urban children and adolescents, feminist theory, and qualitative research methods. She uses sociological and anthropological research methods to analyze educational problems and issues. She is the author of *Teaching Black Girls: Resiliency in Urban Classrooms*, published in 2005. She is also the author and co-author of several journal articles and book chapters.

Jill Ewing Flynn (flyn0103@umn.edu), a former middle/high school English teacher, will earn her Ph.D. in Curriculum and Instruction/Literacy Education from the University of Minnesota in summer 2009. Her research and teaching interests include culturally relevant pedagogy, multicultural literature, and critical literacy. In September 2009, she will join the faculty at University of Delaware as an Assistant Professor of English Education.

David Greenwood (formerly Gruenewald) (greenwood@wsu.edu) is an Associate Professor at Washington State University. His research, teaching, and activism revolve around place-based, environmental, and sustainability education. Widely published in these areas, David recently co-edited the book *Place-Based Education in the Global Age: Local Diversity* (Lawrence Erlbaum, 2008), and recently co-edited Volume 14 (2009) of the *Canadian Journal of Environmental Education*, which explores the theme "Context, Experience, and the Socioecological: Inquiries into Practice."

Susan L. Groenke (sgroenke@utk.edu) is Assistant Professor of Theory and Practice in Teacher Education at the University of Tennessee. She advises and teaches in the graduate English Education program. Her research interests include how adolescents talk about and interpret young adult literature, how new technological literacies can transform teaching and learning, and how English teachers can encourage students to think critically about texts and the world.

J. Amos Hatch (ahatch@utk.edu) is Professor of Theory and Practice in Teacher Education at the University of Tennessee. He teaches graduate courses in early childhood education and qualitative research and works with teacher education students preparing to teach in urban-multicultural settings. He is a qualitative researcher who has published widely in the areas of children's social relationships, teacher philosophies and practices, and urban teacher education.

Nikola Hobbel (hobbel@humboldt.edu) is Associate Professor of English Education at Humboldt State University in California. She studies the intersections of race, curriculum and policy while teaching preservice, graduate and professional development courses. Academic literacy and graphic novels garner her special attention, as do her inspiring students.

John Kambutu (kambutu@uwyo.edu) is an Associate Professor of Educational Studies at the University of Wyoming/Casper College Center. He teaches foundation courses and multicultural education for undergraduate and graduate students. An award-winning educator, Kambutu believes strongly in education that transforms lives. To Kambutu, education is an important tool for liberating humanity from the ills of ignorance, thus enabling them to live a better free life. Kambutu's research focuses on transformative learning. Kambutu has authored several articles and book chapters on a variety of educational issues.

Joe Kincheloe passed away on December 19, 2008. At the time of his death, he was Professor and Canada Research Chair in the Faculty of Education, McGill University in Montreal. Joe wrote or edited scores of books, and he produced hundreds of journal articles and book chapters. His scholarly interests ranged from educational research to popular culture. He was the editor of several important book series, including Springer's *Explorations of Educational Purpose*, of which this book is a part.

Timothy J. Lensmire (lensmire@umn.edu) is an Associate Professor in the Curriculum and Instruction Department at the University of Minnesota. He teaches courses in critical pedagogy, curriculum theory, critical whiteness studies, and the teaching of writing in schools. His writing includes the books *When Children Write* and *Powerful Writing, Responsible Teaching*. His current research focuses on describing and theorizing white racial identity.

Cynthia Lewis (lewis@umn.edu) is Professor of Critical Literacy and English Education at the University of Minnesota. She teaches graduate courses on critical discourse analysis, sociocultural theory, and English education. Her research focuses on the social and cultural dimensions of literacy, with a particular interest in the relationship between social identities and learning in urban schools.

Joellen Maples (jmaples@sjfc.edu) is an Assistant Professor in Literacy Education at St. John Fisher College in Rochester, New York. She previously taught 8th grade reading for 11 years. In her current position, she teaches undergraduate and graduate courses in content area reading and critical literacy. Her research interests include exploring effective strategies for facilitating classroom dialogue and fostering critical literacy through the combined use of young adult literature and new internet technologies in discussion-related tasks.

Wendy B. Meller (Mellerw@rowan.edu) is an Assistant Professor in Early Childhood Education at Rowan University in Glassboro, New Jersey. She teaches undergraduate courses focusing on assessment and diversity in early childhood settings. She is a qualitative researcher interested in teacher preparation, urban education, and literacy development in early childhood settings.

Kate Menken (kmenken@gc.cuny.edu) is an Assistant Professor of Linguistics at Queens College of the City University of New York (CUNY), and a Research Fellow at the Research Institute for the Study of Language in Urban Society at the CUNY Graduate Center. Previously, she was a teacher of English as a second language, and a researcher at the National Clearinghouse for Bilingual Education. Her recent book is entitled *English Learners Left Behind: Standardized Testing as Language Policy* (Multilingual Matters).

Darcy Miller (darcymiller@wsu.edu) is Professor and Director of Teacher Education in the Department of Teaching and Learning at Washington State University. Dr. Miller authored the text *Enhancing Adolescent Competence* and her research interests include teacher education, Fetal Alcohol Spectrum Disorder, and the barriers and challenges faced by students with disabilities.

Karie Mize (mizek@wou.edu) is an Assistant Professor of ESOL/Bilingual Education at Western Oregon University. She coordinates the Bilingual Teacher Initiative, which is an effort to recruit, retain, and recognize bilingual students in teacher preparation programs. Prior to her university experience, Karie taught for nine years in bilingual (Spanish/English) settings. She graduated from the University of San Francisco with a doctorate in International and Multicultural Education and an emphasis in Second Language Acquisition.

Mark Nagasawa (Mark.Nagasawa@asu.edu) is a doctoral candidate in Early Childhood Education at the Mary Lou Fulton College of Education at Arizona State University. His dissertation research is a "biography" of Arizona's state preschool program, which explores the intersections of policy-making, policy texts, and socio-cultural-historical milieu by drawing on the perspectives of informants representing conflicting vantage points in the process.

Lydiah Nganga (lnganga@uwyo.edu) is an Assistant Professor of Elementary and Early Childhood Education at the University of Wyoming/Casper College Center. She teaches Humanities Methods and Early Childhood courses and works with preservice teachers from rural education settings. Her research focuses on multicultural education, social justice and global education. Most recently, Nganga is the author of a children's book entitled *My Sister Kairitu is Sick*, a story intended to create cultural awareness and understanding in a world that is increasingly becoming a global village.

Beth Blue Swadener (Beth.Swadener@asu.edu) is Chair of Early Childhood Education and Professor of Policy Studies at Arizona State University. Her research focuses on social policy, anti-oppressive/ally strategies in early childhood contexts, and global policies linked to local lives in sub-Saharan Africa. She has published nine books, including *Children and Families "At Promise": Deconstructing the Discourse of Risk* and *Power and Voice in Research with Children*. Her current research is a collaborative, cross-national study of children's rights and voice in policies affecting them.

Eileen Dugan Waldschmidt (ewaldsch@unm.edu) was an elementary classroom teacher for 19 years. For the last 11 years she has worked in teacher education at Oregon State University and the University of New Mexico where she is currently the Program Manager of an alternative licensure and master's degree program. Her areas of research are ESOL and bilingual education, social justice, and teacher education.

Author Index

Subject Index

Lightning Source UK Ltd.
Milton Keynes UK
22 August 2009

142961UK00006B/408/P